Making Meaning

Making Meaning

Building Strategies for College Reading

Janeen Myers
University of Central Oklahoma

Evelyn Eskridge
Edmond Public Schools

Patricia Smart Richardson
Rose State College

Barbara Tucker
Oklahoma State University at Oklahoma City

PEARSON
Longman

Boston   New York   San Francisco
Mexico City   Montreal   Toronto   London   Madrid   Munich   Paris
Hong Kong   Singapore   Tokyo   Cape Town   Sydney

Acquisitions Editor: Melanie Craig
Development Editor: Gillian Cook
Senior Supplements Editor: Donna Campion
Marketing Manager: Thomas DeMarco
Production Manager: Bob Ginsberg
Project Coordination, Text Design, and Electronic Page Makeup: Pre-Press Company, Inc.
Senior Cover Design Manager: Nancy Danahy
Cover Designer: Nancy Sacks
Cover Photo: Evelyn Eskridge
Manufacturing Buyer: Roy L. Pickering, Jr.
Printer and Binder: Quebecor World/Dubuque
Cover Printer: Phoenix Color Corporation

For permission to use copyrighted material, grateful acknowledgment is made to the copyright holders on pp. 333–335, which are hereby made part of this copyright page.

Except where noted, all photos courtesy of Evelyn Eskridge.

Visit us at www.ablongman.com

ISBN 0-321-35560-1 (student edition)
ISBN 0-321-43911-2 (annotated instructor's edition)

1 2 3 4 5 6 7 8 9 10—QWD—09 08 07 06

Dedication

Thank you to my husband, John L. Birsner; my children; and my parents, Harry and Daphne Myers, for their encouragement and excitement over this project.

—Janeen Myers

To my parents, Alice and Walter; my in-laws, Martha and Hillis; my husband, Walter; my son Justin and his wife, Valerie; my son Don; and my daughter, Laura: You make my heart sing.

—Evelyn Eskridge

To my husband, Joe Richardson, and my godmother, Mamie Elise Greer Jackson, age 98, who has always been my inspiration.

—Pat Richardson

This book is the direct result of our dear friend and lead author, Janeen Myers. It was her vision and perseverance that helped the rest of us stay focused. She encouraged us continually as we faced one revision after another. It has been an honor for all of us to complete this book, knowing it will strengthen adult readers. My husband, Bob Tucker, listened to my concerns and always encouraged me to believe in our goal. Both of my daughters, Sherri and Patti, were in awe of this undertaking and became my best fans. Thanks to each of you.

—Barbara Tucker

Brief Contents

Detailed Contents

CHAPTER 5   *Discovering Context Clues*   *153*

CHAPTER **8** *Additional Readings* 259

Preface

Making Meaning is designed for college students reading at the fourth- to sixth-grade level and was developed in response to the growing need emerging in technical schools, two-year colleges, and some four-year institutions for a course that accommodates students needing the most basic reading instruction. It seeks to help adult learners acquire the critical thinking and writing skills that will enable them to effectively read, process, analyze, and learn information on their own. *Making Meaning* teaches reading as a way for students to investigate, understand, and respond to the world by including readings, exercises, and activities that are relevant to adult learners. In addition, the book makes explicit how developing effective reading skills will benefit students in their daily lives.

Making Meaning includes a broad range of selections from literature, fiction, newspapers, and magazines, as well as diverse excerpts that relate to everyday life and the concerns and interests of adult learners. It focuses not only on reading but also on the writing process as an integral part of improving reading skills. Reading, writing, speaking, listening, and visual representation are all included in the text as parts of an integrated approach to teaching reading. Students can write about only that which they understand: writing responses and short answers improves their comprehension.

Making Meaning contains numerous photographs and other graphics that illustrate points made in the text, stimulate critical thinking, and teach students to read visual materials. The graphics show students how visuals are used to organize and explain textual information and provide opportunities for them to make meaning from visual information.

The book is also recursive, providing the opportunity in each chapter for students to practice and integrate skills discussed in previous lessons and to apply the reading strategies they have learned to many kinds of texts.

PEDAGOGICAL APPROACH

Making Meaning integrates the teaching of reading, writing, and thinking skills. The format and content are based on four pedagogical elements important for students who are developing readers: a balanced approach to reading, integration of reading and writing, constant reinforcement of skills, and ongoing assessment.

Through the use of a balanced approach, students develop phonological awareness and learn whole-language strategies in the context of content-rich literature-based activities. Research shows this approach allows students—

particularly adults—from a variety of educational backgrounds to build on their strengths and develop effective reading skills. The text also focuses on the writing process as an integral part of improving reading skills. Through the use of the Reader Response writing assignments in each chapter, students identify what they already know, assess what they have learned, and apply what they are learning to thinking critically about the readings. Concise instruction, interspersed with numerous exercises, teaches students basic reading skills. The practices, mastery level exercises, and Looking Back exercises provide ongoing review, reinforcement, and integration of these skills.

Making Meaning emphasizes the importance of students' existing reserves of knowledge, reading abilities, and life experiences. The wide variety of reading selections, ranging from classic fiction to current news stories and excerpts on how to plan a trip or plant a garden were chosen for their relevance and appeal to adult learners and to stimulate critical and imaginative thinking. In addition, readings in content-specific material are included to prepare students for reading-intensive courses at the college level.

Graphs, charts, cartoons, and numerous color and black and white photographs appear throughout the text and are used to help students develop visual literacy skills, as well as to provide visual interest and stimulation.

CONTENT

Chapters 1 through 7 each cover a major reading strategy in depth, allow numerous opportunities for practice and mastery, and build on the preceding chapters. This approach provides ample time for students to practice and fully learn each skill and enables them to integrate and practice skills as they progress through the text. Chapter 8 consists of numerous readings of various lengths, both fiction and nonfiction, with substantial opportunities for students to practice all the reading strategies they learned in the book.

Chapter 1, Preparing to Read, covers the crucial previewing skills of prereading (paying attention to titles, headings, bulleted lists, and other highlighted information in textbooks), connecting what is read to prior knowledge, and predicting what a reading will be about. It also introduces the concept of visual literacy.

Chapter 2, Recognizing Consonants and Vowels, focuses on how letters sound alone and in combination, providing a foundation of information that will aid students in the pronunciation and spelling of both new and familiar words.

Chapter 3, Recognizing Word Parts and Using Syllables, explains how words are formed from root words, prefixes, and suffixes. Learning this information increases comprehension and promotes vocabulary growth. Information on syllables and syllabication is provided to improve decoding and pronunciation skills.

Chapter 4, Using a Dictionary, builds on the preceding three chapters and provides lessons in dictionary use, pronunciation, correct word usage, etymology, and spelling skills.

Chapter 5, Discovering Context Clues, discusses types of context clues (definitions, examples, antonyms, synonyms, and the general sense of the passage) and how to use them to understand unfamiliar words.

Chapter 6, Finding Main Ideas, teaches strategies for recognizing the main idea of paragraphs and longer readings and how to distinguish between main ideas and supporting details.

Chapter 7, Identifying Supporting Details, builds on the preceding chapter and focuses on the types of supporting details, including visual details used in charts and graphs. It also addresses transitional words and phrases and how they are used to link ideas and help readers follow a writer's train of thought.

Chapter 8, Additional Readings, consists of numerous readings from a wide variety of genres, including poetry, fiction, personal narrative, and newspaper articles. These readings increase in length and difficulty through the course of the chapter and may be used throughout the semester or read after students complete the preceding seven chapters. Each reading is accompanied by exercises similar to those presented in the earlier chapters, and a number of Reader Response activities are included.

CHAPTER FORMAT

Each of the seven instructional chapters and the additional readings chapter in *Making Meaning* provides sufficient depth of coverage to allow students to spend several class meetings absorbing and practicing the lessons. The seven instructional chapters have the same format. They open with a section entitled Making Meaning, which uses analogy and other methods to explain the main topic, and an Introduction, which provides an overview of the topic and definitions of terms. Following these openers are Structured Instruction and Exercises, Practicing What You Have Learned, and Mastery Level Exercises sections. Open-ended questions and invitations for students to respond to the readings based on their own experiences in the Reader Response feature provide instructors with discussion choices.

- The **Chapter Preview** appears in a text box at the beginning of each chapter. It introduces the main subject of the chapter and lists the topics that will be covered. Along with the Summary, the Chapter Preview provides a quick reference and review of the skills being taught.

- The **Making Meaning** feature illustrates the main idea of the chapter, using a photograph, an analogy, an exercise, or a brief reading, and demonstrates the importance of the new skill and its relevance to the student's experience.

- The **Introduction** provides a brief overview of the topic of the chapter and definitions of technical terms.

- The **Structured Instruction and Exercises** section includes clear, concise explanations of the topics covered in the chapter and uses various exercises, activities, and reading selections to explain skills and teach students how to apply them.

- **Practicing What You Have Learned** provides ample opportunities for students to practice the skills they have learned through several application exercises related to readings of various types, lengths, and levels of difficulty.

- The **Summary** lists the main points covered in the chapter in a brief format that provides a quick review of chapter content and reinforcement of what students have learned.

- The **Mastery Level Exercises** section provides further opportunities for students to read and interact with diverse kinds of texts and the chance to apply skills that students should now begin to feel confident in using.

- The **Looking Back** sections of Chapters 2 through 7 contain reading selections with exercises and activities that review and reinforce skills learned in earlier chapters. Presenting skills in contexts different from those in the chapters in which they were introduced, Looking Back challenges students to apply what they have learned and integrate skills to read effectively.

- **Reader Response** activities are featured throughout each chapter. These writing exercises offer students the opportunity to think about their life experiences, express themselves in different written formats, respond individually to readings, share their thoughts with the class, keep journals, and demonstrate to the instructor the progress they are making in the course.

USEFUL FEATURES

- **WORDNOTES:** Vocabulary definitions are included under this heading after most readings in all chapters. WORDNOTES vocabulary is also indexed alphabetically at the end of the text with extra space for students to add their own new vocabulary words. This feature is designed to help students increase their working vocabulary and create individual indexed lists of the new words they have learned.

- **Progress Charts:** Each chapter includes an assessment component called a Progress Chart, that students can use to track their scores on mastery level exercises, practices, Looking Back exercises, and self-evaluation questions. The Progress Chart provides instructors with objective scores, enabling them to effectively gauge how well students are learning chapter content. (Instructors can also integrate a percentage factor from the scores into their own grading scale.) The self-evaluation questions allow students to assess their own progress and give instructors information regarding students' attitudes about the progress they are making in the course.

- **Visuals:** The text contains numerous color and black and white photographs, as well as a variety of graphic illustrations (maps, charts, graphs, etc.). The graphics show students how visuals are used to organize and explain textual materials and provide opportunities for them to learn to interpret and use data from visual sources.

- **Text boxes** are used throughout the book to highlight information in the Chapter Preview at the beginning and Summary at the end of each chapter. Other important information such as lists and rules is also contained in text boxes for quick reference for instructors and students.

- **Glossary:** The first time a technical term is mentioned in a chapter, it is printed in boldface. A glossary of these teaching terms is listed alphabetically at the end of the text. The Glossary provides a quick definition and reference to material in the text as students review and move on to new lessons. In order to master using textbooks, students are encouraged to use the glossary and all materials in the book, cover to cover.

Making Meaning is designed with the needs of adult learners in mind. The text contains a wealth of relevant and high-interest readings, fiction and nonfiction, that increase in length and difficulty as the chapters progress and are designed to appeal both to students fresh out of high school and to older learners. The high-interest material engages the reader. Students can enjoy success with shorter selections, which will increase their willingness to meet the challenges of more difficult selections or of genres they have not read before.

ANCILLARY MATERIALS

- The **Annotated Instructor's Edition** is identical to the student text, except that the answers to practices, mastery level exercises, and Looking Back exercises are provided.
- The **Instructor's Manual,** prepared by the authors, offers teaching tips, sample syllabi, and expanded class activities to complement the text.
- The **Instructor's Manual and Answer Key (Instructor/ ISBN 0-321-46166-5)** This supplement accompanies *Making Meaning* and is available to adopters.

SUPPLEMENTS

Longman is pleased to offer a variety of support materials to help make teaching reading easier on teachers and to help students excel in their coursework. Many of our student supplements are available free or at a greatly reduced price when packaged with a Longman reading or study skills textbook. Contact your local Longman sales representative for more information on pricing and how to create a package.

For Instructors

Printed Test Bank for Developmental Reading (Instructor/ISBN 0-321-08596-5)
Offering more than 3,000 questions in all areas of reading, this test bank includes vocabulary, main idea, supporting details, patterns of organization, critical thinking, analytical reasoning, inference, point of view, visual aids, and textbook reading. (An electronic version is also available; see below.)

Electronic Test Bank for Developmental Reading (Instructor/ ISBN CD 0-321-08179-X)
Offering more than 3,000 questions in all areas of reading, this test bank includes vocabulary, main idea, supporting details, patterns of organization, critical thinking, analytical reasoning, inference, point of view, visual aids,

and textbook reading. Instructors simply choose questions, then print out the completed test for distribution *or* offer the test online.

The Longman Instructor's Planner (Instructor/ISBN 0-321-09247-3)

This planner includes weekly and monthly calendars, student attendance and grading rosters, space for contact information, Web references, an almanac, and blank pages for notes.

For Students

Vocabulary Skills Study Card (Student/ISBN 0-321-31802-1)

Colorful, affordable, and packed with useful information, Longman's Vocabulary Skills Study Card is a concise, eight-page reference guide to developing key vocabulary skills, such as learning to recognize context clues, reading a dictionary entry, and recognizing key root words, suffixes, and prefixes. The study card is laminated for durability, so students can keep it for years to come and pull it out whenever they need a quick review.

Reading Skills Study Card (Student/ISBN 0-321-33833-2)

Colorful, affordable, and packed with useful information, Longman's Reading Skills Study Card is a concise, eight-page reference guide to help students develop basic reading skills, such as concept skills, structural skills, language skills, and reasoning skills. The study card is laminated for durability, so students can keep it for years to come and pull it out whenever they need a quick review.

The Longman Textbook Reader, Revised Edition (with answers, Student/ISBN 0-321-11895-2; without answers, Student/ISBN 0-321-12223-2)

Offering five complete chapters from our textbooks in the disciplines of computer science, biology, psychology, communications, and business, this reader's chapters include additional comprehension quizzes, critical thinking questions, and group activities.

The Longman Reader's Portfolio and Student Planner (Student/ISBN 0-321-29610-9)

This unique supplement provides students with a space to plan, think about, and present their work. The portfolio includes a diagnostic area (including a learning-style questionnaire), a working area (including calendars, vocabulary logs, reading response sheets, book clue tips, and other valuable materials), and a display area (including a progress chart, a final table of contents, and a final assessment), as well as a daily planner for students including daily, weekly, and monthly calendars.

The Longman Reader's Journal by Kathleen McWhorter (Student/ISBN 0-321-08843-3)

The first journal for readers, The Longman Reader's Journal offers a place for students to record their reactions to and questions about any reading.

The Longman Planner (Student/ISBN 0-321-04573-4)

Ideal for organizing a busy college life, this planner includes hour-by-hour schedules, monthly and weekly calendars, an address book, and an almanac of tips and useful information.

10 Practices of Highly Effective College Students (Student/ISBN 0-205-30769-8)
This study skills supplement includes topics such as time management, test taking, reading critically, stress, and motivation.

***Newsweek* Discount Subscription Coupon (12 weeks) (Student/ISBN 0-331-08895-6)**
Newsweek gets students reading, writing, and thinking about what's going on in the world around them. The price of the subscription is added to the cost of the book. Instructors receive weekly lesson plans, quizzes, and curriculum guides as well as a complimentary *Newsweek* subscription. The price of the subscription is 59 cents per issue (a total of $7.08 for the subscription). *Package item only.*

Interactive Guide to *Newsweek* (Student/ISBN 0-321-05528-4)
Available with the 12-week subscription to *Newsweek*, this guide serves as a workbook for students who are using the magazine.

Research Navigator Guide for English by H. Eric Branscomb and Linda R. Barr (Student/ISBN 0-321-20277-5)
Designed to teach students how to conduct high-quality online research and to document it properly, Research Navigator guides provide discipline-specific academic resources in addition to helpful tips on the writing process, online research, and finding and citing valid sources. Research Navigator guides include an access code to Research Navigator™—providing access to thousands of academic journals and periodicals, the *New York Times* Search by Subject Archive, Link Library, Library Guides, and more.

Penguin Discount Novel Program
In cooperation with Penguin Putnam, Inc., Longman is proud to offer a variety of Penguin paperbacks at a significant discount when packaged with any Longman title. Excellent additions to any developmental reading course, Penguin titles give students the opportunity to explore contemporary and classical fiction and drama. The available titles include works by authors as diverse as Toni Morrison, Julia Alvarez, Mary Shelley, and Shakespeare. To review the complete list of titles available, visit the Longman-Penguin Putnam website: http://www.ablongman.com/penguin.

The *New American Webster Handy College Dictionary* (Student/ISBN 0-451-18166-2)
This paperback reference text contains more than 100,000 entries.

The *New Oxford American College Dictionary* (Student/ISBN 0-399-14415-3)
Based on the *New Oxford American Dictionary* and drawing on Oxford's unparalleled language resources (including a 200-million-word database), this college dictionary contains more than 75,000 entries and more than 1,000 illustrations, including line drawings, photographs, and maps.

Multimedia Offerings

Interested in incorporating online materials into your course? Longman is happy to help. Our regional technology specialists provide training on all of our multimedia offerings.

MyReadingLab (www.myreadinglab.com)

This exciting new website houses all the media tools developmental English students will need to improve their reading and study skills, all in one easy-to-use place. MyReadingLab for reading and study skills includes:

- **Reading Roadtrip 5.0 Website.** The best-selling reading software available, Reading Roadtrip takes students on a tour of 16 cities and landmarks throughout the United States, with each of the 16 modules corresponding to a reading or study skill. The topics include main idea, vocabulary, understanding patterns of organization, thinking critically, reading rate, note-taking and highlighting, graphics and visual aids, and more. Students can begin their trip by taking a brand-new diagnostics test that provides immediate feedback, guiding them to specific modules for additional help with reading skills. New version 5.0 includes a brand new design, a new Pioneer Level (4th–6th grade level), and new readings.

- **Longman Vocabulary Website.** The Longman Vocabulary Website component of MySkillsLab features hundreds of exercises in 10 topic areas to strengthen vocabulary skills. Students will also benefit from "100 Words That All High School Graduates Should Know," a useful resource that provides definitions for each of the words on this list, vocabulary flashcards, and audio clips to help facilitate pronunciation skills.

- **Longman Study Skills Website.** This site offers hundreds of review strategies for college success, time and stress management skills, study strategies, and more. Students can take a variety of assessment tests to learn about their organizational skills and learning styles, with follow-up quizzes to reinforce the strategies they have learned.

- **Research Navigator.** In addition to providing valuable help to any college student on how to conduct high-quality online research and to document it properly, Research Navigator provides access to thousands of academic journals and periodicals (including the NY Times Archive), allowing reading students to practice with authentic readings from college-level primary sources.

State-Specific Supplements

For Florida Adopters

Thinking Through the Test: A Study Guide for the Florida College Basic Skills Exit Test by D. J. Henry

This workbook helps students strengthen their reading skills in preparation for the Florida College Basic Skills Exit Test. It feature both diagnostic tests to help assess areas that may need improvement and exit tests to help test skill mastery. Detailed explanatory answers have been provided for almost all of the questions. *Package item only—not available for sale.*

Available Versions:

Thinking Through the Test (A Study Guide for the Florida College Basic Skills Exit Tests: Reading and Writing), Third Edition (0-321-38740-6)

Thinking Through the Test (A Study Guide for the Florida College Basic Skills Exit Tests: Reading and Writing), with Answers, Third Edition (0-321-38739-2)

Thinking Through the Test (A Study Guide for the Florida College Basic Skills Exit Tests: Reading), Third Edition (0-321-38738-4)

Thinking Through the Test (A Study Guide for the Florida College Basic Skills Exit Tests: Reading), with Answers, Third Edition (0-321-38737-6)

Reading Skills Summary for the Florida State Exit Exam by D. J. Henry (Student/ISBN 0-321-42062-4)

An excellent study tool for students preparing to take Florida College Basic Skills Exit Test for Reading, this laminated, 4-color reading grid summarizes all the skills tested on the Exit Exam. *Package item only—not available for sale.*

CLAST Test Package, Fourth Edition (Instructor/Print ISBN 0-321-01950-4)

These two 40-item objective tests evaluate students' readiness for the Florida CLAST exams. Strategies for teaching CLAST preparedness are included.

For Texas Adopters

The Longman THEA Study Guide by Jeannette Harris (Student/ISBN 0-321-27240-0)

Created specifically for students in Texas, this study guide includes straight-forward explanations and numerous practice exercises to help students pre-pare for the reading and writing sections of THEA Test. *Package item only—not available for sale.*

TASP Test Package, Third Edition (Instructor/Print ISBN 0-321-01959-8)

These 12 practice pre-tests and post-tests assess the same reading and writing skills covered in the Texas TASP examination.

For New York/CUNY Adopters

Preparing for the CUNY-ACT Reading and Writing Test edited by Patricia Licklider (Student/ISBN 0-321-19608-2)

This booklet, prepared by reading and writing faculty from across the CUNY system, is designed to help students prepare for the CUNY-ACT exit test. It in-cludes test-taking tips, reading passages, typical exam questions, and sample writing prompts to help students become familiar with each portion of the test.

ACKNOWLEDGMENTS

We want to express our thanks to the following reviewers who provided feed-back, useful critiques, and suggestions for improvements, many of which we have integrated into the book:

Lida A. Criner, Southern Arkansas University Tech; Raymond Deleon, California State University, Long Beach; Gail Harrison, Delaware Technical and Community College; Diane Lerma, Palo Alto College; Dina LeVitre, Community College of Rhode Island; Anita van Ouwerkerk, Blinn College; Kathy Riley, Polk Community College; Jeri Thornton, Northeast Texas Community College; and Phyllis Watson, Consumnes Community College.

In addition, we wish to thank our development editor, Gillian Cook, without whom things just would not have come together; Susan Kunchandy for believing in *Making Meaning*; and Melanie Craig, sponsoring editor at Longman.

JANEEN MYERS

EVELYN ESKRIDGE

PATRICIA SMART RICHARDSON

BARBARA TUCKER

Introduction
Making Meaning from What You Read

"It feels like flying!"

"What are you doing?"

"I'm jumping on the trampoline."

"Why?"

"Because it's fun, and it makes me feel like I'm flying."

"Why do you bother, with so many things to do?"

"Because I get just a little higher every time I jump."

"But you're still in the same place."

"No, I'm not. Every time I jump, I feel a little more relaxed, and I trust myself a little more. I get better at it. Besides that, it's great exercise and makes me feel good."

"Maybe I'll try it. Anything I should know before I start?"

"Yeah. Look around you. Make sure you won't hit anything like tree branches when you jump. Stay in the center. Wear comfortable clothes. Don't start with flips. Just jump awhile and relax first. Then I'll teach you some really neat stuff."

READING IS LIKE JUMPING ON A TRAMPOLINE

Reading is a lot like jumping on a trampoline. Take one leap at a time. Practice. The more you read, the easier it will get. You will feel stronger, more relaxed, and confident as you practice the skills you need to become a successful reader. Sometimes it will feel like hard work, but sometimes it will feel like flying. You may not believe it now, but reading can be a rewarding and enjoyable activity. Improving your reading skills will do many important things for you.

- Reading will give you the power to try new things because the skills you learn in this book will help you to understand many different kinds of texts.
- Reading will introduce you to new ideas.
- Reading will help you build your knowledge of the world.
- Reading will teach you about many subjects: science, business, literature, history, and more.
- Reading will help you think clearly and question and analyze what other people have to say.
- Reading will introduce you to the joy of reading for entertainment, relaxation, and stimulation.

BRIEF OVERVIEW OF *MAKING MEANING*

Chapter 1: Preparing to Read introduces the strategy of prereading (previewing) and teaches you what to look for when you first start reading a textbook, story, map, or graph. Prereading involves reading titles, headings, and graphics before reading the main body of a text, asking questions about the information, and predicting what the reading might be about. When you preread, you will understand the text better and organize and remember what you have read.

Chapter 2: Recognizing Consonants and Vowels, Chapter 3: Recognizing Word Parts and Using Syllables and **Chapter 4: Using a Dictionary** cover the basic building blocks of words, consonants and vowels, how to pronounce words using syllables, how to use word parts (prefixes, roots, and suffixes) to work out the meaning of unfamiliar words, and how to use a dictionary. Knowing this basic information about words will help you develop and expand your vocabulary, which is an essential step toward strengthening your reading skills.

Chapter 5: Discovering Context Clues shows you how to use clues in a reading—-definitions, examples, synonyms (words that mean the same as another word), antonyms (words that mean the opposite), and the general sense of the passage—-to help you understand new and unfamiliar words as you read.

Chapter 6: Finding the Main Idea and **Chapter 7: Identifying Supporting Details** will help you develop the skills you need to understand your college reading assignments. You will use your prior knowledge and life experiences to understand what you read. You will learn how to recognize the topic (the general subject of a reading), the main ideas or points the author makes about the topic, the supporting details the author uses to explain and illustrate the main points, and transitional words and phrases that link ideas. Being able to identify the important parts of a reading allows you to understand it better; to organize the information you learn in a logical way; to remember what you have read; and to use what you learn to write essays, discuss what you have read, and answer test questions.

Chapter 8: Additional Readings contains a variety of readings from different disciplines and sources. Each reading is followed by comprehension and skills exercises, similar to the activities in the first seven chapters. Chapter 8 provides you with more practice in everything you have learned in *Making Meaning*, allowing you to sharpen your reading skills and broaden your vocabulary.

HOW EACH CHAPTER WORKS

Each chapter in *Making Meaning* teaches you new reading skills. If you follow the instructions and carefully complete all the activities, you will become a better reader, not only in this class but also in your other classes, at home, at work, and anywhere you have the need to read. All the chapters are set up using the same format:

CHAPTER PREVIEW

In this chapter, you will learn to preread or preview a textbook. **Prereading** is a basic skill that helps you take control of your college reading assignments. Prereading involves paying attention to the following:

- Title, subtitles, and information in bold print, *italics*, or color
- Preface or introduction
- Chapter titles
- Bullets
- Pictures, graphs, and charts
- Glossary and index
- Beginning, middle, and end of the reading selection
- Connecting what you read to prior knowledge
- Predicting what the reading selection will cover

The **Chapter Preview** introduces the main subject of the chapter and lists the topics that will be covered in it.

MAKING MEANING

Would you love to windsurf? What would you do to prepare? An article for beginners explains that you must:

- learn the patterns of boat traffic
- prepare for weather conditions (e.g., wear wetsuit, booties, etc.)
- learn the International Distress Signal
- learn how to read the wind
- stay with your board
- think safety first

What would happen if you didn't prepare for windsurfing? You might run into the beach, damage the board, freeze half to death, or injure yourself or others.

The **Making Meaning** feature illustrates the main idea of the chapter, using a photograph and a brief reading.

The **Introduction** provides a brief overview of the main points of the chapter, definitions of useful terms, and an explanation of how the skills you will learn in the chapter apply to your reading.

INTRODUCTION

You may enjoy reading for pleasure. Maybe you enjoy popular suspense novels or articles in your favorite magazines. You may not enjoy reading for recreation at all but still read the newspaper most mornings. Most of these reading activities probably go fairly smoothly for you. Why is it much harder to read and understand textbooks?

Reading and understanding the material in a textbook is very different from reading fiction or quickly reading an article in a magazine. College textbooks can be challenging to read, but they are definitely predictable! Once you know how to navigate your way through them, you will find they are a source of interesting and useful information. In this chapter, you will learn how to improve the way you read college textbooks by using prereading and active reading skills.

By using a simple system, prereading, reading a textbook can actually be

STRUCTURED INSTRUCTION AND EXERCISES

EXERCISE 3-A   Write a sentence using each of the following words:

1. player

   _____

2. playful

   _____

3. plays

   _____

4. played

   _____

5. replay

   _____

The **Structured Instruction and Exercises** section includes clear explanations of the topics covered in the chapter. You will have many opportunities to learn and practice reading skills by reading various selections and completing the exercises and activities that follow.

In **Practicing What You Have Learned,** you begin to apply what you have learned in a variety of activities related to readings of different types, lengths, and levels of difficulty.

PRACTICING WHAT YOU HAVE LEARNED

PRACTICE 3-1   **Word Parts**

Circle the correct answer.

1. The present-day English language developed from

   a. Old French.

   b. Old English.

   c. Greek.

   d. Latin.

   e. all the above.

SUMMARY

When you preread a textbook assignment, you should use some or all of the following strategies:

- Read the **title** and **subtitle**.
- Read the **preface**. You may not want to read the entire preface. However, you should read the author's reasons for writing the book, the topics covered, and the audience for whom the book is written.
- Read the main headings and subheadings.
- Look for words in **bold** print and *italics*.
- Look for **bullets** that give important information about the topic.
- Look at **pictures, graphs, charts, maps**, and other **graphics** in the chapter that provide additional information in a visual format.
- Look over the **glossary, index**, and other end-of-text features that can help the you understand the text better. Words from the text in **bold** or *italics* are usually found in either the glossary or the index.

The **Summary** lists the main points covered in the chapter in a brief format that you can refer to for a quick review.

The **Mastery Level Exercises** give you further experience in reading and interacting with different kinds of texts and the chance to apply skills that you should now feel confident in using.

MASTERY LEVEL EXERCISES

MASTERY 1-1 **Prereading a History Textbook:** *The Struggle for Civil Rights*

To answer the following questions, refer to the section titled "Lyndon Johnson's Role" that appears page 00.

1. Which president got civil rights laws passed in Congress?

_____

LOOKING BACK

Do you remember reading about the questions you should ask yourself before you start reading? The questions you should ask are:

- Who are the main characters
- What is going on?
- When does the story take place?
- Where does the story take place?
- Why are the characters doing what they are doing?
- How do the characters react in the story, or how does the story end?

If you ask yourself these questions before you start reading, your brain will look for the answers as you read. This is active reading. As a reader, you are thinking about what you are reading by asking and answering those six questions.

The **Looking Back** sections in Chapters 2 through 7 contain readings and activities that give you the opportunity to apply skills you learned in earlier chapters.

Reader Response activities are writing exercises that give you a chance to think about your life experiences and express yourself in different written forms.

READER RESPONSE 1-1

1. Did the title and subtitle help you think about what you already knew about the topic? _____ Name three things you already knew about working in a nursing home:

_____

_____

_____

ONLINE PRACTICE

Go to **MyReadingLab** at www.myreadinglab.com. Click on **Reading Road Trip**, and select your textbook or the **Pioneer Level**.

1. For further practice with **prereading skills**, take a Road Trip to **Rocky Mountain National Park**.
2. For further practice with **active reading strategies**, take a Road Trip to **New Orleans**.

Online Practice guides you to Reading RoadTrip for supplemental reading lessons that correspond with subjects covered in the chapters.

USEFUL FEATURES

There are several features of the book that you will find useful throughout your course.

WORDNOTES

caregivers	people who provide care for others
wail	to cry out in pain or frustration
attendants	those who help or support others
employment	job choices

WORDNOTES are lists of words and their definitions that appear at the end of many of the reading selections in the chapters. Shown in blue print in the readings, these are words that may be new to you. The words and their definitions are also listed in alphabetical order in Appendix A at the end of the book. Appendix A includes extra lines for you to write in words and their definitions that you want to add to your own growing vocabulary.

Progress Charts, printed at the end of each chapter, provide a record of your reading progress throughout the semester. Each one also contains a section that lets you evaluate how you think you are doing.

NAME _____ DATE _____

PROGRESS CHART   CHAPTER **1**

SECTION ONE

Fill out the number of correct answers you have for each item below. Your instructor will tell you how to calculate your percentage score.

PRACTICE 1-1   Number right _____ out of a possible score of 5.   Percentage score _____

PRACTICE 1-2   Number right _____ out of a possible score of 3.   Percentage score _____

PRACTICE 1-3   Number right _____ out of a possible score of 2.   Percentage score _____

STUDY TIP

What to Look for When Prereading

Use the following clues to preread reading assignments in this book and all your college reading assignments:

• Read titles, subtitles, and headings.
• Read bulleted information.
• Check visual information (charts, graphs, photos, etc.).
• Look for important words printed in italics, bold, or color.
• Think about what you already know about the topic.
• Predict what the reading will say before you read it.
• Check your predictions against the information in the reading. Change your predictions as you read new material.

Special **boxes** appear throughout the chapters to highlight important information, for example, rules for spelling words and separating them into syllables. You can refer to these boxes when you need help completing the chapter activities or when you want a quick review.

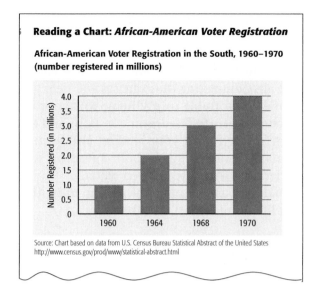

Reading a Chart: *African-American Voter Registration*

African-American Voter Registration in the South, 1960–1970
(number registered in millions)

Number Registered (in millions)

4.0
3.5
3.0
2.5
2.0
1.5
1.0
0.5
0

1960   1964   1968   1970

Source: Chart based on data from U.S. Census Bureau Statistical Abstract of the United States
http://www.census.gov/prod/www/statistical-abstract.html

Visual aids, such as photos, maps, charts, and graphs, are placed throughout the text to make it more interesting, to illustrate the readings, to make points about the topics you are studying, and to provide opportunities for you to practice the skills needed for reading visual material.

The **Glossary** (Appendix B) at the end of the book clearly defines all the words in bold black print from the book that refer to skills, special terms used in reading instruction, and parts of speech. When you see a technical word or phrase in a chapter, you can refer to the Glossary for a quick definition to help you remember and understand the related instruction.

Appendix B

Glossary of Technical Terms

academic   related to school skills

adjective   a word that describes a noun or pronoun

adverb   a word that tells something about a verb, adjective, or another adverb

antonym clue   a word that means the opposite of the unknown word is used

context clues   hints in the text that help the reader understand what unfamiliar words mean

credits   a list of the names of the people whose writing, photography, or artwork have been included in a textbook

READING SELECTIONS

Making Meaning contains many stories, poems, charts, maps, and informative essays. There are also excerpts from newspapers, magazines, and college textbooks similar to the ones you will be using in your classes. The topics they cover range from education and the sciences to stories of real events, past and present. From buffaloes to tornadoes and everything in between, we hope you will enjoy the variety of readings and that you will find the stories relate to your life and interests.

We also encourage you to read all the readings. Some are quite short and easy to read. Others take more time and thought. Some will challenge you to use all the skills you will be learning in class. A variety of exercises and activities, as well as ideas for writing, follow each reading. We encourage you to read, answer, and respond to them all. Completing the exercises will help you practice skills, that, as you become comfortable using them, will improve your reading. Writing or typing your answers to discussion questions and the Reader Response activities will strengthen both your reading and writing skills. Writing helps you make sense of your thoughts about a reading, and also helps you connect to and understand the material even better.

Reading is a powerful tool. *Making Meaning* can enable you to bring this tool into your education and your life. It might just feel like flying!

Preparing to Read

CHAPTER PREVIEW

In this chapter, you will learn to preread or preview a textbook. **Prereading** is a basic skill that helps you take control of your college reading assignments. Prereading involves paying attention to the following:

- **Title, subtitles, and information in bold print, *italics*, or color**
- **Preface or introduction**
- **Chapter titles**
- **Bullets**
- **Pictures, graphs, and charts**
- **Glossary and index**
- **Beginning, middle, and end of the reading selection**
- **Connecting what you read to prior knowledge**
- **Predicting what the reading selection will cover**

MAKING MEANING

Would you love to windsurf? What would you do to prepare? An article for beginners explains that you must:

- learn the patterns of boat traffic
- prepare for weather conditions (e.g., wear wetsuit, booties, etc.)
- learn the International Distress Signal
- learn how to read the wind
- stay with your board
- think safety first

What would happen if you didn't prepare for windsurfing? You might run into the beach, damage the board, freeze half to death, or injure yourself or others.

Just as you should prepare to windsurf, you should prepare to read by prereading. Without prereading, you might not understand the material fully, get frustrated and quit, or waste your time rereading the material several times to make sense of it. Prereading can get you off and sailing, just like the windsurfer in the picture.

INTRODUCTION

You may enjoy reading for pleasure. Maybe you enjoy popular suspense novels or articles in your favorite magazines. You may not enjoy reading for recreation at all but still read the newspaper most mornings. Most of these reading activities probably go fairly smoothly for you. Why is it much harder to read and understand textbooks?

Reading and understanding the material in a textbook is very different from reading fiction or quickly reading an article in a magazine. College textbooks can be challenging to read, but they are definitely predictable! Once you know how to navigate your way through them, you will find they are a source of interesting and useful information. In this chapter, you will learn how to improve the way you read college textbooks by using prereading and active reading skills.

By using a simple system, prereading, reading a textbook can actually be fun and rewarding. **Prereading** means looking over the textbook before beginning to read it word by word. It means reading certain material (titles, introduction, subheads, charts, etc.) in an organized way, asking yourself questions, and predicting what the reading might be about. Prereading helps you form ideas about what you will learn, so when you read the full text you know what to expect. Often you are able to predict some of the information you will read about. Prereading helps you make meaning from the textbook, organize information, recall information, and reduce the stress that often goes along with college reading assignments.

Perhaps reading a textbook—this one or any other—requires work, but it can also be very rewarding. Your reward will be increased knowledge and reading comprehension, to say nothing of higher grades.

STRUCTURED INSTRUCTION AND EXERCISES

PREREADING

Read the following information, which you might find in a book on career choices.

Working in a nursing home is not easy. Making the decision to be part of a team of caregivers demands careful thought on your part. Questions you should ask yourself about working in a nursing home include the following: Do the patients look well cared for? When you enter the nursing home, is there a bad odor? Are the employees full of energy and helpful to each other and to the patients? Does the food look fresh? Do the patients want to eat the food? Do the patients wail for help, and are there enough attendants to support the number of patients? Once you answer these questions about the nursing home and talk to the employees about how they feel about working there, you can make a better decision about your employment options.

When you read this paragraph, did you find it difficult to understand or to remember what you had read? Were you motivated to read the information, or did you just want to be finished with it? Many students hurry through their reading assignments without taking the time to preread them. They don't read and think about the helpful hints that are often included to help readers. Now try prereading the same information in the following reading. Look at all the clues that have been added to help you make meaning from the article.

Choosing a Job in a Nursing Home
Questions to Consider

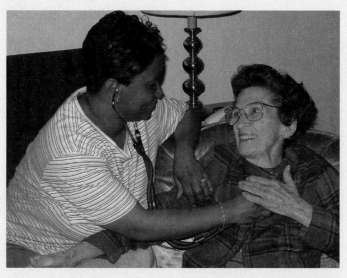

Working in a nursing home is not easy. Making the decision to be part of a team of **caregivers** demands careful thought on your part. Questions you should ask yourself about working in a nursing home include the following:

- Do the patients look well cared for?
- When you enter the nursing home, is there a bad odor?
- Are the employees full of energy and helpful to each other and to the patients?
- Does the food look fresh? Do the patients want to eat the food?
- Do the patients wail for help, and are there enough attendants to support the number of patients?

Once you answer these questions about the nursing home and talk to the employees about how they feel about working there, you can make a better decision about your employment options.

WORDNOTES

caregivers	people who provide care for others
wail	to cry out in pain or frustration
attendants	those who help or support others
employment options	job choices

TITLE, HEADINGS, HIGHLIGHTED PRINT, VISUALS, AND BULLETS

The **title** of the article is the first bit of information you are given. Think about what the title tells you: "Choosing a Job in a Nursing Home" indicates the topic of the article. A **subtitle** (if one is included) can be even more informative. The subtitle in this reading, "Questions to Consider," lets you know there are many questions you should ask about working in a nursing home. Even though you feel like skipping to the body of a reading, don't skip over the title and headings. You might miss something useful.

Next, notice words in the article that are in *italics* or **bold print**; the author is highlighting them to help you understand the reading. Sometimes readings provide definitions of these words as well. In this textbook, words you might be unfamiliar with in the readings are printed in color and defined in the section called WORDNOTES at the end of each reading.

Visual material gives you additional information about a reading. It may consist of a chart, a graph, a cartoon, or a photograph. For example, the photo shown with this article shows a nursing home employee with a resident. From the smiles on their faces, you would judge that they have a close relationship; the employee is enjoying her work, and the resident is relaxed and happy. The photo explains and adds to the meaning of the reading. Be sure to study visuals carefully.

Another helpful visual is a list marked with **bullets**. A bulleted list points out information you need to know. Bullets are easy to find when you see a reading for the first time. In this article, the bulleted list gives the questions to ask that were promised in the subtitle.

CONNECTING TO PRIOR KNOWLEDGE

Early educators believed that students were like empty vases. The teacher's job was to "pour" knowledge into the empty vases and fill students with information. Today, educators understand that students are not empty vases but people full to the brim with knowledge and ideas that they have accumulated (collected) from all their experiences in the past. Educators know now that when students connect what they already know (prior knowledge) to the new information and ideas they are reading about, they can remember and use new ideas better.

Astoria Bridge

When you read, think of yourself as a bridge builder connecting each new idea to existing ones. Ask yourself if the bulleted information in the article is something new you are unfamiliar with or something you already have some knowledge about. What can you remember from your own experiences at this point in your prereading that relates to nursing homes?

PREDICTING WHAT A READING IS ABOUT

As you read, you can often predict what a reading will be about. This process helps you retain what you read. When you read further, you add to your knowledge of a topic. As a result, you might change your predictions about what will come next. By the time you get to the last sentence of the article about working in a nursing home, you should have a good idea of what kind of answers to the questions would make the job a pleasant experience, based on what you have learned.

Now read the article "Choosing a Job in a Nursing Home" again. This time, pay attention to the title, subtitle, bulleted list, and words in color, and take into account what you already know about nursing homes. When you finish, ask yourself what you learned. Did reading the article in this way increase your knowledge or understanding of the topic?

STUDY TIP

What to Look for When Prereading

Use the following clues to preread reading assignments in this book and all your college reading assignments:

- Read titles, subtitles, and headings.
- Read bulleted information.
- Check visual information (charts, graphs, photos, etc.).
- Look for important words printed in italics, bold, or color.
- Think about what you already know about the topic.
- Predict what the reading will say before you read it.
- Check your predictions against the information in the reading. Change your predictions as you read new material.

In this textbook:

- Check the WORDNOTES at the end of the readings to read the definitions of the words printed in color.

READER RESPONSE 1-1

1. Did the title and subtitle help you think about what you already knew about the topic? _____ Name three things you already knew about working in a nursing home:

_____

_____

_____

2. By reading the bulleted information and looking at the photograph, what did you predict that the passage might tell you?

_____

_____

_____

EXERCISE 1-A

1. Write the title of the article: _____

2. Write the subtitle of the article: _____

3. List the words printed in color (WORDNOTES): _____

_____

4. Use two of the words printed in color (WORDNOTES) in sentences:

A. _____

B. _____

5. How did the words printed in color (WORDNOTES) and the bulleted information help you make meaning from the article?

_____

_____

EXERCISE 1-B   What three pieces of information can you recall from the article?

1. _____

2. _____

3. _____

READER RESPONSE 1-2   Write two more questions you could ask if you were considering working in a nursing home:

1. _____

_____

_____

2. _____

_____

_____

EVERYDAY PREREADING

How many times a week do you look at a TV guide? _____

What do you look for? _____

How many times do you look at the movie guide in the newspaper?

_____

What steps do you take to find when and where a movie is playing?

_____

_____

The steps you take to find out this kind of everyday information require prereading. You look at the titles and words printed in bold that tell you things like times and places, and you skim through lots of regular print to find exactly the information you need. You probably do this without thinking much about it. These are the same skills you need to use for reading assignments in college classes. For example, in the schedule that follows Figure 1-1, you can find out when you need to have the assignment ready for each class by looking at the dates printed in bold in the left column.

Figure 1-1 Sample Class Schedule

> ## Class Schedule
>
> **Jan. 20** Introduction to course.
> Write a short paragraph about why you chose to attend this college.
>
> **Jan. 22** Chapter 1 in our text, pp. 20–30. Quiz on vocabulary.
>
> **Jan. 24** Bring newspaper article to class for group work.

PREREADING AND VISUAL MATERIAL

In the same way that you do everyday prereading, you can read tables, maps, graphs, and other visual texts in college textbooks. Like a TV guide and a class schedule, every piece of graphic material has a purpose.

Look at the map of Oklahoma City in Figure 1-2. Using the prereading skills you have learned, what can you predict about the purpose of the map?

_____

_____

_____

_____

This is a map of an area of Oklahoma City, Oklahoma, that many people visit. Within just a few miles, there are five great entertainment attractions for families. Two of these places are famous across the country: the National Cowboy and Western Heritage Museum and the Softball Hall of Fame. Notice the information in **bold** print. What does it tell you about how to find these tourist attractions?

_____

_____

_____

Figure 1-2 Map of Vacation Area of Oklahoma City, Oklahoma

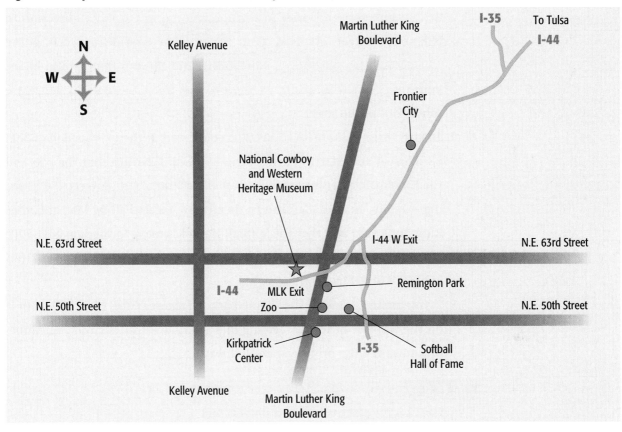

EXERCISE 1-C Complete the following statements. (Some answers are filled in for you. See the WORDNOTES that follow for definitions of the words printed in bold in the exercise.)

1. Finding your way on a map begins with checking the directions. The top of a map is always north. Notice the other directions as well. West is on the left side of the map, east is on the _____ side, and south is at the _____ of the map.

2. There are also highway and street markers. You can see that Interstate Highway 35 (I-35) joins Interstate Highway 44 (I-44) at two points. Streets shown on the map are _____, _____, which run north and _____ and _____, and _____ which run east and _____.

3. To find the National Cowboy and Western Heritage Museum traveling into Oklahoma City from the northeast on I-44 (upper-right corner of map), you would exit on N.E. 63rd Street and drive _____ (direction) to 1700 N.E. 63rd Street. If you are driving into the city from

the west on I-44, you would exit on Martin Luther King Boulevard and drive a very short distance in a _____ direction to N.E. 63rd Street. At N.E. 63rd Street, you would turn left going _____ (direction), and the museum would be on your _____ on the _____ (direction) of the street.

4. To visit three of these locations, you could start at the **intersection** of N.E. 63rd Street and Martin Luther King Boulevard. Notice that the zoo and the Kirkpatrick Center, which includes a **planetarium**, **interactive** learning **exhibits**, an art **gallery**, and a theatre, are located along Martin Luther King Boulevard and that the Softball Hall of Fame is located on N.E. 50th Street. You would travel in a _____ direction from N.E. 63rd Street to see these sights.

5. If you missed going to the theme park at Frontier City, you could visit it on the way out of town traveling in a _____ direction toward Tulsa on Interstate Highway _____ .

WORD NOTES

intersection	a place where two streets cross
exhibits	objects or collections of objects on display
gallery	room or building used to display objects of art
interactive	allowing two-way communication (e.g., an interactive video game)
planetarium	room or building containing a device that projects images of astronomical bodies, such as the solar system, on a curved ceiling

HOW TO PREVIEW (OR PREREAD) A TEXTBOOK

Previewing is another word for prereading. It is a strategy that helps a reader become familiar with a textbook before reading and studying it in detail. This process is very similar to reading a map. There are important and consistent details that will help you get an overall picture of a textbook's content and purpose so that you can find your way around it with confidence.

Title Page

The first piece of information is the **title page**, which lists the full title of the book, the author's name, the publisher of the book, and when the book was published. The date of publication is important. What you learn in college should be based on the most current information, and a recent publication date indicates a book contains up-to-date information.

Figure 1-3 Sample Brief Contents

Brief Contents

Table of Contents

The **table of contents,** which usually follows the title page, gives you an excellent opportunity see what a book covers, which topics are emphasized, in what order the topics are placed, and the special features each chapter contains. Many college textbooks have two tables of contents: a short list of the chapter numbers and titles and a longer list that gives details about everything each chapter covers. The "Brief Contents" in Figure 1-3, from *Fundamentals of Psychology: The Brain, the Person, the World,* gives you valuable hints about what the book is about.

Preface or Introduction

The **preface** or **introduction** to a textbook, often called "To the Student," provides a brief road map to using the book and describes special features of the book. For example, the preface to the psychology textbook gives students information about the field of psychology and what they may expect to learn about it. The preface also describes the organization of the textbook, features in the chapters, and some of the materials that the book offers to students, such as real-life stories, exercises, illustrations, and activities. The preface to a textbook, like the title, is a vital part of the book that you should always consult at the beginning of a college course.

Chapter Structure

Each chapter in a textbook usually starts with an introduction and an outline or list of objectives, which give a brief summary of what is going to be discussed in the chapter. (If you look at the beginning of this chapter, you will see a "Chapter Preview" box that lists what this chapter covers.) Headings within each chapter provide an outline of the material it contains. Other features to look for in a chapter are shown in Figure 1-4, an example from the full contents page of *Fundamentals of Psychology*. The full contents page contains a detailed listing of what is covered in Chapter 1, "Psychology: Yesterday and Today." Within the chapter, main headings are used for major points, and minor headings, or subheadings, further explain those main points. For example, the main heading "Levels of Analysis: The Complete Psychology" is supported by two subheadings, "Events Large and Small" and "All Together Now."

Figure 1-4 Sample Contents

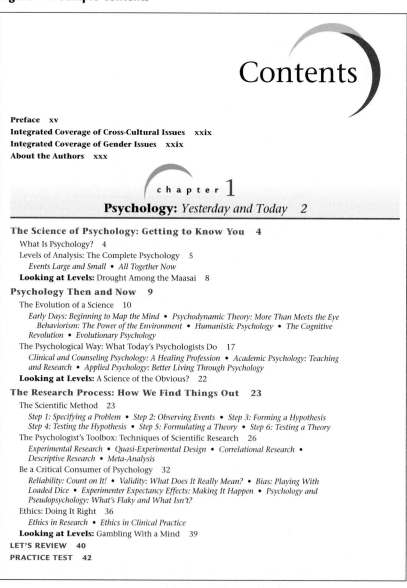

Graphics and Other Aids

Tables and figures, quotes, drawings, photographs, marginal notes, and captions may also be included in a chapter to help you grasp the points the author is making. These guides provide you with additional information about the topics being discussed and offer you help in isolating and understanding the main ideas in the chapter.

Text Boxes

Within each chapter, there may be information set off from the main text. It might be in the form of text boxes containing summaries of important rules, quotations, or helpful tips, notes in the margin (for example, brief definitions of words or technical terms), or shaded text that relates to ideas that connect to themes throughout the book.

Typeface

Particular styles of type will be used to gain your attention as you read. In the psychology textbook, and in *Making Meaning*, important words and terms are shown in **bold** print. In Figure 1-4, the title word, **psychology**, is in bold. It is followed by a definition, "the science of mental processes and behavior." Look in the "Chapter Preview" box at the beginning of this chapter for another example: **prereading** is followed by an extensive definition of the word. *Italics* and underlining are also used to indicate important information. For example, turn ahead to page 28, and see that words in Practice 1-2 are shown in italics as part of the instructions for that exercise. Bulleted lists are brief, useful summaries of important information. Like the list of topics in the "Chapter Preview" section in each chapter of this book, bulleted lists are helpful when you are reviewing a chapter or studying for a test.

EXERCISE 1-D   Although not everything on the following list will be in every book you read, you can learn a lot about what to expect from a text by taking the time to preview and look for these features. Choose a textbook from another class you are taking and use it to practice your prereading skills by answering the following questions. (You can preview *Making Meaning* if you do not have another textbook.)

1. Does Chapter 1 contain an introduction? _____ If so, how many paragraphs does it contain? _____

2. Are the objectives or key topics of the chapter listed at the beginning? _____ If yes, how many are listed? _____

3. What is the first heading in Chapter 1? _____

4. Are there any subheadings after the first heading? _____

   If yes, what are they? _____

   _____

   _____

5. Are photographs included in the chapter? _____ marginal

   notes? _____

Now look for additional visual information:

1. Is any special information set apart inside a box? _____

2. If yes, on which page does the first box appear? _____

3. List any special styles of type used on the first four pages of Chapter 1
   (bold print, italics, capital letters, different fonts, etc.). _____

End-of-Text Features

The end of a textbook also usually contains important information.

Glossary.   Many textbooks include a special dictionary at the end called a **glossary.** The glossary contains words that have particular meaning and importance and need to be explained and learned in order for the reader to understand the content of the book. In Figure 1-5, the term *academic psychologist* is defined as "The type of psychologist who focuses on conducting research and teaching." As you can see, this definition relates to how the word is used in the field of psychology.

Figure 1-5 Sample Glossary

Glossary

Absolute threshold: The smallest amount of a stimulus needed in order to detect that the stimulus is present.

Academic psychologist: The type of psychologist who focuses on conducting research and teaching.

Accommodation (in the eye): Occurs when muscles adjust the shape of the lens so that it focuses light on the retina from objects at different distances.

Accommodation (in Piaget's theory): The process that results in schemas' changing as necessary to cope with a broader range of situations.

Acquisition: The technical name given to the initial learning of the conditioned response (CR).

Action potential: The shifting change in charge that moves down the axon.

Index.   An **index** is an alphabetized list of topics with page numbers to guide you to the page(s) on which each topic appears. You will find that the index at the back of a textbook can be very helpful when you need to look up information quickly on a particular topic. Some textbooks also include an index that lists important people mentioned in the chapters. *Fundamentals of Psychology* has two indexes: a name index and a subject index. Figure 1-6 is an example of a subject index.

Figure 1-6 Sample from Subject Index

AA (Alcoholics Anonymous), 474
Abnormality, defining, 415–419. *See also*
   Psychological disorders
Absolute threshold, 89
Abstinence violation effect, 444
Abuse
   of children, 145
   substance, 358, 399
Academic psychologists, 19–20

Bibliography.   A **bibliography** (sometimes called references) contains a list of the sources an author referred to when preparing a book. It is an alphabetical listing based on authors' last names or, if there is no known author, the first important word of the title of the publication. Other information included for each entry is the name of the publisher, the city and date of publication, and the page numbers of the material cited. Figure 1-7 is an example of a bibliography entry from *Fundamentals of Psychology.*

Figure 1-7 Sample Bibliography Entries

Keith, P. M., & Schafer, R. B. (1991). *Relationships and well-being over the life stages*. New York: Praeger.
Keitner, G. I., Solomon, D. A., Ryan, C. E., Miller, I. W., & Mallinger, A. (1996).
Prodromal and residual symptoms in bipolar I disorder. *Comprehensive Psychiatry, 37,* 362–367.

Appendix.   It is common to have a special section at the back of a textbook called an **appendix.** (Some books have several **Appendices,** which is the plural of *appendix.*) Each appendix contains very specific information or activities related to the course you are taking. For instance, a reading textbook might have an appendix titled "Appendix I: Vocabulary."

Additional Readings or Credits Sections.   Often you will find a section in the back of a textbook that lists other books on topics covered in the textbook. This may be called "Additional Reading Suggestions" or something similar. Also, you will see a section titled "Credits," with a list of the names of people whose writing, photography, or artwork have been included in the book.

EXERCISE 1-E   Using a textbook of your choice, answer the following questions.

1. Does your book have a glossary? _____

2. What is the first word listed in it? _____

3. Look up a topic in the index and write it here. _____
_____

4. On which page(s) does the topic appear in the textbook? _____

5. The bibliography will contain several items. Choose one and write the entire entry here. _____
_____
_____

6. If the textbook has appendices, how many? _____ Write the names of each appendix here. _____
_____
_____
_____

7. List two names from the additional readings list and/or credits sections in your textbook.
_____
_____

Once you are familiar with the organization of the first chapter of a textbook, you will find that the other chapters in the book are often very similar, although some might be organized a little differently because of the subjects they cover. The features of Chapter 1 in this and most of your textbooks will usually be repeated throughout the book, so you can be fairly certain about how the other chapters in the textbook will be organized and confident that you will be able to learn new ideas as they are presented in the book.

READING A TEXTBOOK CHAPTER

Reading a chapter from a textbook is very similar to reading a newspaper and scanning the headlines for major news, checking a TV guide to find movie and TV times, or turning to the sports pages for the baseball scores. Although the subjects in most textbooks are more **academic** (related to school skills), you use the same reading skills. You will find it easier to read, understand, and remember the information in your textbook if you use a system for studying each chapter.

Three Keys to Successful Reading

1. **Preview and skim first**
   In addition to **previewing** a chapter as discussed earlier, you can get an idea of the chapter's content by skimming. **Skimming** is reading for an

overall idea by looking for major ideas and skipping over details. Previewing and skimming help you:

- overcome any hesitations and just get started on whatever assignment you need to complete
- get an overall "feel" for the chapter—a sense of whether it is dry and difficult or light and friendly
- get an overview of the organization and features of the chapter
- get an idea of the content and the major topics discussed
- get an idea of how long the chapter is so you can estimate how much time you need to read it

2. **Read small sections at a time**

In most textbooks, each section within a chapter deals with a specific topic. Reading one section at a time helps you remember what you have read. To break a chapter down into more manageable chunks, you can divide it into sections based on main headings (read from one main heading to the next). When you read a section from a chapter, you should:

- read only the material under *one* heading or subheading at a time
- read the preview and introduction of the section, if provided
- read any subheadings
- look for vocabulary words in **bold** print
- underline words that are **bold**, *italicized*, or Capitalized
- ask yourself, "Do I understand the focus of this section?"

3. **Read actively**

You will get the most out of what you read by being actively involved in reading. There are several ways you can become an involved reader.

- **Ask yourself questions before you read the material.**

Who?	Who is this reading about?
Where?	Where did it take place?
What?	What happened?
Why?	Why did it happen?
When?	When did it happen?
How?	How did it happen?

- **Turn each heading and subtitle in a section into a question.**
  For example, if the heading is End-of-Text Features, you might ask yourself, "What are end-of-text features?"
- **Look for the answers to your questions.**
  As you read, look for answers to the questions you asked when you were prereading. If your question was "What are end-of-text features?" your answer might be "End-of-text features can include a glossary, appendix, bibliography, and additional readings."
- **Read with purpose.**
  For example, are you reading to prepare for a class discussion? An exam? To write a paper? Each of these tasks requires different information, so knowing what you are looking for will make you a more effective reader.

- **Notice supporting details.**
  Look for dates, numbers, facts, or examples that provide additional information about or explanations of the topic (see Chapter 7, "Identifying Supporting Details").

- **Relate what you have just read to your prior knowledge and experience.**
  For example, are you reading about the Civil War? Remember what you already know about it. Perhaps you have seen a film about it recently. Try to recall everything you know or think you know about that time in our country's history. Connecting new information to what you already know helps you understand it better and remember it more easily.

- **Read *ideas*, not just words.**
  Make sure you understand what the author is saying, what the ideas are behind the words used to explain them. If the information is new to you, can you relate it to what you already know? If you can, you will find it easier to understand the new material. What opinions are you beginning to develop about the material based on what you have read?

- **Do something *active* with what you read.**
  Relate to the material in as many ways as you can. Talk about it with other students in your class, think about how it connects to what you already know about the topic, write a brief summary of what you have read, or see how well you can answer the questions you asked when you preread the material.

EXERCISE 1-F   Preview and skim a chapter from the text you have been working with in previous exercises and fill in the following information as completely as you can.

1. Chapter title: _____

2. Subtitle (if any): _____

3. All main headings: _____

   _____

   _____

   _____

4. One main heading and its subheadings: _____

   _____

   _____

   _____

5. Write the first sentence under each of the two subheadings listed in question 4: _____

   _____

   _____

6. Bulleted information (choose one list):

   _____

   _____

   _____

7. Describe any pictures, graphs, maps, or charts:

_____

_____

_____

8. What prior knowledge do you have about the topic discussed in the chapter?

_____

_____

_____

9. Turn two main headings and two subheadings into questions and write them below.

_____

_____

_____

_____

_____

_____

_____

10. What do you predict the reading will tell you?

_____

_____

_____

PRACTICING WHAT YOU HAVE LEARNED

PRACTICE 1-1   **Prereading a History Textbook: *The Struggle for Civil Rights***

First skim and then read the following chapter preview from an American history textbook. Use the prereading and active reading strategies you have just studied.

The Struggle for Civil Rights
The Early 1960s

Chapter Preview

For politicians in the early 1960s, taking a stand on **civil rights** was risky. The white southerners who controlled Congress were clearly against equal rights for African-Americans. They promised to withhold their votes on important farm and foreign policies if civil rights laws were introduced. As the 1960s wore on, however, the voices of **protest** could no longer be ignored in Washington. Two presidents, with much help and pushing from many concerned groups, changed the face of civil rights in America during this time.

Key Concepts

- When he first became president in 1960, **John F. Kennedy** was not sure that he wanted to push the civil rights cause.
- President Kennedy finally took a moral stand on civil rights but was unable to pass his bill through Congress.
- **Martin Luther King, Jr.** spoke with power and passion during the **March on Washington** in August 1963.
- **Freedom Summer,** the voter registration drive in Mississippi in 1964, helped win support for voting rights for African-Americans.
- **President Lyndon Johnson** succeeded in passing the **Civil Rights Act of 1964** and the **Voting Rights Act of 1965.**

Key Terms, People, and Places

John F. Kennedy, Martin Luther King, Jr., Lyndon Johnson, March on Washington, Freedom Summer, Civil Rights Act of 1964, Voting Rights Act of 1965

WORDNOTES

civil rights the rights of citizens to legal, economic, and social opportunity
protest firm objection or disapproval

Answer the following questions.

1. What is the title of this chapter? _____

2. What is the subtitle of this chapter? _____

3. The civil rights movement took place during the _____.

4. Name the presidents who were involved in the civil rights movement.

   _____

5. Name the second national figure you read about in "Key Concepts."

   _____

PRACTICE 1-2 **Prereading a History Textbook:** *The Struggle for Civil Rights*

Now, using your prereading and active reading skills, read each of the following sections of the history textbook. Answer the questions that follow each section.

Introduction

The civil rights movement of the early 1960s forced elected leaders to take a stand. At first, President **John F. Kennedy** did not want to get involved in the civil rights cause. Finally, when protest increased, he provided moral leadership and promised full support for a civil rights bill. The bill was still bottled up in Congress when he died in late 1963. The new president, **Lyndon Johnson,** made the civil rights cause his own. Major civil rights groups helped President Johnson. **Dr. Martin Luther King, Jr.** was a powerful voice for justice and equal rights. The civil rights movement reached its high point in the middle of the 1960s with the passing of the **Civil Rights Act of 1964** and the **Voting Rights Act of 1965.**

WORDNOTES

justice   fair, honest, and moral treatment

Complete the following.

1. Dr. Martin Luther King, Jr. was _____

_____

2. Use the word *protest* in a sentence. _____

_____

3. Use the word *justice* in a sentence. _____

_____

PRACTICE 1-3   **Prereading a History Textbook:** *The Struggle for Civil Rights*

The March on Washington

The March on Washington took place in August 1963. More than 200,000 people came from all over the country to call for jobs and freedom. At the march, **Martin Luther King, Jr.** gave his "I Have a Dream" speech. With power and passion, he spoke to the people at the rally and to the nation at large. He ended his speech with his famous words, "Free at last. Free at last. Thank God Almighty, we are free at last." King's words echoed around the country. Everyone was impressed, even President Kennedy who watched the speech on TV. But the civil rights bill was still stalled in Congress.

Answer the following questions.

1. When did the March on Washington take place? August _____

2. What were Dr. King's famous last words from his "I Have a Dream" speech?

_____

PRACTICE 1-4 **Prereading a History Textbook:** *The Struggle for Civil Rights*

Lyndon Johnson's Role

Three months after the March on Washington, President Kennedy was dead, and his civil rights bill was no closer to passage. When **Lyndon Johnson** became president, he let Congress know that he was going to see the civil rights bill passed, one way or another. Johnson used his political skills and his many years in Congress to gain passage of the bill.

The **Civil Rights Act of 1964** banned discrimination in public places like motels, cafés, and bus stations. It called for an end to school segregation, and it banned hiring practices that discriminated against people based on their race, sex, religion, or national origin.

Johnson was happy, but African-Americans still saw too much inequality in America. Many African-Americans in the south could not vote because of unjust laws. In the summer of 1964, civil rights groups formed a voter registration drive in Mississippi. This drive became known as **Freedom Summer**. The drive was marked by violence. Civil rights workers reported three murders, 35 shootings, 30 firebombings, and 80 mob attacks. Hundreds of workers were arrested. However, this drive pointed to the strong need for voting reform.

The **Voting Rights Act of 1965** focused on six southern states that did not have enough eligible voters registered in 1964. In 1966, 400,000 African-Americans registered to vote in the Deep South. In 1968, the number reached one million. This swelled the total number of registered African-American voters to three million by 1968. The number of African-American voters rose to four million by 1970.

The Voting Rights Act changed southern politics. It formed a new voting population, and it led to African-American representation at local, state, and national levels. The Civil Rights Act of 1964 and the Voting Rights Act of 1965 were landmarks in the history of civil rights in the United States. Both made real changes, and both had a real impact on the future of our country.

WORD NOTES

discrimination	the act of being for or against a person or group based on feelings of prejudice.
segregation	separation from the rest of society

Complete the following.

1. Use the word *segregation* in a sentence. _____

_____

2. What was the Freedom Summer? _____

_____

_____

_____

3. Put these events in the correct order: Freedom Summer, March on Washington, Kennedy became president, Voting Rights Act, Civil Rights Act. (The first one has been done for you.)

a. <u>Kennedy became president</u>

d. _____

b. _____

e. _____

c. _____

4. Define the term *discrimination:* _____

_____

PRACTICE 1-5 **Reading a Chart:** *African-American Voter Registration*

African-American Voter Registration in the South, 1960–1970
(number registered in millions)

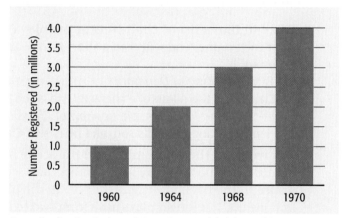

Source: Chart based on data from U.S. Census Bureau *Statistical Abstract of the United States*
http://www.census.gov/prod/www/statistical-abstract.html

1. How many African-American voters were registered in 1960? _____
1970? _____

2 What was the increase in the number of registered voters in the South in the period 1960–1970? _____

3. How many voters were registered in 1964? _____

PREREADING A PLAY

We have discussed important points to remember in reading college textbooks. Prereading activities can also help you understand and make meaning from works of literature you read in college. Plays are commonly found in literature textbooks; therefore, it is important to know how to view and make sense of the structure of a play.

Hamlet is a play by William Shakespeare. Shakespeare wrote many plays and poems. Most of them are very famous. A play is different from a chapter book because in a play, the characters talk to each other. The conversation between characters is called **dialogue**. Sometimes a character talks to him- or herself. The character speaks out loud so that the audience can hear his thoughts. When a character speaks to him- or herself, it is called a **monologue**. The play *Hamlet* has several famous monologues. The text of a play explains the setting for each scene but does not go into the detail you would find in a book. The actors in a play create the characters for the audience. The reader of a play must create the characters in his or her mind.

About the Play *Hamlet*

Hamlet is a play about a young prince named Hamlet. His father, King Hamlet, was murdered while taking a nap in his garden. King Hamlet's ghost appears to Prince Hamlet and wants revenge. Who was the murderer? It was King Hamlet's own brother, Claudius. This play is a tragedy about revenge and human weaknesses.

As you preread the following selection from *Hamlet*, you will notice several things that make a play different from a book:

1. **You will find a list of characters in the play ("Dramatis Personae").** After each name, you will read a short phrase about each character. For example:
   CLAUDIUS, *King of Denmark.*
   (Claudius is the name of a character. He is the King of Denmark.)
   HAMLET, *King Hamlet's son, nephew of Claudius.*
   (Hamlet is King Hamlet's son, and he is also Claudius' nephew.)

2. **You will find the act number and the scene number.** Like chapter numbers in a book, a play's act numbers and scene numbers help the reader and actors know where they are in the play. A short play usually has one act, but longer plays have from two to five acts. The selection from *Hamlet* that you will be reading is from the very beginning of the play. Notice that this selection is in Act I, Scene I.

3. **You will read that Scene I takes place at Elsinore Castle.** Look at the bottom of the page to see if there is any information about Elsinore Castle. Sometimes you will find helpful information at the bottom of each page (footnotes). In this case, you will learn that Elsinore Castle is in Denmark. This lets you know where the play takes place.

4. **You will see a shortened form of each character's name at the beginning of each line, or series of lines, a character says.** If you are reading the play out loud, you will not read the name of the character; you will only read what the character says. Notice the numbers on the right side of the page. They refer to the lines of the play. The first number on the right side is 5. Count backward to determine which lines are numbered 1, 2, 3, and 4. The lines are numbered to help you refer to exact lines in the play.

5. **Look at the bottom of the page for information in footnotes, such as definitions of words or explanations of words and phrases no longer in common use.** This information is numbered so you know which line in the play it refers to.

PRACTICE 1-6   **Prereading a Play: *Hamlet***

Preread the following excerpt from the play *Hamlet*, by William Shakespeare. Pay attention to the following information:

- Title
- Author
- Character list and information about each character
- Act number and scene number
- Line numbers for easy reference to helpful information
- Information at the bottom of each page

    It is also important to *think about what you already know* as you preread. Background or prior knowledge is an important part of reading and will help you make meaning from everything you read. In this case, you will want to think about castles, kings, Denmark, tragedy, soldiers, and keeping watch in the middle of the night.

The Tragedy of Hamlet, Prince of Denmark
By William Shakespeare

Dramatis Personae

CLAUDIUS, *King of Denmark.*
HAMLET, *King Hamlet's son, nephew of Claudius.*
POLONIUS, *counselor to the King.*
HORATIO, *friend to Hamlet*
LAERTES, *son to Polonius*
FORTINBRAS, *Prince of Norway*

GERTRUDE, *Queen of Denmark, mother of Hamlet*
OPHELIA, *daughter to Polonius*
MARCELLUS, *soldier*
BERNARDO, *soldier*
FRANCISCO, *soldier*

ACT I

Scene I. [Elsinore Castle. The platform of the watch.]

BER.   Who's there?
FRAN. Nay, answer me. Stand and unfold yourself.
BER.   Long live the King!
FRAN. Bernardo?
BER.   He.   5
FRAN. You come most carefully upon your hour.
BER.   'Tis now struck twelve. Get thee to bed, Francisco.
FRAN. For this relief much thanks. 'Tis bitter cold, And I am sick at heart.
BER.   Have you had quiet guard?
FRAN. Not a mouse stirring.   10
BER.   Well, good night.
        If you do meet Horatio and Marcellus,
        The rivals of my watch, bid them make haste.

Enter Horatio and Marcellus

FRAN. I think I hear them. Stand! Who's there?   15
HOR.   Friends to this ground.

_____

Dramatis Personae: Latin for "people in the drama"; **Elsinore Castle**: castle in Denmark.
Act I, Scene I: 2. **Nay**: No; **answer me**: give me the password or sign; **unfold yourself**: tell me
who you are; 3. **Long live the King**: the sign or password; 6. **You come . . . hour**: you have arrived exactly on time; 7. **'Tis**: it is; 10. **Not a mouse stirring**: nothing is going on; 13. **rivals**:
partners; **bid them make haste**: tell them to hurry; 16. **Friends . . . ground**: friends of the King
of Denmark

WORDNOTES

tragedy   a serious play with an unhappy ending that is a result of the actions of
            a character or characters

Answer the following questions.

1. Where is Elsinore Castle? _____ (Look at the information
   at the bottom of the excerpt.)

2. What do you know about castles?

   _____

   _____

   _____

3. What does it mean to "unfold yourself" from line 2? _____
   (Look at the information at the bottom of the script.)

4. Who are Bernardo and Francisco? _____
   (Check the cast list.)

5. Have you ever been a soldier? Have you ever guarded an area at night?
   Were you tired or scared? If you have never been a soldier or guard, what
   do you think it would be like?

   _____

   _____

   _____

PRACTICE 1-7   **Prereading a Play: *Hamlet***

Match the word or phrase with the correct definition. (Check the information at the bottom of the excerpt from the play.)

1. _____ nay   a. it is

2. _____ 'tis   b. tell

3. _____ bid   c. a serious play with an unhappy ending

4. _____ not a mouse stirring   d. nothing going on

5. _____ tragedy   e. no

PRACTICE 1-8   Prereading a Play: *Hamlet*

Now read the selection using all the knowledge that you have gained from prereading. Answer the following questions.

1. What are Bernardo and Francisco doing?

_____

2. What is the weather like on the watch? How do you know?

_____

3. Has the watch been quiet? How do you know?

_____

_____

4. Who is Bernardo waiting for?

_____

5. Who speaks in line 15? What does he say?

_____

PRACTICE 1-9   Prereading a Play: *Hamlet*

Now read another excerpt from Act I, Scene I of *Hamlet*, by William Shakespeare.

A Ghost appears clad in armor.

MAR. Peace, break thee off, look where it comes again!   40
BER. In the same figure like the king that's dead.
MAR. Thou art a scholar, speak to it, Horatio.
BER. Looks a' not like the king? Mark it, Horatio.
HOR. Most like, it harrows me with fear and wonder.
BER. It would be spoke to.   45
MAR. Question it, Horatio.
HOR. What art thou that usurp'st this time of night,
      Together with that fair and warlike form
      In which the majesty of buried Denmark
      Did sometimes march? By Heaven I charge thee speak.   50
MAR. It is offended.
BER. See, it stalks away.
HOR. Stay, speak, speak, I charge thee speak.
      (The Ghost vanishes)

_____

clad: dressed; Act I, Scene I: 40. **Peace, break thee off**: Stop talking; 43. **Mark it**: Remember it; 44. **harrows**: scares; 47. **usurp'st**: takes over; 50. **I charge thee speak**: I demand that you talk to us; 52. **stalks**: walks angrily

Answer the following questions.

1. Who demands that the ghost speak to them? In what line did you find this information? _____

2. What does it mean to "stalk away?" _____

3. How is the ghost dressed? _____

4. Whom do they think the ghost looks like? _____

   _____

5. Who is frightened by the ghost? In what line did you find this information?

   _____

SUMMARY

When you preread a textbook assignment, you should use some or all of the following strategies:

- Read the **title** and **subtitle**.
- Read the **preface**. You may not want to read the entire preface. However, you should read the author's reasons for writing the book, the topics covered, and the audience for whom the book is written.
- Read the main headings and subheadings.
- Look for words in **bold** print and *italics*.
- Look for **bullets** that give important information about the topic.
- Look at **pictures, graphs, charts, maps,** and other **graphics** in the chapter that provide additional information in a visual format.
- Look over the **glossary, index,** and other end-of-text features that can help you understand the text better. Words from the text in **bold** or *italics* are usually found in either the glossary or the index.
- Read a few pages at the **beginning, middle,** and **end** of the book. This will give you a sense of the author's style and how difficult the book is.
- **Use your prior knowledge** (what you already know) about a topic to help you understand new material.
- **Predict what the reading will cover** and check the accuracy of your predictions as you read.

MASTERY LEVEL EXERCISES

MASTERY 1-1   Prereading a History Textbook: *The Struggle for Civil Rights*

To answer the following questions, refer to the section titled "Lyndon Johnson's Role" that appears on page 30.

1. Which president got civil rights laws passed in Congress?

_____

2. What three changes came about because of the Civil Rights Act of 1964?

   a. _____

   b. _____

   c. _____

   _____

3. What three changes came about because of the Voting Rights Act of 1965?

   a. _____

   b. _____

   c. _____

4. Why was the civil rights movement of the 1960s so important to our country?

   _____

   _____

Match the following words with their definitions.

1. _____ civil rights   a. fair, honest, and moral treatment

2. _____ protest   b. separation from the rest of society

3. _____ segregation   c. strong objection or disapproval

4. _____ discrimination   d. the rights of citizens to legal, economic, and social opportunity

5. _____ justice   e. the act of being for or against a person or thing based on feelings of prejudice

MASTERY 1-2   Reading a Map: Time Zones of the United States

There are many reasons to read a map: to plan a trip, to learn your way around town, or to find the way to a friend's new house. The map in Figure 1-8 on the following page shows the size and shape of 48 states and the location of several cities in the United States. This is not a highway map to be used to plan a trip. However, the information it shows about time zones would be helpful in making travel plans. Prereading a map involves the same skills you use to begin to understand any kind of text: noticing titles and bold print and using prior knowledge. The first step would be to locate what you already know about a map—perhaps the location of your own home state or city.

There are four time zones in the United States. This is true of the 48 *contiguous* states. Alaska and Hawaii are not considered part of the map in Figure 1-8 on the next page because their borders do not touch these particular states. The four zones are Pacific, Mountain, Central, and Eastern. There is a difference of three hours between the West Coast and the East Coast. Study each of the zones separated by white lines, and then answer the following questions.

1. When it is 4:00 PM in Cheyenne, WY, what time is it in Columbus, OH? _____

2. What time is it in Oklahoma City, OK, when it is 10:00 PM in Charleston, SC? _____

3. In three hours, it will be midnight in Minneapolis, MN. What time is it now in San Francisco, CA? _____

4. If it will be 7:15 A.M. in Helena, Montana in 30 minutes, what time is it now in Portland, OR? _____

5. What is the meaning of the word *contiguous*? Look it up in a dictionary and write the definition. _____ _____

Figure 1-8 TIME ZONES of the United States

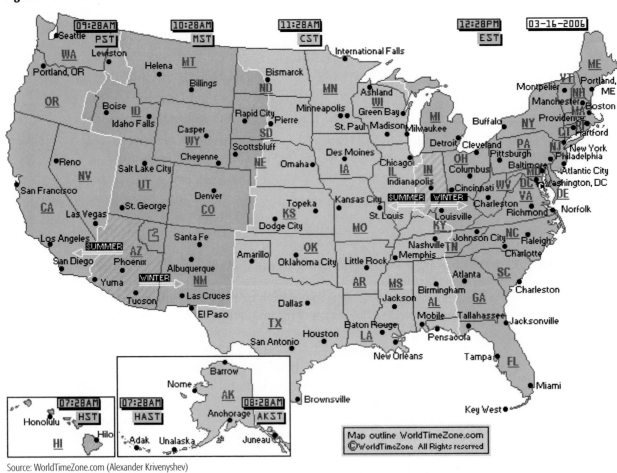

Source: WorldTimeZone.com (Alexander Krivenyshev)

MASTERY 1-3 **Reading a Chart: Stages of Psychosocial Development**

A chart is often used to help a reader make sense of complex or difficult information. Prereading a chart in a reading assignment will help you understand the information. Look over the chart that follows. Sometimes vocabulary words are explained below a chart, in nearby margins, or in the glossary in the back of the book. Always read the definitions of words that you don't know. You can try to figure out what a word means from reading the text, but it is always best to check the definition to see if your idea of what the word means is correct.

The chart in Figure 1-9 on the next page, is an example of the kind of chart you might find in a psychology book. Psychology is the study of how the brain works and how people behave. This example provides information on four of the eight stages of psychosocial development outlined by Erik Erikson. He used these eight stages to help explain how personality develops as a result of important events in a person's life. As you read the chart, think about the important events in your own or your child's life.

Figure 1-9 ERIKSON'S STAGES OF PSYCHOSOCIAL DEVELOPMENT

Stage	Age	Main Event	Tasks
Trust vs. Mistrust	0–18 months	Feeding	Baby forms a loving relationship with caregiver vs. Child does not trust caregiver
Feeling independent vs. Feeling ashamed	18 months–3 years	Toilet training	Child focuses on developing physical skills such as walking and toilet training vs. Child feels shame and doubt
Taking action vs. Feeling guilty	3–6 years	Independence	Child must take more action and explore vs. Child feels guilty choice to take more action
Learning new skills vs. Feeling like a failure	6–12 years	School	Child must learn new skills at school Child makes friends and learns to work in teams vs. Child feels like a failure

Source: Various Internet and print sources

WORDNOTES

independent	taking care of yourself without the help of others
vs.	versus (rather than, as opposed to)
psychosocial	relating to the mind (psycho) and the world around us (social)

Answer the following questions:

1. In what stage is toilet training important? _____

   _____

2. What is the main event in the Trust vs. Mistrust stage? _____

3. What is the main event in the Taking action vs. Feeling guilty stage?

   _____

4. A 3–6 year old child is in what stage? _____

5. How many years does the stage Learning new skills vs. Feeling like a failure last? _____

Match each word or phrase with its correct definition:

1. _____ physical skills
2. _____ feeding
3. _____ independent
4. _____ versus
5. _____ caregiver

a. first stage of psychosocial development
b. taking care of yourself without the help of others
c. walking, toilet training
d. person who cares for others
e. rather than; as opposed to

Read the following paragraph. Use the "Stages of Psychosocial Development" chart to answer the questions that follow.

Carlos is one year old. His father is no longer living in the home, and his mother is working two jobs. Carlos' sister is taking care of him while their mother is at work. Carlos does not always have enough to eat. Sometimes his diaper is not changed for a long time.

1. According to Erikson's stages of development, what is the main event in Carlos's life? _____

2. From what you have read, would you say that Carlos trusts his caregiver? _____ Why or why not?

_____

_____

3. When you look at your own childhood or that of a friend's, did the caregiver make sure that there was enough food to eat at all meals? _____ How did this affect your ability or your friend's ability to trust the caregiver?

_____

_____

_____

_____

_____

MASTERY 1-4 **Reading a Bar Graph: From the Bottom to the Top**

A bar graph is another part of a textbook that you can preread. The bar graph in Figure 1-10 on the next page gives information about the benefits of completing a college education.

1. Using your pre-reading skills, predict the purpose of the graph.

_____

_____

_____

Figure 1-10 Sample Bar Graph *From the Bottom to the Top*

	2000 *From the Bottom to the Top*
	A Comparison Of Average Income Between High School Dropouts and College Graduates in 2000

Average Earnings

Professional Degree	$ 72,337
Master's Degree	$ 48,972
Bachelor's Degree	$ 40,314
High School Dropouts	$ 17,337

Source: Various Internet and print sources.

2. Write the first bit of information (the title). _____

3. Notice the arrow on the graph that points upward from the bottom to the top of the graph. Using your prereading skills, predict what the arrow means.

   _____

   _____

   _____

4. Check the labels in bold print along the bottom of the graph. What does the number represent? _____

5. The other labels at the bottom of the graph are _____

   _____ .

6. Notice that two of the labels at the bottom of the graph are also found in the box on the far right side. The box is called a legend. It defines and explains the information in the graph. In the legend, under the graph's title

is an explanation of what the graph shows. What information is being compared in the graph?

_____

_____

_____

7. There are three amounts for average earnings for college graduates: _____ for a bachelor's degree, _____ for a master's degree, and $72,390 for a _____.

8. The shaded bar to the right of the graph is a list of _____.

9. The bars in the graph refer to _____, as shown in the legend.

10. The information from the legend and the shaded bar are combined in the graph. What does the graph show you about high school dropouts?

_____

_____

_____

_____

READER RESPONSE 1-3

After prereading and reading all the information in "From the Bottom to the Top," write what you think is the purpose of the graph. Be sure to tell why the arrow is important.

_____

_____

_____

_____

_____

MASTERY 1-5   **Reading a Web Page: Recycling**

Todd and Cindy Howell have recently moved to Scott Township, Pennsylvania. Their new neighborhood has a recycling program; however, the Howells have never recycled before. In an effort to become familiar with the program, Todd logged onto the Internet to learn about the program. He went to the following URL: http://www.scott-twp.com/. (See Figure 1-11 on the next page.)

The Howells knew they could recycle glass and newspapers, but they were not sure what else. They also needed to know how to prepare and package recyclables for pickup. From the link "Trash/Recycling Collection," Todd found the information he was looking for.

Figure 1-11a Sample Homepage: Scott Township

Administrative Office
Tax & Real Estate Offices
Code Enforcement Office
Meeting Calendar
Trash / Recycling Collection
Fall/Spring Clean Up
Recent Legislation
Voting Information
F A Q's
Home Occupation Info
Special Events Info
Park Information
Pool Information
Summer Recreation
Scott Twp Police Dept
Scott Twp Fire Dept
Scott Emergency Services
Scott Twp Library

Welcome to the Township of Scott

Scott Township Municipal Building
301 Lindsay Road
Scott Township, PA 15106
(412) 276-5300

Scott Township is located in the Chartiers Valley School District. It has a land area of approximately 3.86 miles and a population of 17,288. It is surrounded by Green Tree Borough, Upper St. Clair Township, Mt. Lebanon Township, Bridgeville Borough, Collier Township, Carnegie Boro, Heidelberg Boro, and the City of Pittsburgh.

To Top I Administrative Offices I Code Enforcement I Tax & Real Estate Offices I Meeting Calendar I Trash/Recycling Collection I
Fall/Spring Clean Up I Recent Legislation I Voting Information I FAQ's I Home Occupation Info I Special Events Info I Park Information I Pool Information I
Summer Recreation I Police Department I Fire Department I Emergency Services I Library

Copyright © 2003

This site was created by **R.M.L. Mere Image & Design**

Figure 1-11b Trash/Recycling Information Webpage

Home
Administrative Offices
Tax & Real Estate Offices
Code Enforcement Office
Meeting Calendar
Fall/Spring Clean Up
Recent Legislation
Voting Information
F A Q's
Home Occupation Info
Special Events Info
Park Information
Pool Information
Summer Recreation
Scott Twp Police Dept
Scott Twp Fire Dept
Scott Emergency Services
Scott Twp Library

TRASH AND RECYCLING COLLECTION INFORMATION

BFI is the Scott Township trash and recycling contactor. For a missed pick-up, please call their customer service toll free number at 1-800-464-2120 or 412-429-2600, Monday through Friday, 7:30 a.m. to 5:00 p.m.

Click here for printable 2006 schedule

Trash Pick-up

Residential Curbside Pick-up:

BFI will take all household rubbish. Items they will NOT pick-up are:

- Building Materials
- Auto body parts
- Medical waste
- Hazardous materials (such as paint, oil & gasoline)

Old paint cans which contain no liquid will be picked up by the hauler if the lid is not on and the can is empty and dry. If the paint can contains paint you should fill it with kitty litter and let it sit until the material is solid.

To dispose of medical waste please call Stericycle at 412-922-8150.

Old refrigerators and air conditioners will only be picked up by the hauler if the Freon is removed by a certified technician and a sticker verifying that the materials have been removed is placed on the appliance. You can contact a local heating/air-conditioning company to have this certification.

Once Todd became familiar with the information on this Web site, he could answer the following questions from information in the chart shown in Figure 1-12.

1. Trash and materials to be recycled are collected in the same truck.

   _____ True   _____ False

2. What is the proper way to prepare the week's collection of newspapers?

   _____

3. Which items cannot be placed in Scott Township's blue recycling bin?

   a. _____

   b. _____

   c. _____

   d. _____

Figure 1-12 Recycling Information Webpage

Recycling Information

Commercial/Municipal Institutional Annual Recycling Report - Click here to download in PDF format.

Notice of Recycling News - Click here to download in PDF format.

Ordinance 1307-90 - Click here to download in PDF format.

Ordinance 1336-91 - Click here to download in PDF format.

Residential Curbside Pickup

Scott Township is mandated by Act 101 to remind residents about the requirements of our recycling programs every six months. The following charts outline proper recycling procedures:

- The Township has provided blue recycling bins for residents' recyclables.
- Items to be commingled in the blue recycling bin are clear and colored glass, Aluminum, Bi-Metal Steel and Tin cans, and #1 – PETE and #2 – HDPE plastics.
- Use twine to bind black & white newspaper or place in brown paper bags
- Place the blue recycling bin out with your trash and they will be picked up on the same day as your trash, but by Recycling Truck.
- Garbage cans and other containers for garbage and recycling may not be placed at curbside until 5:00 pm the previous day of scheduled collection
- Containers must be removed from curbside by 9:00 pm of scheduled collection day

Material	NOT Recyclable	Recyclable	Preparation
Glass Containers	• NO Mix White Glass • NO Plate Glass • NO Light or Fluorescent Bulbs • NO Crystals	• Clear • Amber • Green	• Rinse • Remove metal rings with awl, screwdriver or needle nose pliers
All Metal Cans	• NO Paint Cans	• Aluminum • Bi-Metal Steel • Tin • Beverage Cans	• Rinse • Remove labels

Plastics	• NO #3 PVC markings:
	• some edible oils
	• household cleaners
	• personal care bottles
	• Etc
		• #1 - PETE
		  • soft drinks
		  • peanut butter jars
		  • liquor bottles
		  • edible oil
		  • cleaner bottle
		• #2 - HDPE (natural & colored)
		  • milk & juice
		  • water bottles
		  • detergent & household cleaner
		• personal care bottles
			• Rinse
			
			• Remove labels

Newsprint	• NO Glossy and colored sections	• Black and White Only	• Tie in manageable bundles • Place in brown paper bags

Todd read about plastic recycling on the chart. He was then able to answer the following questions.

1. What category of plastics may not be recycled? _____

   _____

2. Name the two divisions of recyclable plastics:

   a. _____   b. _____

3. In which division would you find soft drink and cleaner bottles? _____

READER RESPONSE 1-4

What is your opinion regarding how the Howells might react to recycling in Scott Township? Do you think they will join the neighborhood efforts and recycle?   Yes _____   No _____

Explain your answer below.

_____

_____

ONLINE PRACTICE

Go to **MyReadingLab** at www.myreadinglab.com. Click on **Reading Road Trip**, and select your textbook or the **Pioneer Level**.

1. For further practice with **prereading skills**, take a Road Trip to **Rocky Mountain National Park**.

2. For further practice with **active reading strategies**, take a Road Trip to **New Orleans**.

3. For further practice **reading graphics and visual aids**, take a Road Trip to **Wall Street, New York City**.

PROGRESS CHART

SECTION ONE

Fill out the number of correct answers you have for each item below. Your instructor will tell you how to calculate your percentage score.

PRACTICE 1-1 Number right _____ out of a possible score of 5.   Percentage score _____

PRACTICE 1-2 Number right _____ out of a possible score of 3.   Percentage score _____

PRACTICE 1-3 Number right _____ out of a possible score of 2.   Percentage score _____

PRACTICE 1-4 Number right _____ out of a possible score of 4.   Percentage score _____

PRACTICE 1-5 Number right _____ out of a possible score of 3.   Percentage score _____

PRACTICE 1-6 Number right _____ out of a possible score of 5.   Percentage score _____

PRACTICE 1-7 Number right _____ out of a possible score of 5.   Percentage score _____

PRACTICE 1-8 Number right _____ out of a possible score of 5.   Percentage score _____

PRACTICE 1-9 Number right _____ out of a possible score of 5.   Percentage score _____

MASTERY 1-1 Number right _____ out of a possible score of 9.   Percentage score_____

MASTERY 1-2 Number right _____ out of a possible score of 5.   Percentage score_____

MASTERY 1-3 Number right _____ out of a possible score of 13.   Percentage score_____

MASTERY 1-4 Number right _____ out of a possible score of 10.   Percentage score_____

MASTERY 1-5 Number right _____ out of a possible score of 6.   Percentage score_____

SECTION TWO

How do you feel? There are no wrong or right answers to how you feel about what you have learned. Circle Yes, Somewhat, or No in response to the following questions.

1. Are you using your prereading skills in other classes?   Yes   Somewhat   No

2. Do you think about what you already know about a topic before you begin reading about it?   Yes   Somewhat   No

3. As you read the title, subtitle, headings, and subheadings, do you think about what they mean?   Yes   Somewhat   No

4. Do you look for a glossary or index that can help you find information quickly? Yes   Somewhat   No

5. Do you predict what the information will cover or what will happen next in what you are reading? Yes   Somewhat   No

6. Do you check out the pictures, graphs, and charts to think about their meaning? Yes   Somewhat   No

7. Do you carefully read the bulleted information? Yes   Somewhat   No

8. Has your reading in other classes improved? Yes   Somewhat   No

9. Are you beginning to use new vocabulary words when you speak and write? Yes   Somewhat   No

SECTION THREE

Take a minute or two to reflect on your reading development. Write a few sentences or discuss with other students how this chapter has changed your reading habits.

_____

_____

_____

_____

_____

_____

_____

_____

_____

_____

Recognizing Consonants and Vowels

CHAPTER PREVIEW

In this chapter, you will learn how to sound out, or decode, words that you don't know by practicing how to pronounce

- **Consonants**
- **Vowels**

MAKING MEANING

Golden Gate Bridge, San Francisco

In this sentence, only the **vowels** in each word are shown. Can you read it?

> I -a—e- o-e- —e -o—e- -a-e —i-e –i— -y –i—e-.

Now try reading the same sentence with only the **consonants** displayed:

> - w-lk-d –v-r th- G-ld-n G-t- Br-dg- w-th m- s-st-r.

Which of these two examples was easier for you to read? For most people, the second sentence, written using only consonants, is more legible because consonants are the backbones of words. They hold words together. To form consonants, you use your lips, teeth, and tongue, which are called your articulators. The articulators work together to produce consonant sounds. The sentence you were trying to read was:

> I walked over the Golden Gate Bridge with my sister.

INTRODUCTION

The English language has 26 letters. Twenty-one letters of the alphabet are called **consonants**: *b, c, d, f, g, h, j, k, l, m, n, p, q, r, s, t, v, w, x, y,* and *z.* Consonants work by themselves and with each other to create many sounds (and sometimes no sound at all). In this chapter, you will practice recognizing several types of consonants:

- **Consonants that make one sound**

  b, f, h, j, k, l, m, n, p, r, t, v, w, y, z

- **Consonants that have to borrow their sounds from other letters**

  c—sounds like *s* or *k*

  q—sounds like *k* and always needs to be followed by the vowel *u*

  x—sounds like *z* or is pronounced by name (*x*-ray)

- **Consonants that make more than one sound**

  d—can sound like *d* or *t* or *j*

  g—can sound like *g* or *j* (also known as hard *g* or soft *g*)

  s—can sound like *s or z*

  z—can sound like *z* or *s*

- **Consonants that work together to create separate but connected sounds, which are called consonant blends (each sound is pronounced). Examples include**

  bl, br, cl, cr, dr, fl, fr

  gl, gr, nd, nk, pl, pr

  sc, scr, sk, sl, sm, sn, sp, spl, spr, st, sw

- **Consonants that work together to create one sound; these combinations are called consonant digraphs**

  ch, ck, gh, ng, ph, sh, th, wh

- **Consonants that can be silent**

  b, c, g, h, k, l, p, t, w

Five of the 26 letters in the alphabet are called **vowels:** *a, e, i, o,* and *u.* In addition, the letter *y* can sometimes be used as a vowel. Like consonants, vowels work alone or with other letters to create the sounds of words. In this chapter, you will learn about the sounds of vowels:

- Long vowel sounds ($\bar{a}$)
- Short vowel sounds ($\breve{a}$)
- Other vowel sounds

In dictionaries, a system of symbols called **diacritical marks** is used to indicate the sounds letters make in a word. For example, *pĭck* and *pīke* show two ways to pronounce the letter *i.* In this chapter, you will learn to use the symbols that indicate the various sounds vowels make depending on the words they are in.

STRUCTURED INSTRUCTION AND EXERCISES

CONSONANTS

Even though there are 21 **consonants** in the alphabet, there are even more consonant sounds. Certain letters have one consonant sound, some have more than one, and others make different sounds when they are combined with other consonants. How many different consonant sounds do you hear when you say each of the following words aloud? Circle the letters or letter combinations that make a consonant sound in each word.

these _____   chocolate _____   combed _____   rent _____

The word *these* has three consonants but only two consonant sounds. The **t** and **h** work together to produce one sound. Consonants that work together to produce one sound are called consonant **digraphs**. *Chocolate* has five consonants but only four consonant sounds. The **c** and **h** work together to produce one sound. This is another example of a digraph. *Combed* has four consonants but only three consonant sounds. The **b** is silent; therefore, it doesn't produce a sound. *Rent* has three consonants and three consonant sounds. The final sounds connect but still produce two separate sounds. These connecting consonants are called a consonant **blend**.

Single-Sound Consonants

Some consonants usually have only one sound:

b, f, h, j, k, l, m, n, r, t, v, w, y

EXERCISE 2-A   Under each word, write a word of your own that has the **bold** consonant in the same place.

Consonant at Beginning	*Consonant in Middle*	*Consonant at End*
1. **b**oat	a**b**out	cra**b**
_____	_____	_____
2. **f**ierce	a**f**ter	sni**ff**
_____	_____	_____
3. **h**orrible	re**h**eat	(not applicable)
_____	_____	
4. **J**upiter	a**j**ar	ra**j**
_____	_____	_____
5. **k**ettle	sti**ck**y	blac**k**
_____	_____	_____
6. **l**over	e**l**ated	tria**l**
_____	_____	_____

Consonant at Beginning	*Consonant in Middle*	*Consonant at End*
7. magnificent	intermediate	alarm
_____	_____	_____
8. nostril	annual	learn
_____	_____	_____
9. private	appendix	develop
_____	_____	_____
10. rapidly	irrigate	longer
_____	_____	_____
11. terrified	brightened	meet
_____	_____	_____
12. vast	aviary	relieve
_____	_____	_____
13. watch	aware	vow
_____	_____	_____
14. yeast	beyond	today
_____	_____	_____
15. zoo	frozen	freeze
_____	_____	_____

Multiple-Sound Consonants

Some consonants have more than one sound:

c, d, g, s, x, z

EXERCISE 2-B Look at the following examples. In each blank provided write your own word that has a consonant sound at the beginning, middle, or end of a word.

	Consonant at Beginning	*Consonant in Middle*	*Consonant at End*
Hard **c** as in	cup	tractor	panic
	_____	_____	_____
Soft **c** as in	city	receipt	juice
	_____	_____	_____
Hard **g** sound as in	ground	anguish	travelogue
	_____	_____	_____

	Consonant at Beginning	*Consonant in Middle*	*Consonant at End*
Soft **g** sound as in	Germany _____	agent _____	manage _____
Hard **d** sound as in	danger _____	redeeming _____	stated _____
D that sounds like *t* (This happens only at the end of the word after an unvoiced sound.)	(not applicable)	(not applicable)	passed _____
D that sounds like *j* (This happens only in the middle of a word.)	(not applicable)	educate _____	(not applicable)
S that sounds like *s* as in	seal _____	messy _____	hops _____
S that sounds like *z* as in	(not applicable)	amusement _____	boys _____
Su that sounds like *zh*. (This happens only in the middle of a word.)	(not applicable)	leisure _____	(not applicable)
X that sounds like *ks*.	(not applicable)	relaxing _____	reflex _____
X that sounds like *gz* as in	existing _____	reexamine _____	(not applicable)

Consonant Blends

Some consonants work together to create separate but connected sounds. Although connected, each sound is pronounced separately. These sounds are called consonant **blends**. Examples include:

bl, br—blend, bright   **cl, cr**—clean, cruel

dr—dress   **fl, fr**—flag, freedom

gl, gr—glass, graze   **nd, nk**—fund, stink

pl, pr—pliers, apricot

sc, scr, sk, sl, sm, sn, sp, spl, spr, squ, st, str, sw—scar, scram, ski, hassle, smudge, spare, splendid, spree, squat, stew, strewn, swat

EXERCISE 2-C Circle the blended sounds that work together but have individual sounds. (Each sound is pronounced separately.)

blue	creature	private	afraid	promote	dunk
ended	frigid	glaring	steak	streak	asked
swivel	scrape	found	approve	drained	gloomy
greasy	fright	acorn	cracker	scorch	swiped

Consonant Digraphs

Some consonants work together to create one new sound. These are called consonant **digraphs**:

ch—chicken   **ph**—phonics (ph usually makes f sound)

ck—crack   **sh**—shout

gh—ghost (hard g) rough   **th**—thought
      (f sound)

ng—ring

EXERCISE 2-D Write examples of your own in the blanks provided. You might want to use your dictionary to find words that fit each category.

	Beginning Digraph	*Middle Digraph*	*Ending Digraph*
ch as in	chick	rancher	reach
	_____	_____	_____
ck as in	(not applicable)	tricky	crack
		_____	_____
gh as in	ghost (hard g sound)	tougher (f sound)	laugh (f sound)
	_____	_____	_____
ng as in	(not applicable)	bringing	whistling
		_____	_____
ph as in	phone (f sound)	amphibian	graph (f sound)
	_____	_____	_____
sh as in	shout	hushed	rush
	_____	_____	_____
th as in	these	mother	breathe
	_____	_____	_____

Silent Consonants

Some consonants or combinations of consonants can be silent:

b, c, g, gh, h, k, l, p, t, w

b   as in *comb*—B is silent when it follows *m*. Pronounce only the *m* sound.

b   as in *subtle*—B is silent when it is before *t*. Pronounce only the *t* sound.

c   as in *quickly*—C is silent when it is before *k*. Pronounce only the *k* sound.

g   as in *gnome*—G is silent when it is before *n*. Pronounce only the *n* sound.

gh   as in *although*—Gh can be silent. Silent *gh* is often found before *t*, as in *fight*.

h   as in *shah*—H is silent at end of some words.

h   as in *hour, heir*—H is silent at beginning of some words. Pronounce beginning vowel sound.

k   as in *knife*—K is silent when it is before *n*. Pronounce only the *n* sound.

l   as in *half*—L can be silent when it is before *f* or *d*. Pronounce only the *f* or *d* sound.

p   as in *psychology, pterodactyl, pneumonia*—P can be silent at the beginning of a word. Pronounce only the next consonant: s, t, n.

t   as in *notch, watch*—T is silent when it is before *ch*. Pronounce only the *ch* sound.

w   as in *write*—W is silent when it is before *r*. Pronounce only the *r* sound.

w   as in *who*—W is sometimes silent before *h*. Pronounce only the *h* sound.

w   as in *two*—In this instance, the *w* is silent. Pronounce only the *t* sound.

EXERCISE 2-E   Circle the silent consonants in the following paragraph.

A Long Night Ahead
By M. C. Dore

The English assignment sat untouched on my desk along with sandwich crumbs and a half-drunk warm soda. I had written several pages, but the right words wouldn't come through to me. The topic had to do with women's rights in

the workplace. What did I know about it? I typed in "women's rights" in the search engine and was surprised by the hundreds of Web sites available to me. I knew it was time to read and write. I had the whole night ahead of me!

EXERCISE 2-F   Make a list of the consonants that can be silent in a word:

_____

VOWELS

Vowels are open-mouth sounds that work with consonants to form sounds in words. There are fewer vowels than consonants—only five—but vowels, like consonants, can have more than one sound and do a mighty job in language. The primary vowels are *a, e, i, o,* and *u.* In some words, *y* functions as a vowel. How do you know how vowels should sound in particular words?

Long vowels

A long vowel sounds the same as its name. When you say the list of vowels, you are pronouncing the long vowel sounds. The long vowel sound is marked in the dictionary with the straight-line **diacritical mark** (called a macron) above the letter. For example, $\bar{a}$ is pronounced as in the word *day.* The long sound of $\bar{e}$ is heard in the word *he.* The long sound of $\bar{\imath}$ is pronounced as in *find.* Long $\bar{o}$ is pronounced as in the word *home.* Long $\bar{u}$ is heard in *united.*

EXERCISE 2-G   Write the word that contains the long vowel sound shown at the beginning of each of the following pairs of words:

1. ā _____ pay, pat   4. ē _____ eat, sell

2. ī _____ pie, pin   5. ō _____ lot, low

3. ū _____ cut, cute

Long vowel sounds can also be made by combinations of vowels, such as the sound the letters *oa* make in the word *coat*, or the sound the letters *ea* make in the word *please*. Only one vowel sound is heard in each word, even though each word contains two vowels.

EXERCISE 2-H   Read each of the following words aloud. For each word, write the symbol for the long vowel sound you hear. Then write a new word that has the same long vowel sound.

	Vowel plus Sound Symbol	*New Word with Same Vowel Sound*
Example: coat	ō	soak
1. leaf	_____	_____
2. rain	_____	_____
3. you	_____	_____
4. boat	_____	_____
5. tie	_____	_____
6. creep	_____	_____
7. rein	_____	_____
8. true	_____	_____
9. float	_____	_____
10. height	_____	_____

Short vowels

A short vowel has a sound different from its name. The **diacritical symbol** of a half circle (called a breve) above the letter indicates a short vowel. A short *ă* is heard in *pat*, and a short *ĕ* is in *pen*. A short *ĭ* sound is in the word *pit*, and a short *ŏ* is heard in *pot*. The short *ŭ* makes the sound heard in *pump*.

EXERCISE 2-I   Write the word in each pair that has the short vowel sound shown at the beginning of the line.

1. ă _____ sat, sale   4. ĕ _____ be, bend

2. ĭ _____ is, ice   5. ŏ _____ shot, show

3. ŭ _____ use, us

EXERCISE 2-J Write the short vowel and symbol for each word.

Example: off ___ŏ___

1. pet _____	6. land _____
2. cut _____	7. less _____
3. rat _____	8. wig _____
4. rot _____	9. box _____
5. it _____	10. uncle _____

Other Vowel Sounds

Some vowel sounds are neither short nor long, such as the sound that *a* makes in the word *car* or the *e* sound in *here*. In both *car* and *here*, the *r* changes the sound of the vowel.

EXERCISE 2-K Write a new word with the same *îr* sound as each of the following words. Then circle the letters with the *îr* sound.

Example: stir _____circle_____

1. turn _____
2. hurt _____
3. her _____
4. birth _____
5. perk _____

Another vowel sound is shown as ə in the dictionary. This is called a **schwa** and is pronounced *uh*, as in *fun*. Any vowel can be pronounced as the schwa sound. The schwa is an unstressed or soft sound in a word. For example, the *uh* sound in the word *label* is made by the letter *e*. Notice that in the strong or stressed syllable, you can hear the long *a* sound, lā-bəl. (You will learn more about the schwa and syllables in Chapter 4, "Using a Dictionary.")

EXERCISE 2-L On the line provided write a new word with the same schwa (ə) sound as each of the following words. Then circle the letters with the schwa sound.

Example: away _____about_____

1. other _____
2. along _____

3. comma _____

4. focus _____

5. giggle _____

Silent Vowels

Some words contain vowels that you don't hear. These vowels are silent. For example, in the word *tape*, you don't hear the final *e*, and in *thief*, you don't hear the *i*.

EXERCISE 2-M Circle the silent letter in each of the following words.

1. stain   6. clue

2. lien   7. soap

3. speak   8. fine

4. grape   9. sleep

5. loaf   10. tube

The Letter *y*

The letter *y* can be a vowel or a consonant. When *y* is the first letter of a word, as in *yard*, it is usually a consonant. A *y* sounds like a long $\bar{\imath}$ when it comes at the end of a one-syllable word, as in *cry* and *fly*. A *y* at the end of a word with two syllables sounds like a long $\bar{e}$, as in *lady* and *tasty*.

EXERCISE 2-N Indicate whether the *y* in each of the following words is pronounced as a consonant, a long $\bar{\imath}$, or a long $\bar{e}$.

Example: yellow (consonant)

1. lately _____   6. year _____

2. by   _____   7. try   _____

3. yellow _____   8. baby _____

4. funny   _____   9. yell _____

5. my   _____   10. crazy _____

PRACTICING WHAT YOU HAVE LEARNED

PRACTICE 2-1 **Consonants:** *The Search Goes On*

Read the following paragraph.

The Search Goes On
By M. C. Dore

We had looked at houses on several weekends. Our Realtor was hoping <u>that</u> we'd made a decision, but we weren't even <u>close</u>. One house had <u>three</u> bedrooms, but they were really <u>small</u>. Another offered a large yard that would require lots of upkeep. We enjoyed gardening but didn't really have enough time to weed, mow, and plant that <u>much</u> yard. A third house was in a nice location but required new <u>plumbing</u> and wiring. That <u>would</u> be a little <u>risky</u>, we thought. Even <u>though</u> we were anxious to buy while the interest rates were low, we decided to look further until we were sure we chose the <u>right</u> house for us.

For each of the following words (which are underlined in the story), place a check mark in the correct column to indicate whether the sounds of the letters in bold print are a blend (consonant sounds that are connected but pronounced separately), a digraph (consonant sounds that combine to form one sound), or silent. The first one has been marked for you.

	Blend	*Digraph*	*Silent*
1. that	_____	X	_____
2. close	_____	_____	_____

	Blend	Digraph	Silent
3. three	_____	_____	_____
4. small	_____	_____	_____
5. much	_____	_____	_____
6. plumbing	_____	_____	_____
7. would	_____	_____	_____
8. risky	_____	_____	_____
9. though	_____	_____	_____
10. right	_____	_____	_____

READER RESPONSE 2-1

Write a paragraph about a house you might like to buy. Make a list of 10 words from your paragraph (as in Practice 2-1). Underline a consonant or a combination of consonants in each word. Write down whether the sound each consonant or combination of consonants makes is a simple consonant sound, blend, digraph, or silent.

PRACTICE 2-2   **Consonants:** *The Evening Dress*

Read the following short story.

The Evening Dress
By Tina Page

When I was about 14, my dad had to go to Washington, D.C., for two months. He had started a new job, and the training was there. While Dad was gone, some members of a local boys' club put up my name for a contest to be their "sweetheart." The contest winner would represent the club at public events.

The contest was like a beauty **pageant** without the swimsuit competition. At first, I thought putting my name in the contest was a mean joke. I was not very pretty. My sister was the beautiful one. When I asked the boys why they nominated me, they said I was nice. So I decided to enter the contest.

I prepared for the contest and practiced my singing. Because we did not have a lot of money and Dad was away on business, I worried about where to get a long evening dress. I had never had one. A week before the contest, my dad mailed a big box to my sister and me. We opened it and found five beautiful evening gowns.

The night of the contest, I wore the yellow gown with ribbons. I felt like a queen when I won. My dad was there that night in spirit.

W O R D N O T E S

pageant   a display or show

For each of the following words (which are underlined in the story), place a check mark in the correct column to indicate whether the sound of the letters in bold print is a blend (consonant sounds that are connected but pronounced separately), a digraph (consonant sounds that combine to form one sound), or silent.

	Blend	*Digraph*	*Silent*
1. **th**e	_____	_____	_____
2. **sw**imsuit	_____	_____	_____
3. **th**ought	_____	_____	_____
4. **pr**epared	_____	_____	_____
5. **wh**ere	_____	_____	_____
6. lo**ng**	_____	_____	_____
7. eve**n**ing	_____	_____	_____
8. ni**gh**t	_____	_____	_____
9. fe**lt**	_____	_____	_____
10. **sp**irit	_____	_____	_____

PRACTICE 2-3   **Comprehension:** *The Evening Dress*

Answer the following questions about the story.

1. Why was Tina's father unable to attend the pageant?

    _____

2. Why did the boys nominate her to be their "sweetheart"?

    _____

3. What did she do for the talent part of the contest?

    _____

PRACTICE 2-4   **Consonants:** *You Entered Me in What?!*

Read the following story.

You Entered Me in What?!
By M. C. Dore

When I was in high school, my mother entered me in a beauty contest. I was embarrassed because I knew that I was bigger than other girls and would never have a chance. My picture was even in our small town's newspaper. A friend's mother cut the picture out and gave it to me. That made me even more uncomfortable. During the contest, we had to answer questions and walk down a runway. Some of the girls had taken modeling lessons, so they knew what to do. I didn't have a clue. Instead of feeling beautiful, I felt like a clumsy ox. I didn't win the contest or even make it into the final 10. I was mortified.

Now that I'm older, I understand that my mother always considered me a <u>winner</u> and was always my biggest fan. <u>She</u> never intended to embarrass me but wanted to show me how proud she was of me. In her eyes, I did win.

WORDNOTES

mortified   very embarrassed

How many consonant sounds are in each of the following words (which are underlined in the story)?

1. when   _____

2. mother   _____

3. that   _____

4. never   _____

5. modeling   _____

6. answer   _____

7. never   _____

8. didn't   _____

9. winner   _____

10. she   _____

PRACTICE 2-5   **Comprehension: *You Entered Me in What?!***

Answer the following questions about the story.

1. Why was the girl embarrassed to be in the contest?

   _____

2. Why did other girls do better on the runway?

   _____

3. Why did the mother enter her daughter in the contest?

   _____

   _____

   _____

4. Create a chart listing details of the two "contest" stories that are the same (comparisons) and details that are different (contrasts).

   Comparisons   *Contrasts*

   _____   _____

   _____   _____

   _____   _____

   _____   _____

   _____   _____

   _____   _____

   _____   _____

READER RESPONSE 2-2

1. Have you dressed up for an important event in your life? Write a short paragraph about the special event and how you felt about it.

2. The author of "The Evening Dress" says that her father was there "in spirit." What does that mean? Write about a time that someone was with you "in spirit."

PRACTICE 2-6 **Vowels:** *At Nighttime*

Read the following poem out loud. Listen for the sounds of the long vowels *a, e, i, o,* and *u.*

> ### At Nighttime
> By Aileen Fisher
>
> At nighttime
> when it's light time,
> and the snow turns blue,
> and maple trees are empty
> as the moon shows through,
> and every star is shiny
> as a silver spike,
> I wonder
> what the weather
> up in space
> is like.
>
> From Aileen Fisher, *I Like Weather* (New York: Crowell, 1963).

How many long vowel sounds did you hear in the poem? _____
Find the words in the poem that match each of the following long vowel sounds, and write them on the line provided. Then write another word with the same long vowel sound.

1. ā _____

2. ē _____

3. ī _____

4. ō _____

5. ū _____

PRACTICE 2-7 **Vowels:** *Marathon Dancing*

Read the following paragraph. In each sentence, circle at least 3 words with short vowel sounds.

Marathon Dancing

(1) In the 1920s, young men and women, hoping to win large cash prizes, entered dance contests to see how long they could stay on their feet. (2) Some marathons lasted a week, and some lasted close to a month, until only one couple was left on the dance floor. (3) The dancers would try to keep each other awake with smelling salts and ice packs. (4) Some would go as far as shaking or jabbing their partners. (5) On occasion, the local government would put a stop to a dance **marathon** to protect the health of the dancers.

WORDNOTES

marathon   a contest of great length that requires endurance

On the following blank lines, write the words you circled in each sentence, and mark the short vowel sound in each word.

1. Sentence 1.

_____

2. Sentence 2.

_____

3. Sentence 3.

_____

4. Sentence 4.

_____

5. Sentence 5.

_____

SUMMARY

- Learning the different sounds of **consonants** and **vowels** can help you decode unfamiliar words.
- **Diacritical marks** are used to tell you how to pronounce letters ($\bar{a}$, $\breve{a}$).
- There are 21 consonants in the alphabet.
  - Consonants can have more than one sound:
  - Consonants that make one sound: *b, f, h, j, k, l, m, n, p, r, t, v, w, y, z*
  - Consonants that have to borrow their sounds from other letters: *c, q, x*
  - Consonants that make more than one sound: *d, g, s, z*
  - Consonant **blends**: combinations of consonants that create separate but connected sounds; for example: *bl, br, cl, cr, dr, fl, fr*
  - Consonant **digraphs**: combinations of consonants that create one sound; for example: *ch, ck, gh, ng, ph, sh, th, wh*
  - **Silent** consonants: *b, c, g, h, k, l, p, t, w*
- There are five vowels in the alphabet: a, e, i, o, u (and sometimes y).
- Vowels can have **long**, **short**, or **schwa** sounds.

MASTERY LEVEL EXERCISES

MASTERY 2-1   Consonants: *Directions to the Party*

Read the following party invitation. Then look at the selected words following the story. Check whether the consonants in bold print are blends, digraphs, or silent.

Directions to the Party

Start by going north on Broadway Extension until U run into the cemetery. Then turn right and head east on Danforth. Go past Coltrane. Turn left on Leawood Drive. (There's no sign, but it's across the street from the Oak Forest addition.) Look for the third house on your right. There will be an old-fashioned car out front! The party starts at 8 p.m. Bring chips and drinks. C U there.

                       Jenn

	Blend	*digraph*	*silent*
1. start	_____	_____	_____
2. north	_____	_____	_____
3. then	_____	_____	_____
4. east	_____	_____	_____
5. there's	_____	_____	_____
6. sign	_____	_____	_____
7. third	_____	_____	_____
8. right	_____	_____	_____
9. chips	_____	_____	_____
10. drinks	_____	_____	_____

MASTERY 2-2   Consonants

Answer the following questions about consonants.

1. In the word *text*, the *x* sounds like _____.

2. Is the *c* hard or soft in the word *cemetery*? _____

3. The *st* in the *forest* is a consonant _____.

4. In the word *triumphant*, what sound does the *ph* make? _____

5. Name three consonants that make more than one sound:

_____

6. Each consonant that can make more than one sound is listed along with some word examples. Write your own words that use each sound on the lines provided.

  a. hard *c*, as in *cat* and *country*; soft *c*, as in *city* and *precinct*

  _____

  b. hard *g*, as in *garage* and *again*; soft *g*, as in *George* and *angel*

  _____

  c. beginning *s* sound, as in *soap*; ending *z* sound, as in *times*

  _____

  d. hard *d*, as in *dog*; *j* sound, as in *soldier*

  _____

  e. sound of *x*, as in *exist*; *ks* sound, as in *reflex*

  _____

MASTERY 2-3   **Consonants and Comprehension:** *Ending Up at the Wrong Hotel in the Wrong Country*

Answer the following question, and then read the entire story that follows.

1. Read the title and the first sentence of the following article. Using just this information, what do you predict will happen in the story?

  _____

  _____

  _____

  _____

Ending Up at the Wrong Hotel in the Wrong Country
By Christina Page

Recently, I got a contract job with a company to help train teachers in Niagara, New York. The job was to last just two weeks, so I chose to stay in a hotel for that time. I went on the Internet to book a room. I found two hotels with the same name, Niagara/Buffalo. I called one of the hotels and asked the receptionist if that hotel was at Niagara Falls. The receptionist said yes, so I booked the hotel for five nights, paying in advance.

I arrived at the Buffalo, New York, airport and got a taxi. I showed the driver the hotel address. We drove about 30 minutes and came to a booth with a woman in a uniform. She asked to see my driver's license and then waved us through the checkpoint. I asked the driver why we had to stop and answer questions. He told me that we had crossed into Canada. When we arrived at the hotel, I went in and found out that I was at the wrong hotel in the wrong country.

I got another taxi, crossed back into the United States, and found the correct hotel. I had spent $50.00 for each taxi. Moreover, I had to write to the president of the Canadian hotel to get my money refunded. This experience taught me to always check a map when I book a hotel.

2. Circle the consonant digraphs in the following paragraph.

"Recently, I got a job with a company to help train teachers in Niagara, New York. The job was to last just two weeks, so I chose to stay in a hotel for that time. I went on the Internet to book a room. I found two hotels with the same name, Niagara/Buffalo. I called one of the hotels and asked the receptionist if that hotel was at Niagara Falls. The receptionist said yes, so I booked the hotel for five nights, paying in advance."

3. List the first five words from the paragraph above that contain blends. Circle the consonant blend in each word.

1. recently   2. company   3. help   4. train   5. fork

4. Were your predictions from question 1 correct?

_____

_____

5. Retell the story in your own words.

_____

_____

_____

_____

_____

_____

_____

MASTERY 2-4   Vowels: *Miss America*

Read the following paragraph.

Miss America

(1) The Miss America contest began in 1921 in Atlantic City, New Jersey. (2) Only eight women entered the first year, but within 10 years the contest was a nationwide event. (3) In those early times, the contestants represented cities instead of states. (4) Winners were chosen for the bathing suit and evening gown

categories. (5) Despite the popularity of the weeklong contest, many people be-lieved the young women were exploited and their costumes indecent and shocking.

WORDNOTES

exploited   taken advantage of, used
indecent   immoral

List the words that contain *y* in each sentence of the paragraph you just read. Write how the *y* in the words is used in each of the numbered sentences—either as a consonant or the sound of long $\bar{e}$ or long $\bar{\imath}$.

Sentence 1. _____

Sentence 2. _____

Sentence 3. _____

Sentence 4. _____

Sentence 5. _____

LOOKING BACK

Do you remember reading about the questions you should ask yourself before you start reading? The questions you should ask are

- Who are the main characters?
- What is going on?
- When does the story take place?
- Where does the story take place?
- Why are the characters doing what they are doing?
- How do the characters react in the story, or how does the story end?

If you ask yourself these questions before you start reading, your brain will look for the answers as you read. This is active reading. As a reader, you are thinking about what you are reading by asking and answering those six questions.

LOOKING BACK 2-1   **Prereading, Vowels, and Comprehension: *Purring Predators***

1. Before reading the following article, what can you learn from the title and

   subtitle?

   _____

   _____

   _____

   _____

2. What do you expect the article to be about?

_____

_____

_____

_____

Purring Predators: Housecats and Their Prey

From David Krough, _Biology: A Guide to the Natural World,_ 3rd ed. (Upper Saddle River, NJ: Pearson Education, 2005), p. 695.

Housecats are famous for bringing home animals they've killed or caught. Curious about the dead animals brought into their own homes in the 1980s, Peter Churcher and John Lawton decided to make a scientific study of the predatory behavior of the **domestic** cat. To do so, they asked for the help of 172 households in the small English village of Bedfordshire, where Churcher lived. The two researchers asked the locals to "bag the remains of any animal the cat caught," and turn the evidence over to them once a week. This went on for a year with full cooperation from the cat owners.

Some of the results were not surprising. Young cats hunt more than older cats; small **mammals**, such as mice, are the favorite prey; and cat hunting is not based purely on hunger—all the cats were fed by their owners and yet all the cats hunted.

What was **remarkable**, however, was the **scale** of the killing. Churcher and Lawton found that cats were responsible for between one-third and one-half of all sparrow deaths in the village, a number they believed no other single predator could match. When they looked at all animals killed (including mice, birds, and other prey), and projected the numbers for the village to the whole country of Great Britain, the researchers calculated that cats were responsible for about 70 million deaths a year.

Since birds total 30 and 50 percent of these kills, this means that cats kill at least 20 million birds a year in Britain. The "at least" here may be an important **qualifier**. An American biologist, the researchers note, found that cats bring home only about half of all the food they catch.

WORDNOTES

predators	animals that live by hunting other animals for food
domestic	tame
mammals	warm-blooded animals that suckle their young
remarkable	worthy of notice, out of the ordinary
scale	a system of measuring or grading
qualifier	something that restricts or limits

3. Find words in the reading that contain the following long vowel sounds and write them on the line beside the appropriate sound. (Use your dictionary if necessary.)

   a. $\bar{a}$ _____

   b. $\bar{e}$ _____

   c. $\bar{i}$ _____

   d. $\bar{o}$ _____

   e. $\bar{u}$ _____

4. What were the results of Churcher and Lawton's scientific study?

   _____

   _____

   _____

5. Why is the qualifier "at least" important in Churcher and Lawton's study?

   _____

   _____

LOOKING BACK 2-2   **Outline: *Purring Predators***

Using the questions who, what, where, when, why, and how, fill in the blanks in the following outline and short summary of "Purring Predators: Housecats and Their Prey."

Outline:

Who: _____

What: _____

Where: _____

When: _____

Why: _____

How: _____

_____

Summary:

Peter Churcher and John Lawton conducted a scientific study of (what)

_____ in (when and where) _____

_____. To determine how many deaths cats are responsible for,

Churcher and Lawton were assisted in their study by cat owners who

(how) _____.

LOOKING BACK 2-3 **Asking Questions:** *When I Was Left Behind*

As a child, were you ever left anywhere by accident? Did your parents drive off and leave you at a store or in an amusement park because they simply thought you were in the car? Read the following story, and then answer the questions that follow.

When I Was Left Behind
By M. C. Dore

My family used to drive to Sunset Lake near Bartlesville, Oklahoma. It was about a 40-minute drive. There were seven of us children, but usually only four or five of us went. The lake was a great place. It had a huge water slide and a trapeze that you could swing on over the water. I loved going there with my brothers and sisters. The place was always packed with people. One lazy Sunday afternoon when I was seven years old, we drove out to Sunset Lake to swim and have a picnic. The day was perfect, but soon it was time to go. Dad had yelled to us to get in the car, but I had to use the bathroom. I ran to the stone building where the restrooms were located. It only took me five minutes, but when I came out, the family was gone. I was shocked. Where were they? Didn't anyone even notice that I was missing? How could they leave me behind?

The lady at the grocery counter near the bathrooms noticed that I was crying. She offered to help me, and I tearfully told her that my family had left without me. She comforted me and told me she was sure that they would return. She gave me a candy bar and a soda. That was really nice of her. I sat quietly on a stone bench and watched the people flying off the trapeze into the water. I watched the ski boats zoom through the water with their wave runners streaking behind them. I was having such a good time eating my candy bar and watching the people in the lake that I was surprised when my dad came rushing up to me. He lifted me into the air and wrapped his arms around me. I felt missed and loved, and I got a free candy bar and a soda out of getting left behind!

While you were reading the story, did you think about the questions who, what, when, where, why, and how?

1. Who was the story about?

   _____

2. What was the story about?

   _____

3. When did the story take place?

   _____

4. Why did the child get left behind?

   _____

5. How did she react to getting left behind?

   _____

6. Who helped her?

   _____

7. What did she do while she waited for her family to return?

   _____

LOOKING BACK 2-4   **Comprehension: *Body Art? Fashion Statement? Tattoos!***

Before reading the following article, think about what you know about tattoos and write a short paragraph on the topic.

_____

_____

_____

_____

_____

_____

_____

Body Art? Fashion Statement? Tattoos!

1   Tattoos have been around a long time. The earliest records tell us tattoos come from **pagan** religions, and there is evidence some American Indians were tattooed. In the recent past, tattoos were not respected. Often criminals or veterans who had traveled around the world were more likely than young adults to have tattoos.

2   Many people have tattoos today, and teenagers and young adults have their own reasons to get tattooed. It can be for spiritual or artistic reasons or to display an important life event. It can even be a form of rebellion. Many symbols are used for tattoos—**fantasy** creatures, religious emblems, **astrological** signs, personal **mementoes**, and names, to name just a few. In some urban areas, teen gang members have their bodies tattooed with the names of gangs they belong to.

3   In the past, for whatever reason a person got a tattoo, he or she would have it for life. The design is applied just under the skin with permanent ink. Although people who consider getting a tattoo are advised to think long and hard about something that cannot be washed off, many decide later they want it removed. Usually, a life change will cause a person to question whether he or she still feels the same way about having a tattoo. Most young people who decide to get rid of their tattoos report that they have trouble getting a job and want to change their image. To distance themselves from violence and danger, gang members have also expressed regret over having their bodies tattooed and seek to hide or remove their tattoos.

4   Removal of tattoos is possible but has been very difficult, painful, and expensive until recently. Technology has gotten better and better at erasing these previously permanent impressions. Procedures such as cutting the tattoo from the skin, freezing and sanding, laser treatments, and heat-light burning are available to someone who is serious about having a tattoo removed.

WORDNOTES

pagan	nature-based primitive religion
fantasy	imaginary, make-believe
astrological	relating to the Zodiac
memento	something given or kept as a reminder of a person or event
permanent	lasting, unchanging
regret	to feel sorry about doing or saying something

2. Why would a person decide to get a tattoo?

_____

_____

3. Why would a person want to have a tattoo removed?

_____

_____

_____

_____

_____

4. Is it possible to have a tattoo removed? _____

5. How? _____

_____

READER RESPONSE 2-3

1. Have you ever thought about getting a tattoo? Describe the process you went through in thinking about whether you would get a tattoo or not.

2. If you have a tattoo, why did you decide to get it?

LOOKING BACK 2-5   **Comprehension: *In Her Footsteps***

In Her Footsteps
By Courtney Angela Brkic
New York Times, Sunday, July 11, 2004

The first thing I noticed about Judy was her red hair. It must have made her an easy target for snipers as a front-line nurse in Croatia and Bosnia. Her New Jersey accent drew attention, too, in Zagreb, where we met two months after the war ended in 1995. I was the American-born daughter of a Croatian immigrant, in Zagreb studying the effects of war on the people there. Judy was a veteran of that war.

"For real?" I asked, completely surprised by this information.

"For real," she said.

I told my family and friends in Zagreb about her. "An American nurse?" they asked. "Are you sure?" They looked at me as if I had just said I had seen a yeti in the city center. Finally, one of my aunts decided: "She must have roots here. Her parents are from Croatia—that must be it." Family, however, had nothing to do with it. "Nope," she told me over dinner, smoking a cigarette with an amused look on her face. "My mother's family was Lithuanian."

Judy had followed the beginning of the war in 1991 from America, including the attacks on Osijek and Vukovar, towns destroyed by the Yugoslav National Army and paramilitary groups. Later, she watched films of Vukovar falling after a vicious three-month battle. Exhausted civilians came out of their cellars to be put in prison, expelled from their own country, or executed. When she saw the shocked faces of people forced to leave the city, something snapped in her. She had wanted to volunteer in Afghanistan during the 1980s. Then she was a recent graduate of nursing school, and decided not to go because of lack of nursing experience and the fears of her family. But she insisted on going to Croatia: "I was talked out of Afghanistan, but not this time."

A few weeks after the fall of Vukovar, she was caring for the wounded and dying and driving around in a battered, damaged ambulance. Off-duty, she lived with a family in Slavonski Brod, a city where mortars fell more regularly than rain and civilian deaths and injuries were very high. I was in awe of her. She was 36. I was 23, but I felt like a child beside her. She was the heroine of books I had read, movies I had seen. I had a secret wish to be her.

Judy has a photo album of her days at war, which she showed me soon after we met. She identified the faces by saying, "He died in February" or "A shell fell on him." There were two pictures of the same man.

"That's him?" I asked, looking from the handsome face to the headless body in the photo.

"Yep," she said. She would come off the front line after two weeks so covered in blood and dirt that gallons of hot water couldn't wash it all away. "A filth you cannot imagine," she said. Judy had been part of a small but fierce group rushing to the country's aid, even as others rushed to get out. Some Croatian parents sent their draft-age sons to live with relatives in other countries or to study at foreign universities. My father worked tirelessly to let people in America know about the war, but he was relieved that my brother and I were safe.

While Judy was on the front line in the early '90s, I was at William and Mary University. I worried about my relatives in Croatia and on most weekends returned home to Arlington, Va., where my father listened to nightly radio reports, tracking towns as they fell. But like other college sophomores, I lived in a different reality. I did not think about joining the war. Had I been older and a nurse, I still wouldn't have. The war was happening over there, and though horrified and angry, I was removed from it. Meeting a nurse who had left her own comfortable American life made me feel ashamed.

People say there is an intensity to front-line life that cannot be found anywhere else. I wouldn't know. My only experience with war was during a 1993 visit to Croatia, when mortars were fired at a train I was traveling in. Passengers were rushed off the train to a filthy basement; I can only remember feeling terror. And yet I could not forget Judy's stories. I was tired of listening and longed for action. A year after the war, I joined an international forensic team digging up mass graves in the ethnically cleansed territory of Republika Srpska. I spent much of 1996 talking to women with missing family members, and their stories had taught me that this work was important. But if I'm honest with myself, I know I wanted to be Judy's equal. So I dug up bodies and helped with autopsies in Bosnia. I went through the pockets of dead men, hoping their few possessions—

pieces of Polaroid pictures, crusts of bread, water-soaked letters—would help identify them. But I lacked the **detachment** of a scientist or the fearlessness of a combat nurse. I lasted only about a month.

WORDNOTES

snipers	hidden shooters
veteran	a person who has served in the armed forces
yeti	Abominable Snowman
paramilitary	trained forces working with the regular army
vicious	very forceful, intense
expelled	driven out
heroine	female hero
filth	foul dirt
intensity	having strong feelings or emotions
forensic	relating to courts of law
ethnically cleansed	words used to describe the killing of people of a certain race or culture
autopsies	examinations of dead bodies to learn the causes of death
detachment	having no interest

1. Notice the names of places in Croatia and Bosnia. How are they similar to the author's name?

_____

_____

2. When did Judy serve in Croatia? _____

3. What was Judy's job in Croatia? _____

4. When did Courtney Brkic meet Judy? _____

5. Why was Judy Courtney's heroine? _____

_____

_____

_____

READER RESPONSE 2-4 From the information given in the article, write a list of what you learned about Judy and another list of what you learned about Courtney. For example, you could begin with Judy's being a nurse who came from New Jersey. Based on your lists, write a short description of each person. You can use the following pattern if you want.

Judy was a (what) _____ who served in (where and when) _____ in ____. She was (how old) __. She decided to go to Croatia because (why)

_____

_____

_____

_____

_____

_____

_____

_____

ONLINE PRACTICE

Go to **MyReadingLab** at www.myreadinglab.com. Click on **Reading Road Trip**, and select your textbook or the **Pioneer Level**.

1. For further practice with **prereading skills**, take a Road Trip to **Rocky Mountain National Park**.

2. For further practice with **active reading strategies**, take a Road Trip to **New Orleans**.

3. For practice using **vocabulary**, take a Road Trip to the **Library of Congress**.

PROGRESS CHART   CHAPTER **2**

SECTION ONE

Fill out the number of correct answers you have for each item below. Your instructor will tell you how to calculate your percentage score.

PRACTICE 2-1 Number right _____ out of a possible score of 10.   Percentage score _____

PRACTICE 2-2 Number right _____ out of a possible score of 10.   Percentage score _____

PRACTICE 2-3 Number right _____ out of a possible score of 3.   Percentage score _____

PRACTICE 2-4 Number right _____ out of a possible score of 10.   Percentage score _____

PRACTICE 2-5 Number right _____ out of a possible score of 4.   Percentage score _____

PRACTICE 2-6 Number right _____ out of a possible score of 5.   Percentage score _____

PRACTICE 2-7 Number right _____ out of a possible score of 5.   Percentage score _____

MASTERY 2-1 Number right _____ out of a possible score of 10.   Percentage score _____

MASTERY 2-2 Number right _____ out of a possible score of 6.   Percentage score _____

MASTERY 2-3 Number right _____ out of a possible score of 5.   Percentage score _____

MASTERY 2-4 Number right _____ out of a possible score of 5.   Percentage score _____

LOOKING BACK 2-1 Number right _____ out of a possible score of 5.   Percentage score _____

LOOKING BACK 2-2 Number right _____ out of a possible score of 7.   Percentage score _____

LOOKING BACK 2-3 Number right _____ out of a possible score of 7.   Percentage score _____

LOOKING BACK 2-4 Number right _____ out of a possible score of 5.   Percentage score _____

LOOKING BACK 2-5 Number right _____ out of a possible score of 5.   Percentage score _____

SECTION TWO

How do you feel? There are no wrong or right answers to how you feel about what you have learned. Circle Yes, Somewhat, or No in response to the following questions.

1. Can you give examples of words with long and short
vowel sounds?   Yes   Somewhat   No

2. Do you know the difference between consonant digraphs and consonant blends?   Yes   Somewhat   No

3. Do you know which consonants can be silent?   Yes   Somewhat   No

4. Can you give examples of words with silent consonants in them?   Yes   Somewhat   No

5. Can you list the primary vowels?   Yes   Somewhat   No

6. Can you give examples of vowels that are neither long nor short?   Yes   Somewhat   No

7. Can you read diacritical symbols?   Yes   Somewhat   No

8. Has your reading in other classes improved?   Yes   Somewhat   No

9. Has your ability to read new words improved?   Yes   Somewhat   No

SECTION THREE

Take a minute or two to reflect on your reading development. Write a few sentences or discuss with other students how this chapter has changed your reading habits.

_____

_____

_____

_____

_____

_____

_____

_____

_____

_____

_____

Recognizing Word Parts and Using Syllables

CHAPTER PREVIEW

Expanding your vocabulary will improve your reading skills. Recognizing how the different parts of words add up to make meaning will help you to figure out words you do not understand. Learning how to break words into syllables will enable you to pronounce words correctly. In this chapter, you will learn about

- **Root words**
- **Prefixes**
- **Suffixes**
- **Syllables**
- **Syllabication**

MAKING MEANING

English: The Equal Opportunity Language

English is popular all over the world because it is so "friendly" to other languages. Of all the words in the *Oxford English Dictionary*, 99 percent were taken from other languages! However, the few words that trace back to Old English are the words we use 62 percent of the time.[1]

Where does the English language come from? The great success story of the English language began long ago. At the beginning of the Middle Ages, around AD 400, several large tribes of sea rovers—the Angles, Saxons, and Jutes—lived along the North Sea coast of Europe. They were a warrior people who invaded and settled the large island of Britannia, bringing with them a language that was later called English (from the word *England,* which means "land of the Angles"). In 1066, new invaders from the northern coast of France, the Normans, arrived in England, bringing with them many French and Latin words. Latin was the language spoken in the ancient Roman Empire, and nearly half of all English words come from Latin. About 500 years

Statue of Achilles

after the Norman conquest, in approximately 1400, the Middle Ages ended, and a new time of learning began called the Renaissance. Educated men and women all over Europe, including England, rediscovered the ancient worlds of Greece and Rome, and many Greek and Latin words entered the English language at that time.

Thus, English developed from Old English, Old French, Latin, and Greek. However, because England and then the United States became economic, military, and scientific superpowers, they came in contact with people and languages from all over the world. As a result, many more foreign words were added to English. The *Oxford English Dictionary* lists 615,000 English words. In comparison, the German language has a vocabulary of about 185,000 words, Russian 130,000, and French fewer than 100,000![2] Today, the English language is truly international. The words listed here demonstrate the varied origins of some commonly used English words.

Some Commonly Used English Words	
algebra: Arabic	caravan: Persian
chorus: Greek	coffee: Turkish
dollar: German	garage: French
polka: Czech	silk: Chinese
boss: Dutch	oasis: Egyptian
shampoo: Hindi	opera: Italian
rodeo: Spanish	ski: Norwegian

NOTES 1. John McWhorter, *The Power of Babel: A Natural History of Language* (New York: Henry Holt, 2001).
2. Richard Lederer, *The Miracle of Language* (New York: Pocket Books, 1991).

INTRODUCTION

Recognizing root words, prefixes, and suffixes will help you increase your vocabulary because you can use them to figure out the meanings of unfamiliar words. A **root word** is the most basic word part. It provides the core meaning of a word and is used to build different words, just as bricks are used to build different buildings.

> *EXAMPLE:* The word *play*, which means "to take part in games, sports, or recreation," is a root word.

A **prefix** is added to the beginning of a root word to change the meaning of the root.

> *EXAMPLE:* The meaning of the root word *play* is changed by the prefix *re-* to *replay* (to play again) and by the prefix *inter-* to *interplay* (to play or act on one another).

A **suffix** is added to the end of a root word and is used to change the root's part of speech, its tense, or, less commonly, its meaning.

> *EXAMPLE:* Adding the suffix *-ful* to the end of the word *play* (noun) makes the adjective *playful* (full of play or fun.) Adding the suffix *-ed* to the end of the word *play* (verb) changes it to the past tense, *played* (as in "she played soccer yesterday").

A word can have both a prefix and a suffix, or more than one prefix or suffix. For example, the word *replaying* contains the prefix *re-* and the suffix *-ing* added to the root word *play*. No matter how many prefixes and suffixes a word has, its meaning always begins with the root word it is built on.

In addition to root words, prefixes, and suffixes, syllables are important when learning new words. A **syllable** is part of a word; each syllable in a word is pronounced separately and contains one vowel sound. Being able to recognize syllables will help you work out the meaning of a word, spell and say a word correctly, and divide a word that breaks across a line.

When you learn about using a dictionary in Chapter 4, you will see that a dictionary divides each word into syllables. For example, the word *future* has two syllables, shown as *fu-ture* in a dictionary.

STRUCTURED INSTRUCTION AND EXERCISES

EXERCISE 3-A   Write a sentence using each of the following words:

1. player

_____

2. playful

_____

3. plays

_____

4. played

_____

5. replay

_____

WORD PARTS

Root Words

Many English words come from Latin or Greek root words. **Root words** provide the core meanings of many familiar words. By learning the definitions of root words, you can often figure out the meanings of words you do not know. For example, the Greek root word *graph* means "write." When you add prefixes to this root, you can make new words, such as the following:

Prefix *auto-* (self) + **root word** *graph* (writing) = *autograph,* meaning "to write with one's own hand"

Prefix *photo-* (light) + **root word** *graph* (writing) = *photograph,* meaning "image created with light"

Prefix *tele-* (working at a distance) + **root word** *graph* (writing) = *telegraph,* meaning "a message sent over a long distance (by wire or radio)

Another Greek root word, *geo,* means *earth.* Try combining *geo* with the suffixes *metry, graphy,* and *ology* to make three words, and write them on the lines provided.

1. _____
2. _____
3. _____

Which word means "writing about the earth"? _____

Which word means "measuring the earth"? _____

Which word means "studying the earth"? _____

The word *geography* means "writing about the earth": root word *geo* (earth) + suffix *-graphy* (writing) = *geography,* meaning "writing about the earth." The word *geometry* literally means "measuring the earth": root word *geo* (earth*)* + suffix *-metry* (measuring) = "measuring the earth." We do not really go out and measure the earth now, but we do measure the lines and angles found in both natural and manufactured objects. The other word may have been a bit harder. *Geology* means "study of the earth": root word *geo* (earth) + suffix *-ology* (word or study). However, we usually think of geology as more "hands-on," more of an applied science, which involves drilling for natural gas or oil, or studying rocks and fossils. So even though the modern meaning of a word may be a little different from the original meaning of the Greek or Latin root word (or words) it is built on, it is still close enough for you to work out what the word means now.

Here is a list of some of the most commonly used root words:

Common Root Words		
Root Word	*Meaning*	*Sample Words*
aud	hear	audience, audio, audible
bio	life	biography, autobiography
cardi	heart	cardiac, cardiologist
cred	believe	credit, incredible
cycle	circle	bicycle, cyclic
derma	skin	dermatitis, dermatologist, dermis
dic	speak	diction, dictionary, dictate
form	shape	uniform, transform, reform
gen	birth, race, family	generation, genealogy, genocide
gyno	woman	gynecologist, gynecology
man	hand	manual, manuscript, manufacture
meter	measure	centimeter, metrics, thermometer
nat	born	native, nation, innate
onym	name	synonym, anonymous, pseudonym
ped	foot	pedal, pedestrian, centipede
phon	sound	telephone, microphone, symphony
quest	ask, seek	inquest, quest, question, request
sim	like	similar, simulation, simultaneous
struct	build	construct, destruct, instruction, structure
terr	land	terrain, territory
therm	heat	thermal, thermometer, thermos
urb	city	urban, suburbs

EXERCISE 3-B Choose the correct word from the sample words listed here to complete the following sentences.

Root Word	Meaning	Sample Words
pac	peace	Pacific Ocean, pacify
port	carry	export, portable
tend, tens	stretch, strain	extend, tension
vac	empty	vacant
mar	sea, pool	marsh
fract, frag	break	fracture, fragment

1. Bill and Wendy have a _____ playpen that can be folded up and carried anywhere.

2. Bill does not let his children play near the old, rundown _____ house.

3. Wendy and Bill spotted a dangerous _____ near their house. It had mosquitoes and wet, smelly grass.

4. The baby girl had an ear infection, so she was very hard to _____ .

5. Even though Wendy had a _____ headache, she was patient with her baby.

6. The _____ of his ankle put Bill out of the basketball game.

Prefixes

A **prefix** is a word part that comes *before* the root word. Because a prefix can have one or more meanings of its own, it changes the meaning of the root word. For example, the word *like,* meaning "in the same or similar way," is changed by the addition of prefixes such as *un* or *dis:*

Prefix *un* (not, the opposite) + root *like* (the same, or similar) = *unlike,* meaning "different from"

Prefix *dis* (do the opposite of) + root *like* (the same, similar) = *dislike,* meaning "feeling of not liking"

Here is a list of some of the most commonly used prefixes:

Common Prefixes		
Prefix	*Meaning*	*Sample Words*
bi-	two	bicycle, biceps
co-	together, with	coauthor, copilot
de-	out, away from	depart, decease
fore-	before, earlier	forecast, forefather
mis-	badly, wrong	mistake, misunderstand, mistrust
mono-	one	monopoly, monotone
non-, un-	not	nonactive, uncoated
post-	after	postwar, postscript
sub-	below, under	submarine, subdivide

EXERCISE 3-C Choose the correct word from the sample words listed here to complete the following sentences.

Prefix	*Meaning*	*Sample Words*
anti-	against	antifreeze, antisocial
ex-	out	exit, exclude
pre-	before	preview, predict
re-	again, back	revise, return
dis-	non, lack of	dishonest, dislikes
in-; im-	not; in, into	inactive, impure; include

1. Is Barbi just shy, or is she really _____?

2. Before we decide to _____ her from our group, we need to know if she really _____ us.

3. Maybe we could invite Barbi to the sneak _____ of *Dumb Blondes III.*

4. I _____ if we _____ Barbi in our group, she will be our friend.

5. Then she might _____ her opinion of us.

EXERCISE 3-D Choose the correct word from the sample words in the "Common Prefixes" box or the list in Exercise 3-C to complete the following sentences.

1. Since the _____called for snow in the mountains, Leon put _____ in his truck.

2. Leon was _____ of a book on _____ Afghanistan.

3. Leon and Iris had to _____ the end of their book.

4. Leon developed ulcers from taking too many _____ aspirins while he was rewriting his book.

5. He should have done more exercises to build up his _____.

Suffixes

Suffixes, like prefixes, are never used alone. A suffix is always added to the end of a root word. A suffix also has one or more meanings of its own. However, a suffix usually does not change the meaning of the root word. In English, a suffix is used to show the part of speech of a word—noun, verb, adjective, or adverb; the tense of a word—whether something happened in the present, past, or future (*call, called, calling*); and if there is more than one of a thing (*book, books*).

Here is a list of some suffixes you will see used often:

Common Suffixes		
Suffix	*Meaning*	*Sample Words*
-ible	able	credible, edible
-ive	to be able to	creative, inventive
-ness	state of	happiness, sadness
-ous	having a certain quality	porous, dangerous
-ism	belief	socialism, communism
-ology	study of	psychology, sociology
-ward	in a certain direction	eastward, downward, forward

Nouns and Verbs

Suffixes allow us to change the parts of speech of words without changing the basic meanings of the words. For example, verbs can be changed into nouns by adding suffixes.

Verb	*Suffix*	*Noun*
teach (to instruct)	+ **er** (one who does)	= teacher (one who teaches)
talk	+ **-er**	= talker (someone who talks)
walk	+ **-er**	= walker (someone who walks)
jump	+ **-er**	= jumper (someone who jumps)
act	+ **-or**	= actor (someone who acts)

EXERCISE 3-E The following words are nouns. Change each word into a verb by taking away the suffix.

1. sailor _____

2. flyer _____

3. farmer _____

4. player _____

5. painter _____

Other suffixes that change verbs into nouns are *-ance*, *-ence*, *-ion*, *-tion*, and *-ment*.

Verb	*Suffix*	*Noun*
create (make)	+ **ion, -tion** (result of)	= creation (something made)
move	+ **-ment**	= movement
place	+ **-ment**	= placement
exist	+ **-ence**	= existence
avoid	+ **-ance**	= avoidance

EXERCISE 3-F The following words are nouns. Change each word into a verb by taking away the suffix.

1. appearance _____

2. establishment _____

3. government _____

4. dictation _____

5. allowance _____

Adjectives and Adverbs

Adjectives can be changed into adverbs by adding *-ly*, which means "like." For example, the adjective *cold* (lacking warmth) becomes the adverb *coldly* (acting in a cold way) when the suffix *-ly* is added. An easy way to find adverbs is to look for words ending in *-ly*. When the suffix *-ly* is added to words that end in *y*, such as *happy*, the *y* changes to *i*, forming the *-ily* ending; for example, *happy* plus *-ly* becomes *happily*.

Here are more examples of the suffix *-ly* added to words:

Adjective	*Suffix*	*Adverb*
slow (taking longer than usual)	+ **-ly** (like)	= slowly (in a slow manner)
quick	+ **-ly**	= quickly
nice	+ **-ly**	= nicely
greedy	+ **-ily**	= greedily
steady	+ **-ily**	= steadily

Verb Tense

The suffix *-ed* added to a verb shows that an action happened in the past, and the suffix *-s* added to a verb shows an action is happening in the present.

Here are some examples:

Past	*Present*
called	calls
talked	talks
walked	walks
added	adds
planned	plans
practiced	practices

Plurals

The suffix *-s* is used at the end of nouns to make them into plural nouns (more than one). These are just a few examples:

books

trees

pictures

computers

courses

teachers

EXERCISE 3-G Fill in the blanks in each of the following sentences by adding the proper suffix to the italicized word. Use the examples listed in the sections on adjectives and adverbs, verb tense, and plurals.

1. Rhonda (*happy*) _____ (*plan*) _____ to study (*computer*) _____.

2. She (*quick*) _____ (*walk*) _____ to the student center to buy her (*book*) _____.

3. Rhonda (*practice*) _____ (*steady*) _____ until she became almost an expert on computers.

4. Rhonda chose Mrs. Brown, who is known as one of the best (*teacher*) _____ because she (*talk*) _____ to each student and knows their names.

5. Rhonda is (*plan*) _____ to do her best in her computer (*course*) _____ to earn high grades.

From what you have learned about suffixes, change the words in italics to fit into the sentences that follow.

6. Juan Carlos will be *(go)* _____ to three *(meeting)* _____ to see other students majoring in computer science.

7. He *(hope)* _____ to graduate in four *(year)* _____.

8. He *(want)* _____ a job that will allow him to earn a good income and *(steady)* _____ advance in his career.

9. He will be *(stay)* _____ at home with his family while he *(complete)* _____ all his *(credit)* _____ for graduation.

10. Juan Carlos has *(serious)* _____ planned on *(graduate)* _____ from college since he first learned to use a computer.

These are other common suffixes:

Suffix	Meaning	Sample Words
-able	able, can do	agreeable, capable
-er	used to compare things	neater, tougher
-less	without	careless, hopeless
-ist	one who	artist, chemist
-ing	an action or process	talking, writing
-ful	full of	careful, helpful

EXERCISE 3-H Choose the correct word from the list of other common suffixes above to complete these sentences.

1. L'Tanya knew that she was _____ of doing better.

2. Her problem was that she was often _____ about her work.

3. She decided that when she was _____ an assignment, she would be more _____.

4. She became _____ with her work, and it paid off.

5. L'Tanya became a successful _____.

SYLLABLES

A **syllable** is a section of a word that is pronounced as a single sound. When you were learning to read, you may have learned to sound out words by tapping syllables out on your desk, clapping them out, or by feeling the movement of your chin. A syllable may be composed of several letters or just one. Every syllable must have one vowel sound, but that vowel sound may be made up of more than one vowel. For example, the word *meat* has two vowels (side by side); however, only one is heard—the $\bar{e}$. The *a* is silent; it does not make a sound in this word. Therefore, the word *meat* has only one syllable because you pronounce only *one vowel sound*. A syllable includes one vowel sound plus any connected consonant sounds around it.

EXERCISE 3-I   Circle the one-syllable words, and then write them on the lines provided.

grind	maybe	friend	chair	lightning	heavily
seventeen	green	garden	lawn	doorway	

1. _____   2. _____   3. _____   4 _____   5. _____

Single-Vowel Syllable

It is possible for a vowel (*a, e, i, o, u*, and *y*) to stand alone as a syllable as long as it represents part of the sound of a complete word. In each of the following examples, a vowel stands alone as a syllable: *a-bout, ra-di-o, i-deal, pit-y*.

EXERCISE 3-J   Rewrite each word listed here on the lines provided and show the syllables by placing a hyphen (-) between them. You will then see how a single vowel can be a complete syllable.

piano	away	Ohio	eclipse	icon	city

Example: ___u-nit___

1. _____   3. _____   5. _____
2. _____   4. _____   6. _____

The Schwa Sound

In English, **schwa** is the name given to the sound made by a vowel in the unstressed (or soft) syllable of the word. The schwa sound is common in the English language, and understanding how it works will help you pronounce new words. The dictionary identifies this sound with an upside-down *e* (ə). The schwa sound is not represented by a letter of the alphabet; it can stand for any of the five vowels or even for a vowel plus the *r* sound.

In words of two or more syllables, one syllable is given more stress, or emphasis, than the others. The word *waiter* is divided into two syllables as follows: *wait-er*. The first syllable, *wait*, is spoken with a heavier accent or emphasis than the second syllable, *er*. It is in this second syllable, the unstressed one, that the schwa sound is heard. It is the weak short *ŭ* sound such as you hear in the *a* in *alone* and the *e* in *happen*. The *a* in *alone* is unstressed, as is the *e* in *happen*.

EXERCISE 3-K   Circle each word listed here that has a syllable making the schwa sound. Then write the words on the lines provided.

color	intern	trouble	magnet	umbrella	group
gallop	sauce	item	piano	tomato	token

1. _____   3. _____   5. _____   7. _____

2. _____   4. _____   6. _____

SYLLABICATION

Syllabication means taking a word with more than one syllable and breaking it into separate syllables. Syllabication helps you decode the word, pronounce the word, and hyphenate it correctly if you need to break the word at the end of a line of text. You can divide words correctly only when you can recognize syllables. Never divide a word that has only one syllable. For example, *cat* (one vowel sound, short *ă*) and *smile* (one vowel sound, long *ī*, because the final *e* is silent) are one-syllable words. Using a dictionary is helpful when you need to divide a word into syllables. (You will learn about using the dictionary in Chapter 4.) However, there are five general rules that will help you separate words into syllables without using a dictionary.

Five Rules for Separating Words into Syllables

Rule 1: Divide a compound word between the two whole words.   A compound word is a combination of two complete words. To break a compound word into syllables, you always divide the word between the two smaller words.

> *EXAMPLE:* The word *bookmark* is divided between the two whole words it contains, *book* and *mark*: *book-mark*.

EXERCISE 3-L   Circle the compound words listed here, and then write them on the lines provided, using a hyphen (-) to separate each word into syllables.

batter	breakfast	railroad	streetcar	tourist
credit	goldfish	workshop	popcorn	message

Example: home-work

1. _____   3. _____   5. _____

2. _____   4. _____   6. _____

Rule 2: Prefixes and suffixes are usually treated as separate syllables. A prefix is a word part added to the beginning of a word. Common prefixes include *com-, de-, dis-, re-, sub-, un-, in-, pre-, non-,* and *ex-*.

> *EXAMPLE:* The word *unfair* is divided between the prefix *un-* and the root word *fair*: *un-fair*.

A suffix is a word part added to the end of a word. Common suffixes include *-ing, -ful, -ness, -tion, -ly, -en, -less, -able, -er, -ment, -al,* and *-ed*.

> *EXAMPLE:* The word *holding* is divided between the root word *hold* and the suffix *-ing: hold-ing*.

EXERCISE 3-M Circle the words containing prefixes and underline the words containing suffixes. Then write the words on the correct lines provided, using a hyphen (-) to separate each word into syllables.

preview	export	jumping	cheapen
dislike	clearly	recall	playful

Prefixes: 1. _____ 2. _____ 3. _____ 4. _____

Suffixes: 1. _____ 2. _____ 3. _____ 4. _____

When a word ends with a *d* or *t*, the suffix *ed* is pronounced as a separate syllable when added to the original word.

> *EXAMPLE:* The words *want, frost, pound,* and *need* all end with *d* or *t*. Adding the suffix *ed* to these words makes the *ed* a separate syllable: *want-ed, frost-ed, pound-ed,* and *need-ed*.

When added to a word not ending in *d* or *t*, the suffix *ed* usually becomes part of the last sound, and the *e* is silent.

> *EXAMPLE:* The word *live* plus the suffix *ed* becomes *lived* and is pronounced "livd."

EXERCISE 3-N Circle the words that end in *d* or *t* and have the suffix *ed* added. Then write those words on the lines provided, using a hyphen (-) to separate each word into syllables.

timed	vented	loved	graded	tied	wooded
proved	scalded	wilted	lifted	hunted	bored

1. _____ 3. _____ 5. _____

2. _____ 4. _____ 6. _____

Rule 3: When two consonants fall between two vowels, VCCV, divide the word between the two consonants VC-CV. In this rule and in rule 4, the letters *C* and *V* are used to label consonants *(C)* and vowels *(V)*. Labeling the consonants and vowels in some words helps you look for certain patterns of consonants and vowels so you can correctly break words into syllables. For rule 3, you are looking for the pattern VCCV. When you find words with that pattern, you divide them between the two consonants: VC-CV.

> *EXAMPLE:* The word *butter* is split between the middle two
> consonants: *but-ter.*

EXERCISE 3-O   Circle the two-syllable words listed here that can be split into syllables using the VC-CV pattern. Write the letters *V* and *C* over the vowels and consonants to find the pattern you are looking for. Then write those words on the lines provided, using a hyphen (-) to separate each word into syllables.

cotton	better	problem	water	light
corner	though	many	pure	goblet

1. cotton _____   3. problem _____   5. corner _____

2. better _____   4. goblet _____

Some words have three consonants in the middle. For example, *monster* has three consonants: *n, s,* and *t.* Usually, the correct division is still between the first two consonants. Thus, *monster* is separated as follows: *mon-ster.*

As discussed in Chapter 2, a **digraph** is a combination of two consonants that produce a single sound unique from that of either of the individual consonants. The consonants in a digraph should always stay together when you divide words into syllables. Because syllables are separated according to sound, the digraph is an exception to rule 1 that says to separate words between two consonants. For example, *ph, sh, th, ch, ck,* and *wh* are digraphs (single sounds) and should never be separated. Therefore, the following words are separated with the digraphs left intact: *fa-ther, ath-lete, ex-change, far-ther.*

EXERCISE 3-P   Circle the words listed here that contain digraphs. Write the words on the lines provided and use a hyphen (-) to separate each word into syllables.

purple	churches	senses	smother	mother
matchbox	between	disclose	checkers	mushroom
constant	forefront	telegram	further	question

Example: _fur-ther_

1. _____   3. _____   5. _____

2. _____   4. _____   6. _____

Rule 4: Divide a word between a single consonant and a single vowel when the pattern is V-CV or VC-V.   For this rule, you are looking for the pattern VCV, a consonant between two vowels. However, a word with this pattern can either be divided between the first vowel and the consonant (V-CV) or between the consonant and the second vowel (VC-V). The best way to determine which way to divide a word with the VCV pattern is to pronounce the word and listen for where you hear the consonant sound.

Try the V-CV pattern first to sound out a word, because it is the more common pattern. If the V-CV pattern does not make sense, then try the VC-V pattern.

EXAMPLE: The word *fever* is split between the first vowel and the first

consonant: *fe-ver*

EXAMPLE: The word *seven* is split between the consonant and the

second vowel: *sev-en*. If you split the word between the first vowel and first consonant you would get *se-ven*. Notice what a difference there is in the way the word sounds when you break it into syllables that way.

EXERCISE 3-Q   The words below match the patterns for dividing words into syllables described in rule 4: V-CV and VC-V. Write the words on the lines provided beside the correct pattern, using a hyphen (-) to separate each word into syllables.

labor	decent	solid	wagon	title
Utah	power	spoken	salad	novel

V-CV: 1. _____   2. _____   3. _____   4. _____   5. _____

VC-V: 1. _____   2. _____   3. _____   4. _____   5. _____

Rule 5: If a word ends in a consonant followed by *le*, the consonant and *le* form the last syllable.

EXAMPLE: The word *handle* is divided into *han-dle*.

An exception to this rule is any word ending in *ckle* or *kle*. These words are divided after *k*.

EXAMPLE: The word *tickle* is divided as follows: *tick-le*

EXERCISE 3-R   Some of the words listed here follow rule 5. Circle these words and write them on the lines provided. Use a hyphen to separate each word into syllables.

table	gargle	pickle	divine
idle	goodness	ripple	division

1. _____   2. _____   3. _____   4. _____   5. _____

PRACTICING WHAT YOU HAVE LEARNED

PRACTICE 3-1   **Word Parts**

Circle the correct answer.

1. The present-day English language developed from
   a. Old French.
   b. Old English.
   c. Greek.
   d. Latin.
   e. all the above.

2. The word *geography*, from the Greek, means
   a. measuring the earth.
   b. planting the earth.
   c. writing about the earth.
   d. reading about the earth.
   e. seeing the earth.

3. The word *algebra* comes from which language?
   a. Hindi
   b. Arabic
   c. English
   d. Chinese
   e. Dutch

4. The root word *pac* means
   a. pack.
   b. war.
   c. peace.
   d. port.
   e. pace.

5. To be *antisocial* means that one
   a. does not like to meet new people.
   b. likes to meet new people.
   c. does not enjoy going to parties.
   d. enjoys going to parties.
   e. a and c.

6. What do the prefixes *in-* and *im-* mean?

    a. before and earlier   d. not and in, into

    b. against and with   e. front and back

    c. in and out

7. What does prefix *post* mean?

    a. in   d. during

    b. after   e. again

    c. before

8. Change the verb *teach* into a noun. _____

9. Change the verb *create* into a noun. _____

10. Change the adjective *steady* into an adverb. _____

PRACTICE 3-2   **Syllabication**

Using the rules for syllabication that you have just learned, divide the following words into syllables. Beside each word, write the number of the rule that applies. Over each letter of the word, write *C* for consonant and *V* for vowel. (Seeing patterns evolve will help you make correct decisions.)

CHECK IT OUT!

Syllabication Rules

Rule 1: Divide a compound word between the two whole words.

    Example: *summer-time*

Rule 2: Prefixes and suffixes are usually treated as separate syllables.

    Examples: *un-usual (prefix), wilt-ed (suffix)*

Rule 3: When two consonants fall between two vowels, VCCV, divide the word between the two consonants, VC-CV.

    Example: *swim-ming*

Rule 4: Divide a word between a single consonant and a single vowel when the pattern is V-CV or VC-C.

    Examples: *e-ven, in-ept*

Rule 5: If a word ends in a consonant followed by le, the consonant and le form the last syllable.

    Example: *trou-ble*

Word	*Divided into Syllables*	*Rule Number*
1. medal	_____	_____
2. birthday	_____	_____
3. success	_____	_____
4. meter	_____	_____
5. tremble	_____	_____
6. return	_____	_____
7. bottom	_____	_____
8. ladybug	_____	_____
9. gentleman	_____	_____
10. formal	_____	_____
11. reading	_____	_____
12. basic	_____	_____

PRACTICE 3-3   **Syllabication, Word Parts, and Comprehension:** *Medicine*

Read the following paragraph and answer the questions.

Medicine

From Palmira Brummett et al., *Civilization: Past & Present, Concise Version.* (New York: Longman, 2001), 73.

Superstitions about the human body held back the growth of medical science until about 420 B.C.E., when Hippocrates, the "Father of Medicine," started a school in which he taught the value of **observation** and the careful **interpretation** of **symptoms**. He believed that disease came from natural, not **supernatural**, causes. The Hippocratic school also gave medicine a sense of service to humanity that it has never lost. All members of the school took the well-known Hippocratic **Oath**, still in use today.

WORDNOTES

Superstitions	beliefs not based on known facts or sensible thinking, especially belief in omens, the supernatural, etc.
observation	a noting and recording of facts as for research
interpretation	explanation
symptoms	signs of illness or disease
supernatural	not explained by known laws of nature; coming from God, ghosts, spirits, etc.
Oath	a statement to God and men that one will speak the truth and/or keep a promise.

1. Look at the word *Hippocrates* divided into syllables and markings for pronunciation: Hi päk'rə tēz. How many syllables? _____ What letter has a long vowel sound? _____

2. Look up Hippocrates in a dictionary? (Hippocrates may be in a special box or section of a dictionary for biographical names.) Write the definition on the line provided.

   _____

3. How was medicine practiced before Hippocrates?

   _____

   How was medicine practiced after Hippocrates?

   _____

4. Find three words in the reading with four syllables and write them on the lines provided, showing the syllables divided with hyphens (-). (Do not use *Hippocrates*.)

   _____

   _____

   _____

5. Choose the correct word from the WORDNOTES to complete the following sentences.

   a. From Jerry's _____ the doctor concluded he had the flu.

   b. The witness took an _____ to tell the judge the truth.

   c. Juanita believes there is a _____ spirit in the barn, but it is only an owl.

   d. Her _____ of the facts is correct.

6. Explain the meaning of the word *disease* by defining the two word parts. You may refer to the list of prefixes in this chapter and your dictionary.

   _____

   _____

7. In the paragraph, find two past-tense verbs with the suffix *d* or *ed* and write them on the line provided.

   _____

8. In the paragraph, find four words that end with the suffix *s*, showing that they are plural (more than one), and write them on the line provided.

   _____

9. Find a compound word in the paragraph and write it as two separate words.

   _____

10. Find four words in the paragraph that have more than three syllables, and write them on the lines provided, separating the syllables with hyphens.

   _____

   _____

SUMMARY

Word Parts

- A **root word** gives the basic meaning of a word. By learning the meaning of one root word, you can figure out the meanings of many other words that contain that root. Many of our root words come from Old English, Old French, Latin, or Greek.

- A **prefix** is placed at the beginning of a root word and changes the meaning of the root.

- A **suffix** is added to the end of a root word and usually does not change the meaning of the root. However, a suffix can indicate when something happened (present, past, future) or if there is more than one of a thing (plurals). Four parts of speech use suffixes: nouns, verbs, adjectives, and adverbs.

- Prefixes and suffixes are never used alone.

Syllables

- **Syllables** are parts of words that are pronounced separately. Every syllable contains a vowel sound.

- **Prefixes** and **suffixes** are separate syllables.

- The **schwa** sound is the weak short ə sound heard in the word *the*. It can stand for any of the five vowels, or even a vowel plus *r*.

- **Syllabication** means dividing a word into separate syllables. It can help you pronounce a word correctly.

Syllabication rules can be used if you do not have a dictionary.

Rule 1: Divide a compound word between the two whole words.

Rule 2: Treat prefixes and suffixes as separate syllables.

Rule 3: When two consonants fall between two vowels (VCCV), divide the syllables between the two consonants (VC-CV).

Rule 4: Divide a word between a single consonant and a single vowel when the pattern is V-CV or VC-V.

Rule 5: If a word ends in a consonant followed by *le*, the consonant and *le* form the last syllable.

MASTERY LEVEL EXERCISES

MASTERY 3-1   Using Words in Sentences

On the lines provided, write 10 sentences, each using one of the following words.

tension	fracture	creation	dishonest	exclude
pacify	agreeable	helpful	export	actor

1. _____

2. _____

3. _____

4. _____

5. _____

6. _____

7. _____

8. _____

9. _____

10. _____

MASTERY 3-2 **Dividing Words into Syllables: *The U.S. Flag***

Read the following paragraph. Answer the questions that follow.

The U.S. Flag

On June 14, 1777, almost a year after the signing of the Declaration of Independence, the Continental Congress adopted a design for the national flag. It resolved that "The flag of the United States shall be thirteen stripes, alternating red and white with stars representing a new constellation." A compromise between this design and that of the continental flag shows the only change was a union of stars to replace the union of crosses of England and Scotland, using the same blue field. Hence, the Stars and Stripes evolved in two stages from the British red ensign.

1. Find six words that cannot be divided into syllables. If there are duplicates, just list the word once.

   a. _____   c. _____   e. _____

   b. _____   d. _____   f. _____

2. Which five words follow rule 2? Circle the prefix or suffix.

   a. _____   c. _____   e. _____

   b. _____   d. _____

3. Which rule is used to divide the word *thirteen* into syllables?

   _____

4. Find two three-syllable words and divide them into syllables using hyphens (-).

   _____

5. Find the word in the last sentence that follows rule 4 (V-CV).

   _____

MASTERY 3-3 **Suffixes: The Double-the-Consonant Rule**

When a one-syllable word ends with a single vowel followed by a consonant, you need to double the final consonant before adding a suffix beginning with a vowel. Here are some examples of what is known as the double-the-consonant rule:

- One-syllable words: *run, hit, push, shoot, jump, fly, spin, eat*
- One-syllable words, each with a single consonant at the end: *run, hit, shoot, spin*
- One-syllable words, each ending with a single vowel followed by a single consonant: *run, hit, spin*

Do you see why some words were eliminated? *Push* and *jump* have two consonants at the end, not one. *Shoot* and *eat* have two vowels in front of the final consonant. These words do not follow the double-the-consonant rule, so you will not double their final consonants when you add a suffix.

Remember that suffixes are usually syllables added to the end of a word to modify the meaning of the original word. Common suffixes include *-ed, -er, -ing, -ly, -ment, -ness, -ful, -ance,* and *-or.* Among these common suffixes, the ones that fit the double-the-consonant rule are *-ed, -er, -ing, -ance,* and *-or.* They fit the description because they begin with vowels.

Practice the double-the-consonant rule by completing the following exercise.

Word	*+ er*	*+ ing*
1. bat	batter	batting
2. fit	fitter	
3. run		
4. trim		
5. skip		

Word	*+ er*	*+ ing*
6. zip		
7. slim		
8. begin		
9. sin		
10. can		

MASTERY 3-4 **Comprehension, Word Parts, and Syllabication:** *In Pain, Gorilla Puts in a Call to the Dentist*

In Pain, Gorilla Puts in a Call to the Dentist
Used with permission of the Associated Press

When Koko the gorilla used American Sign Language for pain and pointed to her mouth, 12 doctors, including three dentists, went into action. Soon, Koko was having her first full medical examination in about 20 years. The infected tooth was removed, and the 33-year-old gorilla got a clean bill of health. About a month ago, Koko, a 300-plus-pound ape who became famous for learning more

than 1,000 signs, began telling the people who care for her at the Gorilla Foundation in Woodside, California, that she was in pain. They quickly made up a pain chart, offering her a scale from 1 to 10, and Koko indicated that her pain was in the 7-to-9 range. Because **anesthesia** would be needed for removal of the tooth, her caregivers decided to give Koko a head-to-toe exam. "She's quite **articulate**," said John Paul Slater, a **volunteer** at the Gorilla Foundation. "She'll tell us how bad she's feeling, how bad the pain is."

The team came to Koko on Sunday, bringing X-ray and ultrasound machines. They set up the machines at her "apartment," which looks like a remodeled boxcar, complete with a makeshift toilet, a television, a DVD player and lots of toys. After four hours of tests—including a **colonoscopy**, a **gynecological** exam, X-rays and ultrasounds—doctors said she was in good health.

Koko needed a checkup. While gorillas in **captivity** are known to live into their 50s, they often have heart and artery disease. Koko and Ndume, her partner of 11 years (he does not know sign language), have not been able to have a baby, and the doctors thought the checkup could tell them if she had any biological problems that kept her from getting pregnant. They found none. Her teacher, Francine Patterson, was at her side when the anesthesiologist came in to put her under in the morning, and Koko asked to meet her doctors. They crowded around her, and Koko asked one woman wearing red to come closer. The woman gave her a business card, which Koko then ate. Otherwise, she was calm, said Dr. David Liang, an assistant professor of medicine at Stanford.

WORDNOTES

anesthesia	loss of feeling, especially from drugs
articulate	able to communicate clearly
volunteer	one who offers to work without pay
colonoscopy	examination of the inside of the large intestine using a fiber-optic device
gynecological	referring to the female reproductive system
captivity	held within bounds

1. Name three unusual things about Koko the gorilla.

   _____

   _____

2. How many signs has Koko learned?

   _____

3. How did the doctors help Koko?

   _____

4. What tests did the doctors give Koko?

   _____

Using information from the story, write down what the following expressions mean:

5. What is "a head-to-toe exam"?

   _____

6. What is "a clean bill of health"?

   _____

7. What does "put her under" mean?

   _____

8. Describe Koko:

   _____

   _____

9. Who taught Koko to use sign language?

   _____

10. Find three compound words. Write them here with hyphens separating the syllables.

    _____

11. For each of the following suffixes, find one word from the reading with that suffix and write it on the line provided.

    Example: -ed   pointed _____

    -s   _____

    _____

    -ed   _____

    _____

    -ing _____

    _____

    -tion _____

    -ly   _____

12. Find one word from the reading for each of the following prefixes.

Example: re-   removal _____

    in-   _____

    re-   _____

13. For each of the following root words, find a word from the reading that contains it.

    bio   _____

    gyn   _____

14. Separate the syllables in each of the following words using hyphens (-).

    pointed   _____

    infected   _____

    needed   _____

    crowded   _____

15. Write five sentences, each using one of the following words.

doctors	indicated	including	examination	quickly

_____

_____

_____

_____

_____

_____

_____

_____

LOOKING BACK

LOOKING BACK 3-1   **Comprehension and Vowels: *William Shakespeare***

William Shakespeare

From Palmira Brummett, et al., *Civilization: Past & Present, Concise Version* (New York: Longman, 2001), 298–299.

The **reign** of Queen Elizabeth I (1558–1603) saw the height of the English **Renaissance** and produced a great number of talented writers. Strongly influenced by the royal court, which was the busy center of intellectual and artistic life, these writers produced works that were emotional, romantic, and often **extravagant** in spite of their **classical** themes.

The most famous writer in Elizabethan literature and perhaps in all Western literature is William Shakespeare (1564–1616). His rich vocabulary and poetic language were matched by his wild imagination. He was a master lyric poet, and many critics have judged him the foremost sonnet writer in the English language.

Shakespeare wrote 37 plays—comedies, histories, tragedies, and romances. His historical plays reflected the patriotic feelings of the English after their defeat of the Spanish Armada in 1588. For his comedies, tragedies, and romances, Shakespeare borrowed many of his stories from earlier writers. His great strength lay in his characters and in his knowledge of human nature that he transformed into dramatic speech and action. Today his comedies still play to interested audiences: *The Taming of the Shrew, As You Like It, A Midsummer Night's Dream,* and *Much Ado About Nothing* are but a few. But it is in his tragedies that the poet-dramatist presents the total range of human emotion and experience.

Shakespeare possessed the Renaissance concern for human beings and the world around them. So his plays deal first and foremost with the human personality, passions, and problems. In such works as *Romeo and Juliet, Measure for Measure,* and *Troilus and Cressida,* the problems of love and sex are studied. Jealousy is analyzed in *Othello,* ambition in *Macbeth* and *Julius Caesar,* family relationships in *King Lear,* and a man's struggle with his own soul in *Hamlet.* Shakespeare's ability to build every fact and action in his plays on the truths of humanity makes his writings as real today as when first presented at the Globe Theater in London.

WORDNOTES

reign	period of rule of a royal leader
Renaissance	great renewal of art and learning in Europe in the 14th to 16th centuries
extravagant	extreme, wasteful
classical	referring to Greece and Rome
foremost	first in place or time
dramatic	action or expression related to theater
dramatist	one who writes plays
ambition	strong desire for fame and power

1. What is the name of the time period written about in the article?

   _____

2. Why was the literature of Shakespeare's time called Elizabethan?

   _____

3. List the types of drama Shakespeare wrote.

   _____

   _____

   _____

   _____

4. Give a title for each type of play Shakespeare wrote.

Comedy

_____

_____

Tragedy

_____

_____

5. In what play does Shakespeare write about jealousy?

_____

6. In what play does Shakespeare write about family relationships?

_____

7. In what London theater were Shakespeare's plays presented?

_____

8. Match the following words to their correct vowel sounds.

$\bar{a}$ _____   a. humanity

$\bar{e}$ _____   b. own, soul

$\bar{\imath}$ _____   c. feeling, dream

$\bar{o}$ _____   d. reign

$\bar{u}$ _____   e. height

9. Find five words with the following silent vowels.

Example: silent *a*   _____deal_____

silent *a*   _____

silent *e*   _____

silent *i*   _____

silent *o*   _____

silent *u*   _____

10. Find five words with the schwa (ə) sound. Circle the schwa sound.

_____

_____

LOOKING BACK 3-2   **Comprehension, Vowels, Consonants, and Vocabulary: *The Guardian***

The following reading is part of an article that appeared in the April 2002 issue of *Town Talk*, a monthly news magazine published by the Oklahoma Municipal Contractors Association. The author, Rick J. Moore, is the executive director of the association. He interviewed Enoch Kelly Haney and wrote the article using Haney's words. The reading reveals that Haney has done many things in his life through education to overcome poverty and poor language skills. To learn more about Enoch Kelly Haney and view some of his art, go to his Web site (http://www.kellyhaney.com).

"The Guardian," Enoch Kelly Haney
By Rick J. Moore

1   People ask when I first got started in art. There's not a time in my memory when I wasn't doing what I call art. My mother tells me I started when I was about two. That's when she noticed I was able to create with crayons what I was able to see. My first sculpture came when I was about five or six years old. I did the head of Abraham Lincoln in the red clay that was in front of our home in Seminole County.

2   I think my **uniqueness** as an artist is because of where I come from. We weren't different from anybody because we were Indians; everybody was in the same boat. We didn't have indoor plumbing, we didn't have running water, I was born at home, and everybody was like that. I think having come from that background was what gave me my **perspective**.

3   When we moved to Shawnee, I remember six family members living in one room, so I know poor. I also came from a bilingual family, and English was very difficult for me at school. I had a wonderful teacher, Mrs. Brown, in my sophomore year at Shawnee High School, who, rather than asking me to write a book report, asked me to draw it. It forced me to go to the library and study several books to be able to do that one sketch. I had to study clothing, architecture, and the **topography** of the land so I could get that book report right.

4   I still use the same system today when I create art. Mrs. Brown made a difference in my life. She took the talent that I had and helped me to build on it. From that beginning I have become a world-**recognized** artist.

6   In 2000, word went out for Oklahoma artists to submit maquettes for the sculpture to top the dome on the State Capitol. I **submitted** my **portfolio** and was one of 6 out of 20 artists selected to submit a maquette, or a model, for **consideration**. They wanted it simple and bold, a Native American male from a **generic** tribe.

7   I must have been driving the day I came up with the concept because the original sketch is on an envelope. I pulled out a pen and in about 15 seconds made some marks so I would not forget the image that was in my mind. Once I decided on a concept, which involves **composition**, **design**, movement, and color, all of those principles that make up art, I began to research, based upon what Mrs. Brown taught me.

8   Let me tell you about that maquette. Once I decided on the design, I did an exact drawing to scale of what I wanted. Then I did a little stick figure. I'm not trained as a sculptor, I just do it, and so I don't have limits on what I can do. Nobody told me I had limits; I just find out by running into them.

9   The most difficult thing was coming up with what a member of a generic tribe would look like. That is very **contradictory** to what I usually do. I spend a great deal of time researching my projects, sometimes even years. I relied on my own historical research on clothing of the native people before the coming of the Europeans for the "generic" tribe member. Beads, for example, were brought into this country from Czechoslovakia. When you think of the Five Civilized Tribes, you think of **turbans** and **gorgets**, but those are actually **imports**. I tried to find an image of a Native American in the native state, untouched by outside influences. I found a Native American model who lived across the street, a young man 18

years old named Derek Roper. He's an athlete at Seminole High School. Derek came over and we took pictures of him, and forever his image, his **anatomy**, will be seen on top of the capitol.

WORD NOTES 1

uniqueness	quality of being one of a kind
perspective	point of view
topography	surface features of land
recognized	noticed, known
submitted	sent in
portfolio	collection of works
consideration	careful thought
generic	general, not specific
composition	shape, structure
design	detailed plan
contradictory	opposite
turban	headdress formed by winding a long scarf around the head
gorgets	fancy collars
imports	goods brought from another country
anatomy	structure of the body

10   I started getting calls from native people saying the statue ought to be facing east. **Theologically** that's very important to us because of the rising sun. Our Indian churches are built facing east; our ceremonies are conducted facing east. However, I am also aware of the traffic pattern at the Capitol—cars come up from the south. So, I decided to **compromise**, and the sculpture is facing east, but his body is turned toward the south. That's why you see a twist in his body. It creates a very nice composition; it gives him life and movement.

11   When I got to the shield, I thought, gee, I'm not very good at cutting out circles, so I went to the kitchen cabinet and found a can with a deep edge on it, and pushed it down into the clay. The next thing I wanted was two round images inside the circle, so I went back to the cupboard and found two cans of food of different sizes that I could make the images with. I started working on my kitchen table years ago, and I always end up working there even though I have a studio out back. My wife kind of has to work around me, but I just feel comfortable there.

12   I needed something for the feathers, and I kept looking around and finally found a paper clip. I thought, yeah, that would work. I straightened it out, put some clay on it, and it worked fine.

13   There are two major **symbols** in the sculpture. One is a group of emblems found within the shield. As an **amateur** theologian I have studied the theology of many tribes across the country. As I looked for similarities, I found that languages are different, customs are different, physical features are different, but the one

thing I could find that tied native theology and **philosophy** together among the tribes is the circle. So on his shield you will find a circle.

14   In the center of the circle, which some tribes call the sacred, or holy, circle, there are two crossed lines, which divide the circle into fourths. This second symbol represents many things: the four seasons, the four directions, even the four cycles of life. The number four is important to native people just like the number seven is to others. Everything that is important comes in fours. That's why I put four feathers on the shield, to honor the sacred number four. Within that shield there is an important theological, philosophical statement about what native people believe.

15   I enjoyed working on his head. For the face I used my oldest son, Kutcha's, forehead, which is like my father's and mine. I used the eyes of my son, William, the cheeks of my grandson, Enoch, the lips of my son, John, and the hands of my grandson, Micco, who is a freshman at Oklahoma University.

16   I submitted the maquette in what is called a blind competition. This means that they took the names of the artists off the sculptures so no one would know what sculpture belonged to what artist. Mine was selected **unanimously**. That meant a lot to me. There was a $50,000 fee attached to the selection, but we as a family made the fee a gift to the State of Oklahoma.

17   I think the silent symbolism of the sculpture means the most to me. The Comanche warrior is a good example, but several tribes share the same attitude. Warriors always cut a leather strap, and when faced with **insurmountable** odds, they strap themselves to the ground with a knife, an arrow, or whatever they have, and say, "This is as far as I'm going, you'll have to come after me. I'm not

moving." That is a statement of standing one's ground. His lance goes through part of his clothing at the bottom of the sculpture. He says he is made from the Dust Bowl and tornadoes to the bombing of the Murrah building and the wars we have faced. Oklahomans have a way of dusting themselves off, standing up, and going on. They make their stand. It also symbolizes, to me, what we at the Capitol ought to be about. That is, standing for and preserving those things that are very important to Oklahoma: family, community, and jobs. All of those things are important to us.

18   That's where the idea came from for his name, "The Guardian."

WORDNOTES 2

Theologically	relating to religion
compromise	settlement by mutual agreement
symbol	something standing for something else, emblem
amateur	one who studies a subject for pleasure instead of pay
philosophy	view of life
unanimously	all in agreement
insurmountable	not able to be overcome

1. According to the article, why did Enoch Kelly Haney struggle in school?

   _____

2. Why is Mrs. Brown important to Enoch Kelly Haney?

   _____

   _____

3. How was Enoch Kelly Haney chosen to create "The Guardian"?

   _____

4. Where is "The Guardian" located?

   _____

5. What Indian tribe does The Guardian represent?

   _____

6. What does the number 4 symbolize to native people?

   _____

7. Native people wanted the statue to face which direction?

   _____

8. What are the two major symbols in the sculpture?

   _____

9. What was Enoch Kelly Haney's first sculpture?

   _____

10. What is the "silent symbolism" mentioned in paragraph 18?

     _____

     _____

11. For each name, write the number of syllables.

     a. Muskogee (Mə-skō´-gē)   _____

     b. Seminole (Sĕ´-mə-nōl)   _____

     c. Shawnee (Shâ-nē´)   _____

     d. Comanche (Cə-măn´-chē)   _____

     e. Tonhawa (Ton´-hə-wâ)   _____

12. How many long vowel sounds are in the names in question 11 a through d, and what are those sounds?

     _____

13. Which names in question 11 have consonant digraphs?

     _____

14. Find one word in the story for each of the following suffixes.

     a. ing   _____

     b. ion/tion _____

     c. ment   _____

     d. ly/ily   _____

     e. ed   _____

15. Review the paragraphs and identify five compound words.

     a. _____

     b. _____

     c. _____

     d. _____

     e. _____

Using information from the article, circle the best definition for the word in italics in questions 16 through 20.

16. In 2000, word went out for Oklahoma artists to submit maquettes for the *sculpture* to top the dome on the State Capitol.

     a. model

     b. figure

     c. symbol

     d. statue

17. I submitted my portfolio and was one of 6 out of 20 artists selected to submit a *maquette* for consideration.

    a. small model for larger work

    b. small stick figure

    c. small bust of clay

    d. small loaf of French bread

18. I must have been driving the day I came up with the *concept* because the original sketch is on an envelope.

    a. question

    b. reason

    c. idea

    d. answer

19. Once I decided on a concept, which involves composition, design, movement, and color, all of those *principles* that make up art, I began to research, based upon what my high school teacher Mrs. Brown taught me.

    a. parts

    b. causes

    c. rules

    d. orders

20. I submitted the maquette in what is called a *blind competition*.

    a. competition for blind students

    b. contest in which artists' names are not known

    c. competition for blind artists

    d. debate for blind students

READER RESPONSE 3-1

What do you remember most about Enoch Kelly Haney's description of "The Guardian"?

_____

_____

_____

_____

ONLINE PRACTICE

Go to **MyReadingLab** at www.myreadinglab.com. Click on **Reading Road Trip**, and select your textbook or the **Pioneer Level**.

1. For further practice using **vocabulary skills**, take a Road Trip to the **Library of Congress**.

2. For practice **using a dictionary**, take a Road Trip to **Historic Boston**.

NAME _____ DATE _____

PROGRESS CHART   CHAPTER **3**

SECTION ONE

Fill out the number of correct answers you have for each item below. Your instructor will tell you how to calculate your percentage score.

PRACTICE 3-1   Number right _____ out of a possible score of 10.   Percentage score _____

PRACTICE 3-2   Number right _____ out of a possible score of 12.   Percentage score _____

PRACTICE 3-3   Number right _____ out of a possible score of 10.   Percentage score _____

MASTERY 3-1   Number right _____ out of a possible score of 10.   Percentage score _____

MASTERY 3-2   Number right _____ out of a possible score of 5.   Percentage score _____

MASTERY 3-3   Number right _____ out of a possible score of 10.   Percentage score _____

MASTERY 3-4   Number right _____ out of a possible score of 20.   Percentage score _____

LOOKING BACK 3-1   Number right _____ out of a possible score of 10.   Percentage score _____

LOOKING BACK 3-2   Number right _____ out of a possible score of 20.   Percentage score _____

SECTION TWO

How do you feel? There are no wrong or right answers to how you feel about what you have learned. Circle Yes, Somewhat, or No in response to the following questions.

1. Do you know the difference between a prefix and a suffix?	Yes	Somewhat	No
2. Do you know how to use suffixes to show changes in verb tense from present tense to past tense?	Yes	Somewhat	No
3. Do you know the definition of *syllable*?	Yes	Somewhat	No
4. Do you know the meanings of at least six prefixes?	Yes	Somewhat	No
5. Do you understand that prefixes and suffixes are separate syllables?	Yes	Somewhat	No
6. Can you find the root word in an unknown word?	Yes	Somewhat	No
7. Can you give examples of words that contain the schwa sound?	Yes	Somewhat	No
8. Has your reading in other classes improved?	Yes	Somewhat	No
9. Are you using new vocabulary in your speaking and writing?	Yes	Somewhat	No

Take a minute or two to reflect on your reading development. Write a few sentences or discuss with other students how this chapter has changed your reading habits.

_____

_____

_____

_____

_____

_____

_____

_____

_____

_____

Using a Dictionary

CHAPTER PREVIEW

In this chapter, you will learn to use a dictionary to improve your vocabulary. With a good vocabulary, you can better understand your courses and improve your reading and writing skills. A dictionary serves many uses and provides the information you need to

- Spell words
- Break them into syllables (syllabication)
- Pronounce words
- Understand their meaning
- Correctly use words in sentences
- Understand how words came into the language

MAKING MEANING

As many as 30 percent of first-year college students end up dropping out of school before their second year begins. One reason for this high dropout rate is that students get discouraged. They come to believe they just can't make it in college. Students who do earn their degrees push through the self-doubt they feel in the first few days or weeks of classes and learn strategies that help them succeed. As you read the following article, you might feel sympathy for this freshman's struggle to gain self-confidence. Maybe you have felt this way yourself. Notice that she found a solution to her problem.

Will I Make It?

By Anita Reyes

Going to college was scary for me: meeting new people, finding my way around a new place, having the proper books and supplies for class, getting used to a school schedule, and keeping up with homework. The biggest fear I had was

whether I was smart enough to do college work. I believed that all the other students in my classes knew more than I did. They hardly looked my way, and they always seemed to understand what was going on. They knew where to go and when. Often they spoke to the teacher as if they were old friends. I was terrified.

One day in psychology class, the very first week of school, the instructor was giving a lecture on information that was not in the book; I was trying to write everything down as fast as I could. I was afraid I would miss something and tried to keep my writing neat enough to read later. Then the teacher said something that stopped me cold—a word I had never heard. No one else in class seemed to notice. I wondered if it was a special word about psychology. Was I the only one who didn't understand it? I felt scared. Maybe it was in the textbook. I could not connect it to anything I knew, and I spelled it as best I could: *e-s-s-o*-something, and it ended in *r-i-c*.

Nothing in the psychology book looked like the word. I looked in the index and the glossary and searched the first two chapters. Not one word came near what I had written. I decided to try my dictionary and went to the *e* section, looking for words beginning with *e-s-s-o*. No luck. What now? I was pretty sure I had correctly written the beginning of the word. Maybe there was just one *s*. I looked back about fifteen words, and there it was! It had to be: *e-s-o-t-e-r-i-c*, pronounced *es'-ə-ter'-ik.* I said it over and over again, trying to remember how it sounded when the instructor used it. I knew I had never heard that word in my life. The definition was "understood by, or intended for, only a select few; secret; mysterious." It was certainly mysterious to me. Now I had to figure out what this meant in my psychology notes.

That was a long time ago. I learned two good lessons that day. One was that I was going to have to work at being a college student. I guess I already knew that. But the other lesson, even more important, was that I could succeed in college by using what I already knew (even though at times it didn't seem like much) and my tools—my textbooks and my dictionary. Becoming a college student didn't have to be an *esoteric* experience for only a select few. I could be successful too.

INTRODUCTION

A **dictionary** is a book that contains an alphabetical listing of the words used in a language. For each word, the dictionary gives a definition, information on the origin of the word (or its **etymology**), how to pronounce it, and what part of speech it is. A dictionary can also contain information on topics like geographical features of the world, commonly used foreign words, basic elements of mathematics, tables of weights and measures, explanations of symbols, and the air distances between major cities.

Owning and being able to use a dictionary is part of going to college. Good-quality paperback dictionaries are available that won't make your book bag too heavy and will be handy for you to have in the classroom. The important thing is to use your dictionary as much as possible.

STRUCTURED INSTRUCTION AND EXERCISES

PREREADING A DICTIONARY

Prereading will help you get the most benefit from your dictionary. The title of the dictionary may include the edition number. For example, the latest edition of *Webster's Compact School and Office Dictionary* is the fourth edition. This information is on the cover and first page of the book. On the reverse side of the title page is the year of publication. The Webster's dictionary just mentioned was published in 2002. What are the title, edition, and publication date of your dictionary? Write the information on the line provided.

"How to Use This Dictionary" Section

Like all college textbooks, dictionaries have a table of contents that outlines what is in the book. Following that is a section with instructions on how to use the dictionary, often called simply "How to Use This Dictionary," "Explanatory Notes," or "Introduction." It is your guide to locating information on how to correctly spell, break into syllables, and pronounce words, as well as how to find their meanings, parts of speech, and origins. It is worthwhile reading that opening section. You will have a deeper understanding of what you find in the entries, and it will save you time in the future when you want information about a word. Look in your own dictionary. What is the title of its introductory section? Write it on the line provided.

Guide Words and Entry Words

Following the first section of the dictionary is the main body of the book—the list of words, their definitions, and other information that helps you understand and begin to use new words as you come across them in your studies.

Guide words are printed in bold at the top of each page. On each left-hand page at the top is the first word listed on that page; on each right-hand page is the last word listed on that page. Any word spelled within the range of the two guide words may be found on those two pages. All the words listed are called **entry words.** For example, the sample dictionary pages below begin with the word *borzoi* (at the top of the left-hand page) and end with the word *brainwash* (at the bottom of the right-hand page) contain the word *boy* because the spelling of this entry word comes between the guide words in alphabetical order.

borzoi ► 58

bor·zoi (bôr′zoi′) ***n.*** ⟦Russ *borzój,* swift⟧ a large dog with a narrow head, long legs, and silky coat
bosh (bäsh) ***n., interj.*** ⟦Turk, empty⟧ [Inf.] nonsense
Bos·ni·a and Her·ze·go·vi·na (bäz′nē ə and hert′sə gō vē′nə) country in SE Europe: 19,741 sq. mi.; pop. 4,366,000 —**Bos′ni·an *adj., n.***
bos·om (booz′əm; *also* bōō′zəm) ***n.*** ⟦OE *bosm*⟧ **1** the human breast **2** the breast regarded as the source of feelings **3** the inside; midst *[in the bosom of one's family]* **4** the part of a garment that covers the breast —***adj.*** close; intimate *[a bosom friend]*
bos′om·y *adj.* having large breasts
bos·on (bō′sän) ***n.*** ⟦after S. N. *Bose* (1894-1974), Indian physicist + -ON⟧ any of certain subatomic particles, including photons and mesons
boss[1] (bôs, bäs) ***n.*** ⟦Du *baas,* a master⟧ **1** an employer or manager **2** one who controls a political organization —***vt.*** **1** to act as boss of **2** [Inf.] to order (a person) about —***adj.*** [Slang] excellent
boss[2] (bôs, bäs) ***n.*** ⟦OFr *boce,* a swelling⟧ a protruding ornament or projecting knob
boss′y *adj.* -i·er, -i·est [Inf.] domineering —**boss′i·ness *n.***
Bos·ton (bôs′tən, bäs′-) seaport & capital of Massachusetts: pop. 574,000 —**Bos·to′ni·an** (-tō′nē ən) ***adj., n.***
bo·sun (bō′sən) ***n.*** *phonetic sp. of* BOATSWAIN
bot·a·ny (bät′'n ē) ***n.*** ⟦< Gr *botanē,* a plant⟧ the science that deals with plants and plant life —**bo·tan·i·cal** (bə tan′i kəl) or **bo·tan′ic *adj.*** —**bot′a·nist *n.***
botch (bäch) ***vt.*** ⟦ME *bocchen,* to repair < ?⟧ to bungle —***n.*** a bungled piece of work —**botch′er *n.***
bot·fly (bät′flī′) ***n.,*** *pl.* **-flies′** a fly resembling a small bumblebee
both (bōth) ***adj., pron.*** ⟦OE *ba tha,* both these⟧ the two *[both birds sang loudly]* —***conj., adv.*** together; equally *[both tired and hungry]*
both·er (bäth′ər) ***vt., vi.*** ⟦prob. < *pother*⟧ **1** to worry; harass **2** to concern (oneself) —***n.*** **1** worry; trouble **2** one who gives trouble —**both′er·some** (-səm) ***adj.***
Bot·swa·na (bät swä′nə) country in S Africa: 224,607 sq. mi.; pop. 1,327,000
Bot·ti·cel·li (bät′ə chel′ē; *It* bôt′tē chel′ē), **San·dro** (sän′drô) 1445?-1510; It. painter
bot·tle (bät′'l) ***n.*** ⟦< LL *buttis,* a cask⟧ **1** a narrow-necked container for liquids, usually of glass **2** its contents —***vt.*** **-tled, -tling** to put into a bottle —**bottle up** to restrain —**hit the bottle** [Slang] to drink much alcoholic liquor —**bot′tler *n.***
bot′tle·neck′ *n.* **1** a narrow passage or road where traffic is slowed or stopped **2** any similar hindrance to movement or progress
bot·tom (bät′əm) ***n.*** ⟦OE *botm,* ground⟧ **1** the lowest part or place **2** the part on which something rests **3** the side underneath **4** the seat of a chair **5** the ground beneath a body of water **6** basis; cause; source **7** [Inf.] the buttocks —***adj.*** lowest; last; basic —**at bottom** fundamentally —**bot′tom·less *adj.***
bottom line **1** [Inf.] profits or losses, as of a business **2** [Slang] *a*) the basic factor, etc. *b*) the final statement, decision, etc.
bot·u·lism (bäch′ə liz′əm) ***n.*** ⟦< L *botulus,* sausage⟧ poisoning, often fatal, by the toxin produced by a bacterium sometimes found in foods improperly canned or preserved
bou·doir (bōō dwär′, bōō′dwär′) ***n.*** ⟦< Fr, lit., pouting room⟧ a woman's private room
bouf·fant (bōō fänt′) ***adj.*** ⟦< Fr *bouffer,* puff out⟧ puffed out; full
bou·gain·vil·le·a or **bou·gain·vil·lae·a** (bōō′gən vil′ē ə, -vil′yə, -vē′yə) ***n.*** ⟦ModL⟧ a woody tropical vine having large, showy purple or red bracts
bough (bou) ***n.*** ⟦OE *bog,* shoulder or arm⟧ a main branch of a tree
bought (bôt) ***vt.*** *pt. & pp. of* BUY
bouil·lon (bool′yän′, -yən) ***n.*** ⟦< Fr *bouillir,* to boil⟧ a clear broth
boul·der (bōl′dər) ***n.*** ⟦< ME *bulderston,* noisy stone⟧ a large rock worn by weather and water
bou·le·vard (bool′ə värd′) ***n.*** ⟦Fr < MDu *bolwerc,* bulwark⟧ a broad street lined with trees, etc.
bounce (bouns) ***vi.*** **bounced, bounc′ing** ⟦ME *bounsen,* to thump⟧ **1** to spring back, as upon impact; rebound **2** to spring; leap **3** [Slang] to be returned: said of a worthless check —***vt.*** **1** to cause (a ball, etc.) to bounce **2** [Slang] to put (a person) out by force **3** [Slang] to fire from a job —***n.*** **1** *a*) a bouncing; rebound *b*) a leap or jump **2** capacity for bouncing **3** [Inf.] energy, zest, etc. —**the bounce** [Slang] dismissal —**bounc′y *adj.***
bounc′er *n.* [Slang] a person hired to remove disorderly people from a nightclub, restaurant, etc.
bounc′ing *adj.* big, healthy, etc.
bound[1] (bound) ***vi.*** ⟦< OFr *bondir,* to leap⟧ **1** to move with a leap or leaps **2** to bounce; rebound —***vt.*** to cause to bound or bounce —***n.*** **1** a jump; leap **2** a bounce; rebound
bound[2] (bound) ***vt., vi.*** *pt. & pp. of* BIND —***adj.*** **1** tied **2** closely connected **3** certain; sure *[bound to lose]* **4** obliged **5** having a binding: said as of a book **6** [Inf.] determined; resolved
bound[3] (bound) ***adj.*** ⟦< ON *bua,* prepare⟧ going; headed *[bound for home]*
bound[4] (bound) ***n.*** ⟦< ML *butina,* boundary⟧ **1** a boundary **2** [*pl.*] an area near a boundary —***vt.*** **1** to limit **2** to be a limit or boundary to **3** to name the boundaries of —**out of bounds** **1** beyond the boundaries **2** forbidden
bound·a·ry (boun′drē, -də rē) ***n.,*** *pl.* **-ries** anything marking a limit; bound
bound′en *adj.* ⟦old pp. of BIND⟧ **1** [Archaic] obligated; indebted **2** obligatory *[one's bounden duty]*
bound′er *n.* ⟦< BOUND[1]⟧ [Inf., Chiefly Brit.] a cad
bound′less *adj.* unlimited; vast
boun·te·ous (boun′tē əs) ***adj.*** ⟦see BOUNTY⟧ **1** generous **2** plentiful —**boun′te·ous·ly *adv.***
boun′ti·ful (-tə fəl) ***adj.*** BOUNTEOUS
boun′ty (-tē) ***n.,*** *pl.* **-ties** ⟦< L *bonus,* good⟧ **1** generosity **2** a generous gift **3** a reward or premium
bou·quet (bō kā′; *for 2, usually* bōō-) ***n.*** ⟦Fr⟧ **1** a bunch of flowers **2** aroma, as of wine
bour·bon (bur′bən) ***n.*** ⟦after *Bourbon* County, KY⟧ [*sometimes* **B-**] a whiskey distilled from corn mash
bour·geois (boor zhwä′) ***n.,*** *pl.* **-geois′** ⟦Fr < OFr *borc,* town⟧ a member of the bourgeoisie —***adj.*** of the bourgeoisie: used variously to mean conventional, smug, materialistic, etc.
bour·geoi·sie (boor′zhwä zē′) ***n.*** [*with sing. or pl. v.*] the social class between the very wealthy and the working class; middle class
bout (bout) ***n.*** ⟦ME *bught*⟧ **1** a struggle or contest **2** a period of some activity, as a spell of illness
bou·tique (bōō tēk′; *occas.,* bō-) ***n.*** ⟦Fr < L *apotheca,* storehouse⟧ a small shop where fashionable articles are sold
bou·ton·niere or **bou·ton·nière** (bōō′tə nir′, -tən yer′) ***n.*** ⟦Fr, buttonhole⟧ a flower worn in a buttonhole
bo·vine (bō′vīn′, -vēn′) ***adj.*** ⟦< L *bos,* ox⟧ **1** of an ox, cow, etc. **2** slow, dull, stupid, etc.
bow[1] (bou) ***vi.*** ⟦< OE *bugan,* to bend⟧ **1** to bend down the head or body in respect, agreement, etc. **2** to give in —***vt.*** **1** to bend (the head or body) down in respect, etc. **2** to weigh (*down*) —***n.*** a bending down of the head or body, as in respect or greeting —**take a bow** to acknowledge applause, etc.
bow[2] (bō) ***n.*** ⟦OE *boga*⟧ **1** anything curved *[a rainbow]* **2** a curve; bend **3** a flexible, curved strip of wood with a cord connecting the two ends, for shooting arrows **4** a slender stick strung with horsehairs, as for playing a violin **5** a decorative knot, as a bowknot —***adj.*** curved —***vt., vi.*** **1** to bend; curve **2** to play (a violin, etc.) with a bow
bow[3] (bou) ***n.*** ⟦< LowG *būg*⟧ the front part of a ship, etc.
bowd·ler·ize (boud′lər īz′) ***vt.*** **-ized′, -iz′ing** ⟦after T. *Bowdler* (1754-1825), Eng editor⟧ to expurgate —**bowd′ler·ism′ *n.*** —**bowd′ler·i·za′tion *n.***
bow·el (bou′əl) ***n.*** ⟦< L *botulus,* sausage⟧ **1** an intestine, esp. of a human being **2** [*pl.*] the inner part —**move one's bowels** to defecate
bow·er (bou′ər) ***n.*** ⟦< OE *bur,* dwelling⟧ a place enclosed by boughs or vines; arbor
bow·ie knife (bōō′ē, bō′-) ⟦after Col. J. *Bowie* (1799?-1836)⟧ a long single-edged hunting knife

BOWIE KNIFE

bow·knot (bō′nät′) ***n.*** a decorative knot, usually with two loops and two ends
bowl[1] (bōl) ***n.*** ⟦OE *bolla*⟧ **1** a deep, rounded dish **2** the contents of a bowl **3** a bowl-like thing or part **4** an amphitheater or stadium —**bowl′like′ *adj.***
bowl[2] (bōl) ***n.*** ⟦< L *bulla,* bubble⟧ **1** the wooden ball used in the game of lawn bowling **2** a roll of the ball in bowling —***vi.*** **1** to roll a ball or participate in bowling **2** to move swiftly and smoothly —**bowl over** **1** to knock over **2** [Inf.] to astonish —**bowl′er *n.***
bowl·der (bōl′der) ***n.*** *alt. sp. of* BOULDER
bow·leg (bō′leg′) ***n.*** a leg with outward curvature —**bow′leg′ged** (-leg′id, -legd′) ***adj.***
bowl′ing *n.* **1** a game in which a heavy ball is rolled along a wooden lane (**bowling alley**) at ten wooden pins **2** LAWN BOWLING
bowling green a lawn for lawn bowling
bowls (bōlz) ***n.*** LAWN BOWLING
bow·man (bō′mən) ***n.,*** *pl.* **-men** (-mən) an archer
bow·sprit (bou′sprit′, bō′-) ***n.*** ⟦prob. < Du⟧ a tapered spar extending forward from the bow of a sailing ship
bow tie (bō) a necktie tied in a bow
box[1] (bäks) ***n.*** ⟦< Gr *pyxos,* BOX[3]⟧ **1** a container, usually rectangular and lidded; case **2** the contents of a box **3** a boxlike thing or space *[a jury box]* **4** a small, enclosed group of seats, as in a theater **5** a booth *[a sentry box]* **6** *Baseball* an area designated for the batter, catcher, etc. —***vt.*** to put into a box —**box in** (or **up**) to shut in or keep in; surround or confine —**in a box** [Inf.] in difficulty —**box′like′ *adj.*** —**box′y, -i·er, -i·est, *adj.***
box[2] (bäks) ***n.*** ⟦< ?⟧ a blow struck with the hand —***vt.*** **1** to strike with such a blow **2** to engage in boxing with —***vi.*** to fight with the fists
box[3] (bäks) ***n.*** ⟦< Gr *pyxos*⟧ an evergreen shrub with small leathery leaves: also **box′wood′**
box′car′ *n.* a fully enclosed railroad freight car
box′er *n.* **1** one who boxes; prizefighter **2** a medium-sized dog with a sturdy body and a smooth coat
box′ing *n.* the skill or sport of fighting with the fists, esp. in padded leather mittens (**boxing gloves**)
box office **1** a place where admission tickets are sold, as in a theater **2** [Inf.] the power of a show or performer to attract a paying audience
box wrench a wrench with an enclosed head
boy (boi) ***n.*** ⟦ME *boie*⟧ **1** a male child **2** any man: familiar term **3** a male servant: a patronizing term —***interj.*** [Slang] used to express pleasure, surprise, etc.: often **oh, boy!** —**boy′hood′ *n.*** —**boy′ish *adj.***
boy·cott (boi′kät′) ***vt.*** ⟦after Capt. *Boycott,* Irish land agent so treated in 1880⟧ to join together in refusing to deal with, buy, etc. so as to punish or coerce —***n.*** a boycotting
boy′friend′ *n.* [Inf.] **1** a sweetheart or escort of a girl or woman **2** a boy who is someone's friend
Boy Scout a member of the **Boy Scouts,** a boys' organization that stresses outdoor life and service to others

59 **◄ brainwash**

boy·sen·ber·ry (boi′zən ber′ē) ***n.,*** *pl.* **-ries** ⟦after R. *Boysen,* U.S. horticulturist, developer (*c.* 1935)⟧ a berry that is a cross of the raspberry, loganberry, and blackberry
Br[1] *abbrev.* **1** Branch **2** British **3** Brother
Br[2] *Chem. symbol for* bromine
bra (brä) ***n.*** ⟦< BRASSIERE⟧ a woman's undergarment for supporting the breasts
brace (brās) ***vt.*** **braced, brac′ing** ⟦< Gr *brachiōn,* arm⟧ **1** to bind **2** to strengthen by supporting the weight of, etc. **3** to make ready for an impact, shock, etc. **4** to stimulate; invigorate —***n.*** **1** a couple; pair **2** a thing that clasps or connects **3** [*pl.*] [Brit.] suspenders **4** a device for setting up or maintaining tension **5** either of the signs { }, used to connect words, lines, etc. **6** any propping device **7** *a*) a device for supporting a weak part of the body *b*) [*often pl.*] a device worn for straightening teeth **8** a tool for holding a drilling bit —**brace up** to call forth one's courage, etc.
brace and bit a tool for boring, consisting of a removable drill (*bit*) in a rotating handle (*brace*)
brace·let (brās′lit) ***n.*** ⟦< Gr *brachiōn,* arm⟧ an ornamental band or chain worn around the wrist or arm —**brace′let·ed *adj.***
brack·en (brak′ən) ***n.*** ⟦ME *braken*⟧ a large, weedy fern found in meadows, woods, etc.
brack·et (brak′it) ***n.*** ⟦< Fr *brague,* knee pants⟧ **1** a support projecting from a wall, etc. **2** any angle-shaped support **3** either of the signs [ ], used to enclose a word, etc. **4** the part of a classified grouping within certain limits *[high income bracket]* —***vt.*** **1** to support with brackets **2** to enclose within brackets **3** to classify together
brack·ish (brak′ish) ***adj.*** ⟦< MDu *brak*⟧ **1** salty **2** nauseating —**brack′ish·ness *n.***
bract (brakt) ***n.*** ⟦L *bractea,* thin metal plate⟧ a modified leaf growing at the base of a flower or on its stalk
brad (brad) ***n.*** ⟦ON *broddr,* arrow⟧ a thin wire nail with a small head
brae (brā, brē) ***n.*** ⟦ON *bra,* brow⟧ [Scot.] a sloping bank; hillside
brag (brag) ***vt., vi.*** **bragged, brag′ging** ⟦ME *braggen* < ?⟧ to boast —***n.*** boastful talk —**brag′ger *n.***
brag′gart (-ərt) ***n.*** an offensively boastful person —***adj.*** boastful
Brah·ma (brä′mə) ***n.*** Hindu god regarded as the creator of the universe
Brah·man (brä′mən) ***n.,*** *pl.* **-mans** ⟦Hindi < Sans, worship⟧ **1** a member of the Hindu priestly caste **2** a breed of domestic cattle developed from the zebu of India and having a large hump
Brahms (brämz), **Jo·han·nes** (yō hän′əs) 1833-97; Ger. composer
braid (brād) ***vt.*** ⟦< OE *bregdan,* to move quickly⟧ **1** to interweave three or more strands of (hair, straw, etc.) **2** to make by such interweaving —***n.*** **1** a length of hair, etc. formed by braiding **2** a woven band of cloth, etc., used to bind or decorate clothing
Braille (brāl) ***n.*** ⟦after L. *Braille* (1809-52), its Fr inventor⟧ [*also* **b-**] a system of printing for the blind, using raised dots felt with the fingers
brain (brān) ***n.*** ⟦OE *brægen*⟧ **1** the mass of nerve tissue in the cranium of vertebrates **2** [*often pl.*] intelligence **3** [Inf.] an intelligent person —***vt.*** [Slang] to hit hard on the head
brain′child′ *n.* [Inf.] an idea, plan, etc. produced by a person's own mental labor
brain drain [Inf.] an exhausting of the intellectual or professional resources of a country, region, etc., esp. through emigration
brain′less *adj.* foolish or stupid
brain′storm′ *n.* [Inf.] a sudden inspiration, idea, or plan —***vi.*** to engage in brainstorming
brain′storm′ing *n.* the unrestrained offering of ideas by all members of a group to seek solutions to problems
brain′wash′ *vt.* [Inf.] to indoctrinate so thor-

Michael Agnes and Andrew N. Sparks, eds., *Webster's New World Compact School and Office Dictionary, Fourth Edition* (New York: Hungry Minds, 2002), 58–59.

SPELLING

A dictionary is a valuable resource when it comes to spelling words. However, anyone who has had difficulty spelling a word correctly knows the frustration of being told to "just look it up in the dictionary." This is not an easy answer to the problem of correcting a misspelled word because many letters have more than one sound. Also, the spelling of a word in a dictionary is the Standard American English spelling. Sometimes an alternative spelling (often British) may appear after the American one; however, the first one is always preferred in the United States. For example, the words *practice* (American English) and *practise* (British English) are usually both shown in a dictionary. The first spelling, *practice*, is preferred in this country.

STUDY TIP

Are You a Misspeller?

Do you struggle to find words in a dictionary because you are not sure how to look them up when you don't know how to spell them? If you are a misspeller, and many of us are, you might want to take a look at a special dictionary that has words listed the way they are often incorrectly spelled. For example, you could find out how to correctly spell the word *midnight* by looking up the possible spelling *midnite*. *Webster's Bad Speller's Dictionary* is just one of several of these special dictionaries available with helpful instructions on how to look up words. Dictionaries for those of us who are "spelling impaired" can also be found in electronic form and on the Internet. See http://www. answers.com/library/Misspeller's%20Dictionary.

Four Methods for Finding the Correct Spelling of a Word

Method 1: Think about how the word sounds. Pronounce the word slowly and listen to the letter sounds in the word. Then write the word you are searching for, spelling it as accurately as you can. Look in your dictionary for an entry word containing the letters you hear. Always look for the initial or first sound to begin your search. Often a silent letter will make a difference in how a word sounds and how it is spelled. For example, the word *psychology* sounds like it would be spelled *sikology*, but it will not be found under *s*. This might be the time to check a misspeller's dictionary, or try method 2.

Method 2: If the word is not in the dictionary as you have written it, then check the consonants you have used to spell it. Try a single consonant instead of a double one, or try doubling a consonant if you wrote a single one. For example, the word for a notebook with important dates and reminders sounds as though it is spelled *planer*, but the word *planer* means something else altogether. If you double the consonant *n* and look for the word again, you will see that the correct spelling for the notebook is *planner*. If you don't find your word by doubling or removing a consonant, try method 3.

Method 3: Because vowels can sound alike, try putting another vowel in the place of a vowel you have written in your word. If you have spelled your word with an *i*, try an *e* or another vowel. For example, *English* is correct, but *Inglish* is not. If you cannot find your word after checking each possible vowel, then try Method 4.

Method 4: Try a consonant or a group of consonants from Chapter Two that sound like those used in your word but use different letters to make the sound. Examples are *c/k, c/s,* or *sh/ch.* Try finding the word in your dictionary by changing these letters. For example, the words *shampane* and *champagne* both start with the same sound, but the dictionary shows that *champagne* is the correct spelling.

EXERCISE 4-A   Find the correct spelling of each of the following words in your dictionary, note the page number, and rewrite the word correctly.

1. sherrif, sheriff, or sherif   Page # _____   Correct spelling _____

2. recieve, receeve, receive   Page # _____   Correct spelling _____

3. sylablle, syllable, sylleble   Page # _____   Correct spelling _____

4. comfert, cumford, comfort   Page # _____   Correct spelling _____

5. nickel, nikel, nickle   Page # _____   Correct spelling _____

Words That Sound Alike

Some words sound alike but are spelled differently to indicate different meanings. For example, the words *reed* and *read* sound the same, but *reed* means "a kind of hollow grass" and *read* means "to get the meaning of something by interpreting characters or signs." Look up the word you want according to the way you think it is spelled. Note the definition. If the definition of the word does not match the sense of the passage, think of another way the word might be spelled.

EXERCISE 4-B   Put a check mark beside the correct definition for each of the following words. Both answers sound the same but have different meanings. Use your dictionary if necessary.

1. a plant   _____ been   _____ bean

2. a fine, powdered grain   _____ flower   _____ flour

3. a single thing   _____ one   _____ won

4. loved   _____ deer   _____ dear

5. to shut   _____ close   _____ clothes

Spelling and Root Words

Many of the entry words listed in alphabetical order in the dictionary are root words. If you are looking for a word that has a suffix, like *-ed* or *-ing,* you may not find it listed as an entry word. For example, the entry word *write* also includes *written* and *writing,* new words formed by adding suffixes (endings) to the root word *write.* The correct spelling for these new words (*written, writing*) is found by looking up the entry word *write.*

EXERCISE 4-C   The following words are made from root words with suffixes added to them. In your dictionary, find the root word for each word, and notice its correct spelling (without a suffix). Record the page number where you found the word and the correct spelling of the root word.

1. sleeping   Page # _____   Root word _____

2. skipped   Page # _____   Root word _____

3. committing   Page # _____   Root word _____

4. hopeful   Page # _____   Root word _____

5. lengthy   Page # _____   Root word _____

Spelling and Plurals

Most nouns can be made plural (to indicate more than one) by adding an *s* or *es*. For example, the word *box* becomes *boxes* in its plural form. However, some nouns have completely different spellings or don't change at all when they become plural. Look up the word *mouse* in your dictionary. Note that the word is followed with the abbreviation *pl*, showing that the plural form of the noun is to follow. The plural form of *mouse* is *mice*.

EXERCISE 4-D   This exercise will help you spell correctly the plural forms of the following nouns.

Locate each noun in your dictionary, record the page number, and write the correct spelling of its plural form.

1. passerby   Page # _____   Plural form _____

2. louse   Page # _____   Plural form _____

3. deer   Page # _____   Plural form _____

4. index   Page # _____   Plural form _____

5. son-in-law   Page # _____   Plural form _____

Spelling and Word Processors

If you use a word processor to write your papers, the spell-checker feature can be helpful. However, using a spell-checker is not without problems. If you type the word *personel*, for example, the spell-checker might suggest *personnel* or *personal*, two words with quite different meanings, and you are still faced with choosing the correct word for your paper. If you are not certain, a dictionary is the answer because you can check both spellings and chose the one with the correct meaning for your paper. Small handheld computer dictionaries are also available, but they provide limited information because of their size. They can be useful when you need a fast reference but should not be used as a serious study tool.

EXERCISE 4-E   Use your dictionary to find the correct spelling of each of the following words. Remember the four steps mentioned earlier in this section to help you find the correct spelling.

Misspelled Word	*Dictionary Page #*	*Correct Spelling*
1. reseptiv	_____	_____
2. sertainte	_____	_____
3. sivil	_____	_____
4. enkorage	_____	_____
5. publik	_____	_____
6. disgrasful	_____	_____
7. horibul	_____	_____
8. akseptanse	_____	_____
9. konfuson	_____	_____
10. fotograf	_____	_____

SYLLABLES AND SYLLABICATION

A dictionary can help you pronounce words correctly, too. As you learned in Chapter 3, a **syllable** is a part of a word that is pronounced as a single sound. The number of syllables in a word depends on the way the word is pronounced, not the way it is written. For example, only two syllables are pronounced in the word *million*. The word is written with three vowels: *i, i,* and *o*. However, in the second syllable, the *i* and *o* actually make only one sound. Thus, the word has two syllables. A word may have one or more syllables; the number of syllables depends on the number of vowel sounds. Unlike vowel sounds, the sounds made by more than one consonant do not produce separate syllables.

Recall from Chapter 3 that **syllabication** means dividing a word into its separate syllables. Entry words in the dictionary that have more than one syllable are divided into syllables by dots, dashes, or spaces. For example, *gallery* may be written *gal•ler•y, gal-ler-y* or *gal ler y*. A one-syllable word cannot be divided into syllables.

A dictionary also shows you whether a word is written as a compound word (like *bloodhound*), as a hyphenated word (like *blood-red*), or as two words (like *blood bank*.)

EXERCISE 4-F   Look up each of the following words in your dictionary and use the method indicated to divide it into syllables.

irresistible (use dots)	_____
dictionary (use dashes)	_____
discipline (use spaces)	_____

EXERCISE 4-G Use your dictionary to locate the following words and complete the chart.

Entry Word	Dictionary Page #	Number of Syllables	Word Rewritten as Separate Syllables
1. American	_____	_____	_____
2. threaten	_____	_____	_____
3. discourage	_____	_____	_____
4. psychology	_____	_____	_____
5. experience	_____	_____	_____
6. reverse	_____	_____	_____
7. valuable	_____	_____	_____
8. alternative	_____	_____	_____
9. initial	_____	_____	_____
10. gesture	_____	_____	_____

PRONUNCIATION

As mentioned earlier, a dictionary helps you to pronounce words correctly. In your dictionary, look at the section called "Guide to Pronunciation," or something similar, and you will find a list of vowels with symbols showing how each one sounds. The following box shows a sample of what you will see in your dictionary.

a as in **fat**	$\bar{o}$ as in **note**
$\bar{a}$ as in **fate**	oo as in **spoon**
ä as in **far**	oi as in **oil**
e as in **met**	ow as in **owl**
$\bar{e}$ as in **mete**	$\bar{u}$ as in **mute**
i as in **pin**	u as in **up**
$\bar{i}$ as in **pine**	ŭ as in **pull**
	ə as in **comm**a

EXERCISE 4-H Look up the following italicized words in your dictionary. For each word, write the word from the preceding box that has the same vowel sound.

1. Sally went to a *dude* ranch in Colorado. _____

2. Joe is in the *infantry*. _____

3. Don't *spoil* your supper! _____

4. This party is for the *adults*. _____

5. Did you drop your *knife*? _____

In addition to the symbols that represent the sounds of vowels (and consonants), there are marks that show which syllable to stress more sharply when saying a word. For example, the word *total* is pronounced with the stress on the first syllable. It is shown in the dictionary as *to'təl*. Notice the bold stress mark. This is the strongest stress; a lighter mark would be a slight stress in words of more than two syllables, as in the word *esoteric,* which appears as *es'ə-ter'ik* in the dictionary.

EXERCISE 4-1 Using your dictionary, find each of the following words, and write them below using the pronunciation symbols and the strong stress marks shown in the dictionary.

Entry Word	*Word Rewritten with Pronunciation Symbols and Stresses*
1. American	_____
2. threaten	_____
3. discourage	_____
4. psychology	_____
5. experience	_____
6. reverse	_____
7. valuable	_____
8. alternative	_____
9. initial	_____
10. gesture	_____

MEANING

Sometimes you might get lucky. You might look up a word in the dictionary and find only one definition. But most words have more than one definition. You must choose the definition that helps you make meaning from the text you are reading. Read the following paragraph and pay particular attention to the words in bold print. Then read the dictionary definitions that follow and decide which definition, if there is more than one, best explains each word.

Moments to Remember

The **legendary** play was about to begin. As the lights dimmed, the audience settled down, and those who had come in late quickly **located** their seats. I was **tingling** with excitement. We were sitting in Her Majesty's Theatre in London, and The **Phantom** of the **Opera** was about to **commence**. I was **overwhelmed** by the sight of the beautiful **chandelier**, which I knew played an important part in the play. Although we were seated in the balcony, the theater provided an **intimate** setting because of its small size compared with other theaters. The music of the pipe organ **swelled** in my ears, and the famous love story came to life.

EXERCISE 4-J For each word in bold print, write the definition that best fits the overall meaning of the paragraph.

1. **leg′end**—*n.* **1** a widely accepted but unverified story **2** an inscription; a caption; a written key

   _____

2. **lo′ cate**—*v.t.* **1** discover or describe the place or locality of **2** establish in a particular place, settle

   _____

3. **tin′ gle**—*v.i.* have a prickling or stinging sensation; cause such a sensation

   _____

4. **phan′ tom**—*n.* **1** an apparition; specter; something unreal **2** a representation of something abstract or ideal

   _____

5. **op′ er a**—*n.* **1** a drama wholly sung **2** pl. of *opus*

   _____

6. **com mence′**—*v.t. & i.* **1** begin **2** to have or make meaning

   _____

7. **o″ ver whelm′**—*v.t.* **1** cover, bury, load, or weigh upon overpoweringly; crush; oppress **2** overcome with emotion

   _____

8. **chan″ de lier′**—*n.* a branched cluster of lights hung from the ceiling

   _____

9. **in′ ti mate**—*adj.* **1** close in personal relations; familiar, closely allied **2** personal; private **3** pertaining to the inmost part or essential nature

   _____

10. **swell**—*v.i. & t.* **1** grow in bulk; bulge; expand **2** rise, as a wave **3** show elation

    _____

As you noticed, many of the words in Exercise 4-J were different forms of the words from those in the text. For example, you had to use the definition of *legend* to understand the meaning of the word *legendary* because the word *legendary* is not defined in many dictionaries. Dictionaries often provide the most useful words in the English language rather than every word because of lack of space. Often other forms of the word are listed after the definition of the more commonly used word. The adjective *legendary* is provided at the end of the definition for the noun *legend*:

> leg'end—*n* **1** a widely accepted but unverified story **2** an inscription; a caption; a written key (leg' end ar' y) *adj.*

Several of the words in bold print in the "Moments to Remember" paragraph are past tense verbs: *located, overwhelmed,* and *swelled.* To find the definitions of these words, you would have to look up the present tense of the verbs in the dictionary: *locate, overwhelm,* and *swell.* Regular past-tense verbs are usually not included as entry words in the dictionary. The following spelling rules for changing verbs from present tense to past tense will help you locate the correct meanings of words in your dictionary. (Information about verb tenses can usually be found in the "How to Use This Dictionary" section in the introductory pages of most dictionaries.)

CHECK IT OUT!

Rules for Changing Verb Tenses

- When changing a regular verb that already ends in *e* from present to past tense, add a *d*.

  grade
  graded

- To change verbs ending in a consonant from present to past tense, add ed.

  benefit
  benefited

- When changing a regular verb that ends in *y* to past tense, change the *y* to *i* and add *ed.*

  defy
  defied

Note: Some verbs ending in a consonant are changed from present tense to past tense by doubling the final consonant and adding *ed.* To be sure, check the entry word of the present-tense verb in the dictionary.

EXERCISE 4-K   Change the following verbs from past to present tense.

1. frustrated   _____

2. disposed   _____

3. imposed   _____

4. faded   _____

5. berated   _____

EXERCISE 4-L Change the following verbs from past tense to present tense.

1. prevented _____
2. destroyed _____
3. invented _____
4. treated _____
5. grounded _____

EXERCISE 4-M Change the following verbs from past tense to present tense.

1. supplied _____
2. terrified _____
3. multiplied _____
4. relied _____
5. amplified _____

EXERCISE 4-N Change the following verbs from past tense to present tense.

1. bragged _____
2. prodded _____
3. swatted _____
4. plotted _____
5. clogged _____

PARTS OF SPEECH

All the words in the English language have been divided into eight groups. These word groups are called the **parts of speech**: nouns, pronouns, verbs, adjectives, adverbs, prepositions, interjections, and conjunctions. The dictionary tells you what part of speech a word is. Many words may be used as more than one part of speech. In a dictionary, the part of speech is indicated by an abbreviation in *italics* that comes either before or after the meaning of the word. The abbreviations for the eight parts of speech are:

n.	noun
pron.	pronoun
v.i.	verb (intransitive)
v.t.	verb (transitive)
prep.	preposition
adv.	adverb
interj.	interjection
adj.	adjective
conj.	conjunction

For example, the dictionary entry for the word *aardvark* is **aard′ vark′** (ärd′ värk′) *n.* an African ant-eating mammal; groundhog. Notice the small, italicized *n.* after the pronunciation of the word. The *n.* means that the word *aardvark* is a noun.

EXERCISE 4-O

1. The abbreviation for *preposition* is _____.

2. Look up the word *abroad. Abroad* can be a preposition. It can also be an

_____.

Each of the following words has more than one part of speech. For each word, list the parts of speech given in your dictionary.

3. daily   _____

4. just   _____

5. Write a sentence using the word *load* as a noun.

_____

CHECK IT OUT!

Reviewing the Parts of Speech

1. **Noun:** names a person, place, thing, or idea (e.g., *Delores, cup*).

   Delores has learned how to hold a *cup*.

2. **Pronoun:** used in place of a noun (e.g., *I, me, you*).

   Let *me* tell *you* what *I* think *we* should do.

3. **Verb:** expresses action or a state of being (e.g., *is, are, play, walk*).

   We *are walking* our dog, Gypsy.

4. **Adjective:** describes a noun or pronoun (e.g., *pretty, short, nice*).

   Shanny is *pretty*.

5. **Adverb:** tells something about a verb, an adjective, or another adverb. (e.g., *easily, very, fast, soon*).

   Larry is *very* handsome.

6. **Preposition:** shows how a noun is related to another word in a sentence (e.g., *on, near, from*).

   Larry and I went *to* a play *on* my birthday.

7. **Interjection:** shows emotion or surprise (e.g., *Wow, Oh*).

   Wow, that is really cool!

8. **Conjunction:** connects words or groups of words (e.g., *and, or, but, so*).

   Connie had a good job, *but* she had trouble getting to work on time.

WORD ORIGINS

The **origin of a word** is a word's history, or **etymology**. The history of a word tells you how a word has changed through different languages and many years to become the word we know today. In most dictionaries, the origin of a word is set off in square brackets **[ ]** in the entry. You will find a section at the beginning of your dictionary that lists the various symbols used and what they mean. Often the language of origin is abbreviated in the dictionary entry. Some of the most common abbreviations are shown below:

AF	Anglo-French	**G**	German
Afr	African	**Gk**	Greek
AmerInd	American Indian	**It**	Italian
Ar	Arabic	**L**	Latin
Celt	Celtic	**ME**	Middle English
Du	Dutch	**OE**	Old English
F	French	**Sp**	Spanish

Many people never notice the abbreviations that indicate the language or languages of origin for words. If they do notice, they do not know the meaning of the abbreviations they see. It is important to take the time to learn about where words come from. After reading about a word's background, you will probably remember the history of the word you looked up, and that will help you remember its meaning. The following two entries show samples of word origin information from *Webster's New World Compact School and Office Dictionary* (see the sample pages from the dictionary shown on page 120 of this chapter). The information about word origins appears in bold print here. Sometimes a word is traced back to more than one language.

> **boss** (bôs, bos) *n.* **[Du *baas*, a master]** **1** an employer or manager **2** one who controls a political organization—*v.t.* **1** to act as boss of **2** *Informal*, to order a person about

> **braid** (brād) *v.t.* **[< OE *bregdan*, to move quickly]** **1** to interweave three or more strands (of hair, straw, etc.) **2** to make by such interweaving —*n.* **1** a length of hair, etc., formed by braiding **2** a woven band of cloth, etc., used to bind or decorate clothing

EXERCISE 4-P
1. If a dictionary has the abbreviation Gk after a definition, the word origin is _____.

2. Find the word *cushy* in your dictionary. It is originally from the _____ language.

3. The origin of the word *diaper* is _____.

4. The word *rock* has two meanings: "to sway" comes from _____; "mass," as in a heavy object, comes from _____.

5. *Dismal* comes from Latin and means "evil days." Use the word *dismal* in a sentence _____

_____

PRACTICING WHAT YOU HAVE LEARNED

PRACTICE 4-1 **Dictionary Skills**

Use your dictionary to locate the following words and complete the chart.

Entry Word	Dictionary Page #	Number of Syllables	Word Rewritten as Separate Syllables
1. constitution	_____	_____	_____
2. paradox	_____	_____	_____
3. celebration	_____	_____	_____
4. thorough	_____	_____	_____
5. erroneously	_____	_____	_____
6. stupendous	_____	_____	_____
7. matriculation	_____	_____	_____
8. ebony	_____	_____	_____
9. allegiance	_____	_____	_____
10. hurricane	_____	_____	_____

PRACTICE 4-2 **Dictionary Skills**

Using your dictionary, find each of the following words and write the pronunciation symbols and strong and slight stress marks shown in the dictionary for each.

Entry Word	Word Rewritten with Pronunciation Symbols and Stresses
1. constitution	_____
2. paradox	_____
3. celebration	_____

4. thorough _____

5. erroneously _____

6. stupendous _____

7. matriculation _____

8. ebony _____

9. allegiance _____

10. hurricane _____

PRACTICE 4-3 **Dictionary Skills**

Look up the following words in your dictionary, and write them with the correct stress marks.

1. fumble _____

2. theater _____

3. bubble _____

4. triangle _____

5. lipstick _____

PRACTICE 4-4 **Dictionary Skills**

Put a check mark next to the correct definition for each word in the list below. Use your dictionary if necessary.

1. uncovered _____ bear _____ bare

2. moisture _____ dew _____ do

3. negative answer _____ know _____ no

4. to purchase _____ by _____ buy

5. correct _____ write _____ right

6. mother's sister _____ aunt _____ ant

7. total _____ some _____ sum

8. number after 7 _____ ate _____ eight

9. a fragrant flower _____ rose _____ rows

10. middle of body _____ waste _____ waist

PRACTICE 4-5 **Dictionary Skills**

Change the following verbs from present tense to past tense.

1. elate _____ 3. integrate _____

2. revolve _____ 4. practice _____

5. revise _____   8. change _____

6. create _____   9. bake _____

7. love _____   10. locate _____

PRACTICE 4-6 **Dictionary Skills**

Change the following verbs from past tense to present tense.

1. layered _____   6. predicted _____

2. covered _____   7. talked _____

3. cooked _____   8. presented _____

4. listened _____   9. elected _____

5. walked _____   10. followed _____

PRACTICE 4-7 **Dictionary Skills**

Change the following verbs from past tense to present tense.

1. studied _____   6. varied _____

2. readied _____   7. gratified _____

3. levied _____   8. spied _____

4. carried _____   9. married _____

5. worried _____   10. fried _____

PRACTICE 4-8 **Dictionary Skills**

Change the following verbs from past tense to present tense.

1. grabbed _____   6. compelled _____

2. committed _____   7. concurred _____

3. occurred _____   8. jabbed _____

4. trotted _____   9. matted _____

5. batted _____   10. propelled _____

PRACTICE 4-9 **Dictionary Skills**

Using your dictionary, find the correct meanings of the verbs in bold print in the following sentences. On the lines provided, write the meaning of each word and write the present-tense verb you located in your dictionary to help you find the meaning of the past-tense verb.

1 He **bleached** his hair by being in the sun all summer.

bleached: _____

2. I **gargled** with warm salt water when I was sick.

gargled: _____

3. The pirates **scanned** the horizon for enemy ships.

   scanned: _____

4. The bus driver **horrified** the passengers when he hit the deer.

   horrified: _____

5. The automotive store **itemized** the bill so I could see exactly what I was paying for.

   itemized: _____

PRACTICE 4-10   **Dictionary Skills: *Beauty from a Distance***

Read the following paragraph.

> ### Beauty from a Distance
>
> I was **infatuated** with her, but she wouldn't even **glance** my way. My friends and I had taken an **excursion** on the *Maid of the Mist* to view the **magnificent** Niagara Falls. We had **departed** from the Canadian side decked in blue rainproof **ponchos** that looked a lot like garbage bags. As I pushed my way toward the bow of the ship, I saw her, and her sparkling eyes and **radiant** smile made my heart beat faster. **Unfortunately**, she was smiling at another fellow instead of at me. Suddenly, the spray from the falls landed in our faces, and the boat leaped up and over the **turbulent** waves. Those people not holding on to the rail were thrown to one side and then another. I saw her lose her balance and fall **dramatically** into the arms of another man. Why couldn't it have been me!

Use the dictionary to find the definitions of the words in bold print. If a word has more than one definition, write the one that best matches how the word is used in the paragraph. Write the word that you looked up in order to find the meaning of each boldfaced word.

1. infatuated: _____

   _____

2. glance: _____

   _____

3. excursion: _____

   _____

4. magnificent: _____

   _____

5. departed: _____

   _____

6. ponchos: _____

   _____

7. radiant: _____

_____

8. unfortunately: _____

_____

9. turbulent: _____

_____

10. dramatically: _____

_____

PRACTICE 4-11 **Parts of Speech:** *Marly*

Write the correct part of speech beside each word printed in bold.

Marly

Marly (1) **slammed** (_____) the phone onto its holder. (2) **Her** (_____) (3) **sister** (_____) Suzanne sometimes made her so mad. Marly had been talking to Carla, one of her sister's (4) **best** (_____) friends. (5) **Carla** (_____) had (6) **jokingly** (_____) told Suzanne that Marly had stood her up (7) **for** (_____) a lunch date. Suzanne, thinking the worst about her irresponsible (8) **little** (_____) sister, had had a major meltdown before Carla could explain. Carla then told Suzanne that Marly had called (9) **and** (_____) canceled ahead (10) **of** (_____) time. (11) **She** (_____) had not (12) **really** (_____) stood her up for a luncheon date. (13) "Wow", (_____) said Carla. "I told her to chill, to not get so upset about little things. After all, you are an adult." Marly (14) **barely** (_____) heard Carla say good-bye. She was too busy (15) **planning** (_____) how to best get even with her sister.

PRACTICE 4-12 **Language of Origin:** *André*

Write the language of origin beside each word printed in bold.

André

My nephew André is a little (1) **devil** (_____). He runs (2) **amok** (_____) the entire day. Last (3) **Thursday** (_____), he ran at full speed into an outside corner of his little sister's play (4) **cottage** (_____) while playing (5) **soldiers** (_____). We had to rush

him to the (6) **hospital** (_____) by (7) **ambulance** (_____).
He was in (8) **surgery** (_____) for over an hour getting stitches. He is so (9)
spoiled (_____), but we (10) **love** (_____) him.

SUMMARY

- A **dictionary** contains an alphabetical listing of words with their **definitions** (meanings); many words have more than one definition.

- A dictionary tells you what **part of speech** a word is (noun, verb, adjective, adverb, preposition, conjunction). Many words may be used as more than one part of speech.

- A dictionary often provides information on the **etymology**, or origin, of words. The language of origin is abbreviated in the dictionary entry.

- A dictionary helps you pronounce words by dividing them into syllables and marking which syllables to stress. **Syllables** are parts of words that carry separate sounds. Every syllable must include a vowel sound.

- A dictionary shows you how to spell words correctly. .

- There are **four methods** for finding the correct spelling of a word:

Method 1: Think about how the word sounds.

Method 2: If the word is not in the dictionary as you have written it, check the consonants you have used to spell it.

Method 3: Try putting another vowel in the place of a vowel you have written in the word.

Method 4: Try a consonant or a group of consonants that sound like those used in the word but which use different letters to make the sound.

- Special **misspellers dictionaries** list words the way they are often incorrectly spelled.

MASTERY LEVEL EXERCISES

MASTERY 4-1 **Spelling**

Read the following paragraph about the Pledge of Allegiance and complete the questions following the reading.

(1) Frances Bellamy, a former Baptist minnister, wrote the Pledge of Allegiance in 1892. (2) It was first printed on September 8, 1892, and appeared in the children's magazine *The Youth's Companion.* (3) The pledge was modified on June 14, 1923, by substituting the words "the flag of the United States" instead of "my flag." (4) In 1924, the words "of America" were added when Congres adopted the pledge. (5) The last change in the pledge occured June 14 (Flag Day), 1953, when President Eisenhower approved adding the words "under God." (6) Millions of Americans have memorized and treasured the Pledge of Alegiance that Frances Bellamy wrote. (7) The auther could not have known how much controversy the patriotic pledge would create in the years that followed its publication.

Sentence 1. Which word is misspelled? _____, which is on page _____ in your dictionary.

Sentence 2. *Children* is the plural form of the noun _____, which appears on page _____ in your dictionary.

Sentence 3. To find the meaning of the word *substituting*, you would look up the word _____, which is on page _____ in your dictionary.

Sentence 4. Find the misspelled word and respell it correctly _____. Which page is it on in your dictionary?_____

Sentence 5. The misspelled word, respelled correctly, is _____, which is on page _____ in your dictionary.

READER RESPONSE 4-1

Can you find the misspelled words in sentences 6 and 7? Write them below using the correct spelling. Include the number of the pages they appeared on in your dictionary.

_____

_____

MASTERY 4-2 **Syllables**

Read the following paragraph about St. Patrick's Day.

(1) Ireland claims the shamrock as its national symbol. (2) The three-leafed plant was used by St. Patrick, as popular legend declares, to explain the doctrine of the Trinity as he converted the Irish people from paganism to Christianity. (3) The legend says St. Patrick used the herb in the fifth century; however, historians have never been able to prove this story. (4) The shamrock was considered a sacred plant in ancient Ireland, too, because it signaled the rebirth of spring. (5) It became popular to display the shamrock as a symbol of Irish nationalism during the seventeenth century. (6) Stories about the shamrock continue to charm today's generation, even though most of these stories are only legends.

Follow the directions to show the number of syllables requested.

Sentence 2. Divide *leafed* into syllables. _____

Sentence 3. Divide *historians* into syllables. _____

Sentence 4. Find a three-syllable word. _____

Sentence 5. How many syllables are in the word *nationalism*? _____

Sentence 6. Find a four-syllable word and divide it properly. _____

READER RESPONSE 4-2

Study the cartoon on the next page. Make a list of the things you notice.

_____

_____

_____

_____

What is your response to the cartoon?

_____

_____

_____

_____

MASTERY 4-3 **Pronunciation:** *Obesity*

Read the following paragraph.

Obesity

Obesity has become a major health problem in America. Most doctors, **educators**, and even the government agree that about one-third of the **population** is **severely** overweight. This **trend** is caused by people eating food high in fat and sugar and not exercising enough. Many young people suffer from obesity and are at risk for serious illness when they reach **adulthood**. Diseases caused by weighing too much include **diabetes**, heart disease, high blood pressure, and **arthritis**. Parents should set a good example for their children by being **physically** active and eating and serving a diet with lots of fresh **vegetables** and fruits instead of sweet snacks and pop.

Look up each of the following words in your dictionary. Write the word, showing the syllables, the pronunciation symbols, and the definitions. Then write a sentence using the word.

1. obesity: _____

_____

_____

2. educators: _____

_____

_____

3. population: _____

_____

_____

4. severely: _____

_____

_____

5. trend: _____

_____

_____

6. adulthood: _____

_____

_____

7. diabetes: _____

_____

_____

8. arthritis: _____

_____

_____

9. physically: _____

_____

_____

10. vegetables: _____

_____

_____

MASTERY 4-4 **Vocabulary: *Job Hunting***

Read the following story.

Job Hunting

On Wednesday, Jill decided to look for a job. She had found several jobs in the past by working for friends of her parents. This was the first time she had to find a job on her own. She checked the classified ads in the newspaper and circled some possibilities that interested her. The Internet offered her even more choices. She found several online application forms. The problem for Jill was that she wasn't sure she could fill out an application correctly. Some of the words on the online application forms didn't make any sense to her. So Jill stopped by a department store in the mall and got two applications from the same store. She planned to use one as a guide for filling out other applications. First, though, she had to learn the meanings of the unknown words. The dictionary was the best place to start. After learning what all the words meant and gathering all the necessary information, she was able to transfer the information onto each application form. This process saved her time and gave her a practice sheet for completing future applications. Understanding the words on the application form would also help her perform well in interviews.

Here is a list of words that Jill didn't understand. Use your dictionary to help you match each word with its correct meaning.

1. _____ current
2. _____ benefits
3. _____ eligible
4. _____ chronological
5. _____ previous
6. _____ permanent
7. _____ duties
8. _____ references
9. _____ résumé
10. _____ dismiss

a. The order in which events happen

b. Insurance plans or other extras an employer provides

c. Fit to be chosen (providing information such as a driver's license or Social Security card is one way to prove fitness)

d. Happening before the present time

e. Happening in the present time

f. A summary of a person's experience and history

g. To send someone away

h. Letters of support, usually written by former employers

i. Tasks a person must do

j. Lasting a long time

After Jill looked up the words in the dictionary, she felt more comfortable filling out the application forms. She also knew that she would now know how to answer some of the questions in an interview. Read the following dialogue with a partner. This dialogue is an example of an interview between an employer, Ms. Fern, and Jill.

MS. FERN: Jill, did you bring a résumé with you?

JILL: Yes. My résumé lists my experiences and contact information.

MS. FERN: Does this include your permanent address and phone number?

JILL: Yes, that's the best place to reach me.

MS. FERN: This looks fine. Tell me about your previous job.

JILL: I worked at the front desk for a dentist named Ms. Ground. My duties included answering the telephone, making appointments, and keeping good records. Ms. Ground wrote a reference for me which I included with my résumé.

MS. FERN: Why did you leave that job? You weren't dismissed, were you?

JILL: No, I wasn't fired! I wanted to return to school, and Ms. Ground needed someone to help full time.

MS. FERN: Are you currently employed?

JILL: Not at this time, but I am very interested in working part time while I go to school.

MS. FERN: Full-time employees receive benefits including medical insurance and paid holidays. Part-time employees receive no benefits. Do you understand?

JILL: Yes, I understand.

MS. FERN: We have our own application form that you will need to fill out. Be sure to list your previous experience in chronological order. I will need to see two forms of identification to prove your eligibility for this position. Just leave the application at the front desk. I'll read over your résumé and reference letter, and we'll see if you would be a good fit for this job. OK?

JILL: Yes, thank you. I look forward to visiting with you again, Ms. Fern.

Jill's understanding of the vocabulary on the application form was helpful to her during the interview process. Using your dictionary, find the meanings of the words in bold print in the following sentences. Write the definition that best applies to an interview.

11. Writing on an application form must be **legible**.

    legible: _____

12. As an employee, you will receive an **evaluation** every six months.

    evaluation: _____

13. You will work as an **apprentice** under a more experienced employee for the first three months.

    apprentice: _____

14. Your **salary** will be based on your experience and abilities.

    salary: _____

15. An employee can be **terminated** for arriving late on the job.

    terminated:_____

READER RESPONSE 4-3

Write a dialogue between an employer and a person wanting a job. Use at least six of the words listed in the box.

apprentice	termination	duties	current	benefits
eligible	chronological	previous	references	salary
résumé	permanent	dismiss	evaluation	

_____

_____

_____

_____

_____

_____

_____

_____

_____

_____

_____

_____

_____

_____

_____

_____

_____

_____

_____

_____

MASTERY 4-5   **Comprehension: *Appointment in Samarra***

Read the first sentence of the passage on the next page and then stop and answer question 1 before you read the rest of the story.

1. From reading the first sentence, write three events you predict will happen in the story.

   a. _____

   b. _____

   c. _____

Appointment in Samarra
By W. Somerset Maugham

There was a **merchant** in Bagdad who sent his servant to market to buy **provisions**, and in a little while the servant came back, white and trembling, and said, "Master, just now when I was in the marketplace I was **jostled** by a woman in the crowd and when I turned I saw it was Death that jostled me. She looked at me and made a **threatening gesture**; now, lend me your horse, and I will ride away from this city and **avoid** my fate. I will go to Samarra and there Death will not find me." The merchant lent him his horse, and the servant mounted it, and he dug his spurs in its flanks and as fast as the horse could gallop he went. Then the merchant went down to the marketplace and he saw Death standing in the crowd and he came to Death and said, "Why did you make a threatening gesture to my servant when you saw him this morning?" "That was not a threatening gesture," Death said, "It was only a start of surprise. I was astonished to see him in Bagdad, for I had an appointment with him tonight in Samarra."

WORDNOTES

merchant	one who buys and sells
provisions	supplies
jostled	bumped or pushed against
threatening	intending to harm
gesture	movement
avoid	keep away from

2. How many people are in the story? _____

3. Who are they? _____

4. What is your dictionary's definition of the word *astonished*?

   _____

5. How does your dictionary define *marketplace*?

   _____

6. After reading the story, look up the word *fate* in your dictionary. Then write your own definition of the word.

   _____

   _____

   _____

7. What was the servant's fate? _____

8. Was the servant able to escape from Death? Why or why not?

   _____

MASTERY 4-6 **Parts of Speech**

Underline the part or parts of speech in the following sentences that match the part of speech in bold at the beginning of each sentence. The example sentence has three nouns.

Example: **Nouns:** Kendall told Olivia the secret.

1. **Pronouns:** Jackie dropped her jacket on her bed.
2. **Pronouns:** We made a funny get-well card for him.
3. **Verb:** Carlotta threw a pop-bottle rocket.
4. **Verb:** Andy watched the entire basketball game.
5. **Adjectives:** Male cardinals have beautiful red feathers.
6. **Preposition:** The first pitch curved inside the batting area.
7. **Adverb:** Chase hit the next pitch hard.
8. **Preposition:** Our cat likes sleeping in a desk drawer.
9. **Conjunction:** We can fish now or in the morning.
10. **Interjection:** Hey! Can you keep this car between the lines?

MASTERY 4-7 **Origins of Words**

Use your dictionary to find the origins of the following words.

1. saltcellar _____
2. manor _____
3. chapel _____
4. hospital _____
5. cue _____
6. disaster _____
7. finance _____
8. dismal _____
9. record _____
10. tulip _____

READER RESPONSE 4-4

Choose five words from Mastery 4-7, and write a sentence or sentences using the words. You may use more than one of the listed words in the same sentence.

1. _____
2. _____
3. _____
4. _____
5. _____

MASTERY 4-8   Prereading: *Big Mac Attack*

1. Before reading the following essay from *An Introduction to Human Geography*, write your own definition of a *Big Mac Attack*.

_____

2. What do you know about the Big Mac?

_____

_____

MASTERY 4-9   Comprehension and Word Parts: *Big Mac Attack*

Now read the article and then answer the following questions.

Big Mac Attack

From James M. Rubenstein, *An Introduction to Human Geography,* 8th ed. (Upper Saddle River, NJ: Prentice Hall, 2005), 4.

If when driving across the United States on an interstate highway you begin to feel hungry, you probably will not be thinking about geography. At the next interchange you look for fast-food restaurant signs, but there are none. Now very hungry, you drive by the second interchange. No luck there. Finally, as you approach the third interchange, you see a familiar image—McDonald's "golden arches."

When you drive off the highway to the local road, you have a choice of a half-dozen fast-food restaurants. You wonder why none of these were located at the two interchanges you just passed. Why locate a half dozen at a single interchange instead of one or two at each interchange? Now you are asking questions about geography. Geographers ask where things are located and why.

Geographers are interested in the location of McDonald's restaurants around the world, not just around a U.S. interstate exit. The spread of McDonald's from a single restaurant in Des Plaines, Illinois, in 1955, to more than 25,000 worldwide shows what for many human geographers was the most important trend of the late twentieth century: globalization of economy and culture. Human geographers are interested in the economic and cultural conditions that saw companies such as McDonald's spread across the world in the last 50 years. Especially significant for some human geographers is the fact that American companies, from Coca-Cola and Ford to Microsoft and MTV, began to be seen across the globe and were recognized and even changed in their new locations.

Human geographers also know that just because American companies like McDonald's are in other countries, each location respects its own different economy and culture. Local restaurants offer menu items for local tastes—such as Japan's Teriyaki McBurger (with sausage and teriyaki sauce) and Chile's McPalta (with avocado)—and the company avoids countries where few people can afford its meals.

Human geography is an exciting subject in the twenty-first century because of the interaction between the common and the exotic, between global forces and local character. Every McDonald's—every place on Earth—is in some way tied to the global economy and culture, yet at the same time reflects certain characteristics specific to the culture or place they are in.

WORD NOTES

interchange	a meeting between highways where cars may enter and exit
familiar	common, ordinary, often met or seen
trend	a general movement
globalization	bringing together common interests over the globe
economy	system of managing monies and resources of a country
culture	habits, preferences, behaviors of people in a given place and time
interaction	ongoing exchange of information
exotic	foreign
character	type or kind of behavior of a certain group

1. What questions do geographers ask?

   _____

2. When did McDonald's begin?

   _____

3. How many McDonald's restaurants are there in the world today?

   _____

4. For human geographers, what is the most important trend in the late twentieth century?

   _____

5. What American companies besides McDonald's are globalizing?

   _____

6. Why is McDonald's interesting to geographers?

   _____

   _____

   _____

7. For each of the following suffixes, find a word from the reading that uses it.

   ic _____

   al _____

   er _____

   tion _____

   istics _____

8. Find five examples of past-tense verbs. Write the past tense and present tense of each word.

a. _____

b. _____

c. _____

d. _____

e. _____

READER RESPONSE 4-5

Have you ever been to a McDonald's outside the United States? _____

How was it different from a McDonald's in the United States?

_____

_____

How was it the same? _____

_____

_____

LOOKING BACK

The "Looking Back" sections in this and the remaining chapters will help you remember and practice skills that you have learned in the text so far. To complete the exercises, you will need to use the skills you have learned from this and previous chapters.

LOOKING BACK 4-1   **Prereading; *After the Suspect***

Describe what you think the following paragraph will be about when you read the title, "After the Suspect." What do you already know that will help you gain meaning from text?

_____

_____

_____

After the Suspect

The room was dirty; I didn't even want to go in there. It stunk of old food and urine. This was my first day on the job, and the reality of the situation was scaring me to death. I had seen plenty of drug busts on TV and had prepared for this kind of scenario at the police academy. But now it was real. The door was halfway off its hinges, so I could see through to the kitchen area. No one was around. My partner motioned to me that she would slip around to the back door. We were expecting backup at any moment. I peered again into the filthy room and yelled, "Police!" The silence seemed threatening.

LOOKING BACK 4-2   **Parts of Speech and Root Words**

For each of the following words, write its part of speech as it is used in the paragraph, its root word, and its suffix.

	Part of Speech	Root Word	Suffix
1. dirty	_____	_____	_____
2. prepared	_____	_____	_____
3. expecting	_____	_____	_____
4. filthy	_____	_____	_____
5. threatening	_____	_____	_____

LOOKING BACK 4-3   **Consonants**

Place a check mark in the correct column to show whether each underlined consonant or pair of consonants is a blend (sounds that are connected, but each one is pronounced), a digraph (sounds that combine to form one sound), or silent.

	Blend	Digraph	Silent
1. wa<u>nt</u>	_____	_____	_____
2. firs<u>t</u>	_____	_____	_____
3. kit<u>ch</u>en	_____	_____	_____
4. woul<u>d</u>	_____	_____	_____
5. fil<u>th</u>y	_____	_____	_____

LOOKING BACK 4-4   **Vowel Sounds**

Write the vowel sound you hear in the underlined letters in each of the following words (using the correct symbols). Then write a new word that has the same vowel sound.

	Vowel Sound	New Word
Example: fl<u>oa</u>t	ō	boat
1. l<u>a</u>ke	_____	_____
2. n<u>e</u>ws	_____	_____
3. p<u>ee</u>red	_____	_____
4. s<u>i</u>lence	_____	_____
5. t<u>i</u>me	_____	_____
6. p<u>e</u>t	_____	_____
7. <u>u</u>p	_____	_____
8. l<u>au</u>gh	_____	_____
9. c<u>o</u>st	_____	_____
10. l<u>i</u>ve	_____	_____

READER RESPONSE 4-6

How did your predictions for "After the Suspect" match the actual content of the article?

_____

_____

_____

_____

_____

_____

ONLINE PRACTICE

Go to **MyReadingLab** at www.myreadinglab.com. Click on **Reading Road Trip**, and select your textbook or the **Pioneer Level**.

1. For further practice using a **dictionary**, Take a Road Trip to **Historic Boston**.

2. For further practice using **vocabulary skills**, Take a Road Trip to the **Library of Congress**.

PROGRESS CHART

SECTION ONE

Fill out the number of correct answers you have for each item below. Your instructor will tell you how to calculate your percentage score.

PRACTICE 4-1   Number right _____ out of a possible score of 10.   Percentage score _____

PRACTICE 4-2   Number right _____ out of a possible score of 10.   Percentage score _____

PRACTICE 4-3   Number right _____ out of a possible score of 5.   Percentage score _____

PRACTICE 4-4   Number right _____ out of a possible score of 10.   Percentage score _____

PRACTICE 4-5   Number right _____ out of a possible score of 10.   Percentage score _____

PRACTICE 4-6   Number right _____ out of a possible score of 10.   Percentage score _____

PRACTICE 4-7   Number right _____ out of a possible score of 10.   Percentage score _____

PRACTICE 4-8   Number right _____ out of a possible score of 10.   Percentage score _____

PRACTICE 4-9   Number right _____ out of a possible score of 5.   Percentage score _____

PRACTICE 4-10   Number right _____ out of a possible score of 10.   Percentage score _____

PRACTICE 4-11   Number right _____ out of a possible score of 15.   Percentage score _____

PRACTICE 4-12   Number right _____ out of a possible score of 10.   Percentage score _____

MASTERY 4-1   Number right _____ out of a possible score of 5.   Percentage score _____

MASTERY 4-2   Number right _____ out of a possible score of 5.   Percentage score _____

MASTERY 4-3   Number right _____ out of a possible score of 10.   Percentage score _____

MASTERY 4-4   Number right _____ out of a possible score of 15.   Percentage score _____

MASTERY 4-5   Number right _____ out of a possible score of 8.   Percentage score _____

MASTERY 4-6   Number right _____ out of a possible score of 10.   Percentage score _____

MASTERY 4-7   Number right _____ out of a possible score of 10.   Percentage score _____

MASTERY 4-8   Number right _____ out of a possible score of 2.   Percentage score _____

MASTERY 4-9   Number right _____ out of a possible score of 8.   Percentage score _____

LOOKING BACK 4-2   Number right _____ out of a possible score of 5.   Percentage score _____

LOOKING BACK 4-3   Number right _____ out of a possible score of 5.   Percentage score _____

LOOKING BACK 4-4   Number right _____ out of a possible score of 10.   Percentage score _____

SECTION TWO

How do you feel? There are no wrong or right answers to how you feel about what you have learned. Circle Yes, Somewhat, or No in response to the following questions.

1. Before you studied this chapter about using a dictionary, were you confident about searching for correct spellings?   Yes   Somewhat   No

2. Do you understand how a dictionary can be used to get many kinds of information?   Yes   Somewhat   No

3. Are you convinced that carrying at least a paperback dictionary in your book bag is necessary to improve your reading vocabulary?   Yes   Somewhat   No

4. If a fellow student asked you, "How can a dictionary help when I can't look for the word unless I can spell it?" could you explain how to search for a correct spelling?   Yes   Somewhat   No

5. Did you add at least five new words to your vocabulary log after reading this chapter on dictionary skills?   Yes   Somewhat   No

6. Do you believe learning to use a dictionary will help you in at least one other class?   Yes   Somewhat   No

SECTION THREE

Take a minute or two to reflect on your reading development. Write a few sentences or discuss with other students how this chapter has changed your reading habits.

_____

_____

_____

_____

_____

_____

_____

_____

_____

_____

Discovering Context Clues

CHAPTER PREVIEW

In this chapter, you will learn about context clues. Context clues are hints in the text that help you understand what words or phrases mean so you can make sense of what you are reading. Clues to the meaning of a word may come before or after the word or phrase that is unknown to you. Here are the types of context clues you will learn to recognize and use:

- **Definition clues**
- **Example clues**
- **Antonym clues**
- **Synonym clues**
- **General sense of the passage**

MAKING MEANING

Northhead Lighthouse

A lighthouse is like a context clue. It sends a signal to ships that might be lost at sea. The lighthouse often has a foghorn that is also used (and is extremely loud!) to help mariners know where they are in relation to the rocky cliffs or sandbars that could wreck their ships.

Context clues help readers find their way through unknown words and phrases so they can understand them and find meaning in what they are reading.

INTRODUCTION

Context clues are hints in the text that help you understand what unfamiliar words mean. Although you have learned several strategies you can use to make sense of words you do not understand, like sounding them out and looking them up in your dictionary, context clues can help you figure out what words mean *as you read*.

Read all of the following paragraph once. Then, as you read it a second time, fill in the blanks. Decide which words to put in the blanks by using the other words in the paragraph as clues.

Refinancing Your Car

What is the **interest rate** you are paying on your car loan? If your interest rate is too high, then it might be a good idea to **refinance** your loan at a _____ rate. If you are now paying a high rate on your car, check other banks to see if they can offer you a rate that is lower. Refinancing could save you hundreds of _____ over the life of your _____.

WORDNOTES

interest rate   the amount paid for the use of money
refinance   replace a loan with another at a better interest rate

What words did you write in the blanks? Did you write *lower* in the first blank, *dollars* in the second blank, and *loan* in the third blank? You were probably able to insert these or similar words into each of the blanks because the context of the paragraph gave you clues about the missing words.

Read the following paragraph, and then fill in the blanks. Use the context clues in the paragraph to help you work out what the missing words should be.

The Economy: Good or Poor

When the economy is good, people buy more products. Unemployment is low, and the sale of new homes is _____. In a good or thriving economy, people feel comfortable spending _____, and new _____ are often created because businesses are growing.

On the other hand, in a poor or depressed economy, people do not buy products. Unemployment is high because people are losing their _____. A _____ economy often means money problems for many people. Currently, would you say we are living in a good or _____ economic time? Why do you think so?

Look at the bottom of page 158 for some words you could have used to fill in the blanks. Did you come up with the same or similar words to complete the sentences? _____ How did the context (the other words in the text) of the paragraph help you choose the missing words?

_____

_____

_____

READER RESPONSE 5-1

Currently, would you say we are living in a good or poor economic period? Why do you think so?

_____

_____

_____

_____

_____

_____

STRUCTURED INSTRUCTION AND EXERCISES

Using **context clues** helps you to make sense of what you are reading without having to stop and consult a dictionary. When you are looking for context clues, read the sentence that contains the unknown word or phrase as well as the next few sentences. Sometimes it is helpful to look back at previous sentences, too. Instead of just focusing on the unfamiliar word, the idea is to read around the word and look for clues that might help you understand what it means and how it relates to the other words in the text.

TYPES OF CONTEXT CLUES

These are the five kinds of context clues you'll want to look for and use as you read.

1. **Definition clues:** The unknown word is defined following its use.
2. **Example clues:** The unknown word is followed by one or more examples that help you understand the meaning of the word.
3. **Antonym clues:** A word that means the opposite of the unknown word is used.
4. **Synonym clues:** A word that means the same as the unknown word is used.
5. **General sense of the passage:** Other words in the sentence or in the sentences before or after the unknown word give you a general sense of what the word means based on your knowledge and experience.

DEFINITION CLUES

Writers sometimes define a word immediately after using it. The words *which, or,* and *by* can indicate that a definition or example will follow a word. Sometimes the definition will follow in parentheses. In the following examples, the unknown words are printed in bold, and the definitions (the context clues) are underlined.

EXAMPLE 1: Yujing was studying **criminology**, <u>which is the study of crime.</u> In this sentence, *criminology* means "the study of crime."

EXAMPLE 2: My parents-in-law mailed us an **itinerary** for their vacation. The itinerary listed <u>where they would be going, and what they would be doing on each day of their vacation.</u> In this sentence, *itinerary* means "where you go and what you do on a trip."

EXERCISE 5-A   Underline the words in the sentences that helped you understand the words in bold print.

1. My teacher asked me to **elaborate** by going into more detail than I had before.
2. Misha **modeled** good handwriting skills by carefully making her letters on the chalkboard for her students to copy.
3. Joe was asked to take a **polygraph** test, which tracks blood pressure and other body signals to see if a person is lying.
4. I don't think that I can **predict** (foretell) the future.
5. I can't **concentrate** on this assignment today. It's too nice an afternoon to focus on the assignment.

EXAMPLE CLUES

One way writers provide clues to what words mean is by providing examples that illustrate them. You might find one or more examples in the same sentence as the unknown word, or they may follow in the next sentence. Examples are often introduced by the key words *by, like, for example, such as, include,* or *is.* Examples like the following are often used in textbooks:

> Examples of **past tense verbs** include *laughed, cried, and sang.*
>
> An example of a **geometric formula** is *area = length x width.*

In some textbooks and other types of writing, examples are not always so obviously marked, as these examples below demonstrate. In each of the following examples, the unknown word is in bold, and the example is underlined.

> *EXAMPLE 1:* The **detritus** from the flood, which included <u>sand, gravel, leaves, and tree branches</u>, was piled all over the front lawn.
>
> In this sentence, *detritus* means "debris or waste" ("sand, gravel, leaves, and tree branches").
>
> *EXAMPLE 2:* Because the appointment time was **indefinite**, <u>Jerry didn't know when to show up for the interview</u>.
>
> In this sentence, *indefinite* means "unclear or vague" (Jerry didn't know when to show up).

EXERCISE 5-B   In each of the following sentences, underline the words that helped you understand the meaning of the word in bold.

Example: **Oblivious** to the camera phone pointed in my direction, <u>I continued to dance and sing in my yard</u>.

1. Martin had acted in a **juvenile** manner. Yelling, screaming, and calling the bank teller names had been childish and immature.
2. **Overwhelmed** by the destruction of his home in the hurricane, Jorge wept.
3. Joel was **preoccupied** and missed his road. He had been thinking about calling a girl he just met when he missed his exit.
4. She had baked him a spinach **soufflé**, which is like a fluffy quiche.
5. After a tornado in Martin's neighborhood, **debris**, such as shingles, siding, and pieces of wood, was scattered in his yard.

ANTONYM CLUES

An **antonym** is a word or short phrase that is the opposite of another word. The opposite of *happy* is *sad,* and the opposite of *empty* is *full.* Writers often define unknown words by including their antonyms. The antonym might consist of one word or several words. Key words such as *while, but,* and *on the other hand* often indicate that an antonym (opposite) will follow. In each of the following examples, the unknown word is in bold, and the antonym is underlined.

> *EXAMPLE 1:* Miesha threw his clothes around the dorm room in a **haphazard** manner while Guillermo carefully hung each piece of clothing in a special location.
>
> In this sentence, *haphazard* means "lack of order or plan" (not neat and orderly).

> *EXAMPLE 2:* Angela **frantically** searched for the concert tickets, but Alex calmly looked in all the places they might have left them.
>
> In this sentence, *frantically* means "greatly excited, frenzied" (not calm—at rest, undisturbed, quiet).

EXERCISE 5-C   In each of the following sentences, underline the words that helped you understand the meaning of the word in bold.

1. Charles was a **gourmet** chef, while Robert was a simple cook who liked to make macaroni and cheese.
2. Charles loved his life of **leisure**, while Robert worked 40 to 50 hours a week.
3. Jackie was usually **tolerant** of other drivers; on the other hand, Sungbin had no respect for other drivers on the road and often yelled at them.
4. Alondra exercised **regularly**, but Diana hardly ever did any physical activity.
5. Angel was **punctual**, but E-Roo never got anywhere on time.

SYNONYM CLUES

A **synonym** is a word or short phrase that means the same, or nearly the same, as another word. Sometimes writers use a synonym as a way to indicate the meaning of a word they have used. Synonyms can appear in the same sentence as the unknown word or in sentences that follow it. In each of the following examples, the unknown word is in bold, and the synonym is underlined.

> *EXAMPLE 1:* The history course **concentrated** on the Vietnam War. Our attention was drawn to the Viet Cong, the North Vietnamese Army, and the supply line called the Ho Chi Minh Trail (pronounced "Ho Chee Men").
>
> In this sentence, *concentrated* means "directed towards a common center, focused."

Answers to "The Economy: Good or Poor" fill-in exercise on page 155: *high, money, jobs, jobs, poor, poor.*

> *EXAMPLE 2:* France and Germany were **opposed** to the Iraqi War. They made it clear to the United States that they were against going to war with Iraq.
>
> *Opposed* means "to be against something or someone."

EXERCISE 5-D In each of the following sentences, underline the words that helped you understand the meaning of the word in bold.

1. As **commanding** general, General Westmoreland was leader of the entire military offensive.

2. **Patriotic** men and women served in the Vietnam War. They proudly served their country.

3. After 9/11, airport security was **scrutinized**. Most luggage is now checked very carefully.

4. Many people feel that the government has an **obligation** to the survivors of 9/11 because the United States has a responsibility to protect and care for its people.

5. I cannot **underscore** enough the heroic work of the police and firefighters on 9/11. It is important that we emphasize the work and courage of these men and women who died attempting to save the lives of others.

GENERAL SENSE OF THE PASSAGE

Another way to work out the meaning of a word you do not recognize is to look for other information in a passage that gives you a sense of what the unknown word means. When using this kind of context clue, you need to draw from your own knowledge and experiences. As you read the text, make connections between the new information you are learning about a topic and what you already know about it.

EXAMPLE 1: My boss told me I was an **indispensable** member of the team. He said the team couldn't do without me because I was so important.
Indispensable is an adjective that means "absolutely necessary."

EXAMPLE 2: I'm planning to update my **résumé** so that employers will see that I have gained lots of experience over the years.
Résumé is a noun that means "a document that includes a person's work experiences."

EXERCISE 5-E Underline the words that helped you understand the meaning of word in bold in each of the following sentences.

1. At home, Donna had **creative** ideas; she enjoyed painting a castle on her child's bedroom wall.

2. Jeanna had a strong work **ethic**. Honesty and integrity were important to her in the workplace.

3. Kim was never **lethargic**. He completed his duties and never wasted time.

4. On the road, Jorge loved to take pictures. He was definitely a **shutterbug**.

5. Christina had one **phobia**, though. Spiders terrified her.

EXERCISE 5-F Use your own words to fill in the blanks so that the paragraph below makes sense.

A Time to Relax

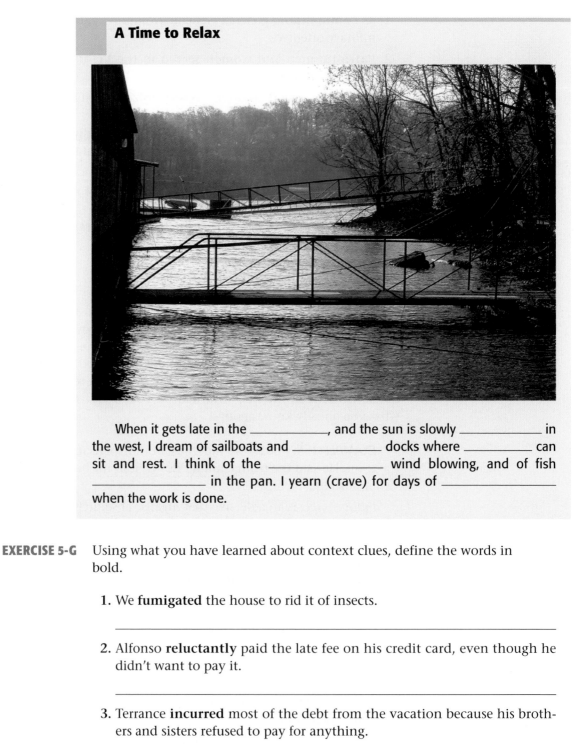

When it gets late in the _____, and the sun is slowly _____ in the west, I dream of sailboats and _____ docks where _____ can sit and rest. I think of the _____ wind blowing, and of fish _____ in the pan. I yearn (crave) for days of _____ when the work is done.

EXERCISE 5-G Using what you have learned about context clues, define the words in bold.

1. We **fumigated** the house to rid it of insects.

   _____

2. Alfonso **reluctantly** paid the late fee on his credit card, even though he didn't want to pay it.

   _____

3. Terrance **incurred** most of the debt from the vacation because his brothers and sisters refused to pay for anything.

   _____

4. The **pungent** odor in the cave caused me to rush back out.

   _____

5. I didn't want to be responsible for harming an **endangered** animal that could be one of the last of its kind.

STUDY TIP

Guidelines for Deciding Whether a Word Is Important for Your Reading Comprehension

How do you know if a word is important for your reading comprehension? Here are a few guidelines to help you decide.

- If you cannot understand the **main idea** of a passage without understanding a particular word, then that word is important.
- If a word is in the **title, subtitle,** or **heading** of a chapter, it is probably important.
- If a word is the **subject** or **main verb** of a sentence, it is often important.
- If you feel uncomfortable not knowing what a particular word means, then it is important you find out, so use context clues, look it up, or ask someone for help!

EXERCISE 5-H   Fill in the blanks in the following paragraph from a history text about Egypt and the Nile River Valley by choosing the correct words from the box.

food	Nile River Valley	fell	migrated	dried
water	desert	moved	fertile	

Egypt and the Nile River Valley

From Iftikhar Ahmad, Herbert Brodsky, Marylee Susan Crofts, and Elizabeth Susan Gaynor, *World Cultures: A Global Mosaic* (Englewood Cliffs, NJ: Prentice-Hall, 1996), p.73.

About 4,000 years ago, the climate of the Sahara was changing. Less rain _____. Lakes and rivers _____ up. Without _____, grasses no longer grew. Animal herds _____ to other parts of Africa to find _____. The people who hunted those animals also _____. Some people _____ to the Nile River Valley. Now, 96 percent of the Sahara is _____. The Nile River Valley is a strip of _____ land that contrasts sharply with the land around it. Most people in Egypt live in or very close to the _____.

You probably had little trouble choosing words to fill in the blanks to make sense of the sentences because of the help you got from the context clues in the passage. As you noticed, the words *moved* or *migrated* are used more than once. Notice as well that the words *migrated* and *moved* can be substituted for one another. Also, the animals moved to find food *or* water. Either word would be correct because both words express the idea that the Sahara became a place that could not support life. The words *fertile, green,* or *lush* could describe the strip of land around the Nile. It makes sense that most of the people in Egypt live in the Nile River Valley, because that is where there is water for animals and crops.

EXERCISE 5-I In each of the following sentences, write a word that may be used in place of the one in bold type.

Example: When I **ponder** (think about) the life of the Egyptians, I am happier with my own life.

1. Even before the Sahara dried up, people in various parts of the world had learned to **raise** (_____) crops.

2. A belief in life after death was **central** (_____) to Egyptian religion.

3. The pharaoh had **total** (_____) power over the lives of the people.

4. Egyptian doctors studied the human body; they set **fractured** (_____) bones, treated spinal injuries, and **performed** (_____) some types of surgery.

5. Egyptian civilization **survived** (_____) for thousands of years.

EXERCISE 5-J In the following sentences, fill in the blanks using your own words. Several different words might be correct for each blank.

1. Before the people of Cairo marched hundreds of servants carrying golden staffs and wearing gold jewelry; hundreds of camels _____ by loaded with gold. The Egyptians gazed in _____ at the procession.

2. At the head of the _____ rode the owner of all this wealth— Mansa Musa of Mali.

3. Mali was a _____ and powerful empire in West Africa during the 1300s.

4. In 1324, the mansa, or _____, traveled almost 3,000 miles across the Sahara Desert to Mecca, the holy city of Islam.

5. It was his _____ as a Muslim to make a _____ to Mecca.

CHECK IT OUT!

Remember the Five Types of Context Clues

1. **Definition clues:** The unknown word is defined following its use.

2. **Example clues:** The unknown word is followed by examples that help you understand the meaning of the word.

3. **Antonym clues:** A word that means the opposite of the unknown word is used.

4. **Synonym clues:** A word that means the same as the unknown word is used.

5. **General sense of the passage:** Other words in the sentence or in the sentences before or after the unknown word give you a general sense of what the word means based on your knowledge and experience.

PRACTICING WHAT YOU HAVE LEARNED

PRACTICE 5-1   **Context Clues:** *How Cold Is It? Part One*

Here is an excerpt (a passage from a longer piece of writing) taken from a journal entry by Han Rue. Read the excerpt carefully. Then do the exercise that follows.

How Cold Is It? Part One
By Han Rue

My family went on a float trip down the Colorado River in Arizona last summer. In the summer, Arizona can be hot, really boiling hot. You would think that the Colorado River that runs through Arizona would be warm water because of the **scorching** heat. Well, I got a big surprise!

My surprise came in two parts. The first surprise was that I fell into the river without meaning to. The **second shocker** was that the water was not warm. It was so cold you wouldn't believe it.

The events that led up to my falling into the river were really pretty simple. There were 20 people and John, our guide, on the boat. Sometimes we were on a part of the river where the wind was **blustery** and strong. We came to a place like that, and a **gust of wind** blew someone's hat off.

My son called out, "Oh no! Someone's hat blew away!" Our guide quickly **maneuvered** the boat around so that we could go back to get the hat out of the river. As the boat got nearer to the hat, I could see that it was near the **starboard,** or right side, of the boat where I was sitting. I kept my legs in the

Colorado River

boat and leaned over the side toward the hat. As the boat moved closer to the hat, I leaned even further to grab it. Just as I thought I had it in my hand, I got the first big surprise. Splash, I was in the water! I couldn't believe it; I was in the river. I did not plan that.

For each word or phrase, write in the clue, or clues, to its meaning, and then write your definition of what the word means.

Example: Unknown word: **scorching**

↓

Clue(s): The paragraph talks about how hot it is in Arizona.

↓

Definition: Scorching must mean really hot.

1. Unknown words: **second shocker**

↓

Clue(s): _____

_____

↓

Definition: _____

2. Unknown words: **blustery, gust of wind**

↓

Clue(s): _____

_____

↓

Definition: _____

3. Unknown word: **maneuvered**

↓

Clue(s): _____

_____

↓

Definition: _____

4. Unknown word: **starboard**

↓

Clue(s): _____

_____

↓

Definition: _____

READER RESPONSE 5-2

From reading the journal entry, what do you know about Arizona and the Colorado River in the summer?

_____

From reading the journal entry, what have you learned about Han?

_____

_____

PRACTICE 5-2   **Context Clues and Comprehension:** *How Cold Is It? Part Two*

Read the next excerpt from Han's journal. Then answer the questions that follow the reading.

How Cold Is It? Part Two
By Han Rue

We had been told that the river water was cold. We had been told that by more than one person. I had heard what they had said, but I had not felt the water. I had only been told about the cold water. Well, I sure was feeling that **frigid** water just as soon as I fell into it. Think about the last time that you were not ready for something. That is how I felt. I was not ready for the strong reaction that I got from the cold, cold water. Think of the coldest thing that you have ever felt. This water was that cold, maybe colder. Soon I felt something else. I noticed that I was not breathing. I knew that I was not breathing because my body was as **astounded** by the cold water as my mind was, maybe more. You have to breathe, don't you? I have to breathe; you have to breathe, but I was not breathing. I had to get out of that freezing water fast! Also I had to be sure that I did not sink down to where the water was over my head. I was not sure how long I could keep my head above water because my body did not seem to be working very well at that time. I didn't want to **submerge** completely because I was afraid of ending up underneath the boat.

1. What does the word *frigid* mean? How do you know?

   _____

   _____

2. What does the word *astounded* mean? How did Han's body react to the shock of the cold water?

   _____

   _____

3. What was Han afraid of doing?

   _____

   _____

4. If Han submerged completely, what might happen to him?

   _____

   _____

READER RESPONSE 5-3   Describe how you would feel if you fell out of a boat.

   _____

   _____

   _____

PRACTICE 5-3   **Context Clues and Comprehension:** *How Cold It It? Part Three*

Here is a third excerpt from Han's journal. Read it carefully, and then answer the questions that follow.

How Cold Is It? Part Three
By Han Rue

Before we had started our float trip, our guide had told all of us that if one of us fell out of the boat, we could grab hold of a rope that went all along the side of the boat. I was lucky that the guide had explained that because now I needed a rope to **hoist** myself onto the boat. I looked up, and just as he had said, the rope was there. I reached up, grabbed the rope, and held it in my fist. I pulled on the rope to lift myself up, but my body was not working very well. My body was feeling the first effects of **hypothermia**. I could not get back up by myself, but at least I could keep myself from submerging.

Next I saw my daughter, Lynn, and our guide, John, leaning over the side of the boat. Each of them reached down to me with an open hand. I grabbed John's hand with my left hand and Lynn's hand with my right hand. They hoisted me up into the boat. I was **relieved** to be back up there because I knew that the cold water was taking away my strength very fast.

I saw that I was not the only person in the boat who was surprised that I had fallen overboard. Everyone was looking at me, and their eyes were really big. But soon, they could see that **all was right with the world,** and John started the motor again. We went on our way down the Colorado River, the deep, green, cold Colorado River.

1. **Hypothermia** can cause death. What do you know about hypothermia? How did what you already know about hypothermia help you understand the story?

   _____

   _____

   _____

2. What does **relieved** mean?

   _____

3. "All was right with the world" is an expression that is commonly used. What does it mean?

   _____

4. Write two sentences, each using one of the boldfaced words in the passage you just read. (For example, I was **relieved** when I got a good grade in class!)

   a. _____

   b. _____

READER RESPONSE 5-4

Write five sentences using the new vocabulary words you have learned from Han's journal excerpts.

1. _____
2. _____
3. _____
4. _____
5. _____

PRACTICE 5-4   **Context Clues: *Small Steps***

The following is an excerpt from the prologue, or introduction, to the book *Small Steps: The Year I Got Polio*, by Peg Kehret. The book is autobiographical because it is about the author's life—specifically, her experiences as a victim of polio. In the prologue, Kehret describes the polio epidemic that hit the United States in 1949. Read the prologue and think about what the words in bold print might mean, using the context of the reading.

> ### Small Steps
> From Peg Kehret, *Small Steps: The Year I Got Polio* (Morton Grove, IL: Albert Whitman, 1996), Prologue, pp. 9–10.
>
> Before a polio vaccine was developed, polio killed or crippled thousands of people each year. A president of the United States, Franklin Delano Roosevelt, got polio as a young father. He spent the rest of his life in a wheelchair, using hip-high leg braces and a cane when he needed to stand to make a speech.
>
> Children, however, are more likely to get polio than adults are. It is a highly **contagious** disease, and in 1949 there were 42,033 cases reported in the United States. There was only one case **diagnosed** that year in Austin, Minnesota: a twelve-year-old girl, Peg Schulze. Me.
>
> The disease's full name is poliomyelitis, or **infantile** paralysis, but it is usually called polio. The polio virus attacks the nerve cells that control the muscles of the body.
>
> If damage to the nerve cells is slight, the muscle weakness will be **temporary**. If the virus kills many nerve cells, the **paralysis** will be extensive and possibly permanent.

Using your knowledge of context clues, underline the best definition for the words in bold print.

1. contagious
   - a. catching
   - b. difficult to catch
   - c. humorous
   - d. deadly

2. diagnosed
   - a. talked about
   - b. identified a disease
   - c. discussed
   - d. discovered

3. **infantile**
   a. related to infants
   b. related to adults
   c. related to animals
   d. related to polio

4. **temporary**
   a. last forever
   b. hard to deal with
   c. last a short time
   d. will be extensive

5. **paralysis**
   a. inability to move
   b. childhood illness
   c. ability to walk
   d. damage to nerve cells

PRACTICE 5-5   **Context Clues: *Small Steps***

Now read another excerpt (a short selection) from the prologue to *Small Steps* (Prologue, p. 10).

> There is no **cure** for polio. There are no miracle medicines to stop the damage to nerve cells or repair those already damaged.
>
> When I began to write about my polio days, long forgotten memories bubbled to the surface. I was astonished by the intense **emotions** these memories brought with them. Those months, more than any other time in my life, molded my personality.
>
> Since I have no transcript of these events, the dialogue is not strictly **accurate,** but the people mentioned are all real people. The **incidents** all happened, and the voices are as close to reality as I can make them.
>
> Although I used fictional techniques to write this book, I can **verify** my feelings about everything that happened—and feelings are the most important part of any story.

Using the context clues in the passage, underline the word or phrase that gives the best meaning of each of the words in bold print.

1. **cure**
   a. hope
   b. technique
   c. restorative measure
   d. success story

2. **emotions**
   a. pictures
   b. feelings
   c. speech patterns
   d. ideas

3. **accurate**
   a. true
   b. false
   c. silly
   d. make-believe

4. **incidents**
   a. conversations
   b. events
   c. mistakes
   d. frustrations

5. **verify**
   a. prove the truth of
   b. tell the story of
   c. add to the story
   d. write the story of

PRACTICE 5-6 **Context Clues:** *Small Steps*

Using the context clues in the following sentences, choose words from the box to fill in the blanks.

verify	incidents	accurate	paralyzed	infantile

1. I was so scared that I could not move. It was as though I were

_____.

2. The police asked me to _____ that I saw the attack on the young man.

3. I gave a truthful and _____ statement about the terrible event.

4. The _____ leading up to the attack were confusing.

5. I know my feelings were _____, but I was so scared that I just wanted to go home and cry like a baby.

PRACTICE 5-7 **Context Clues:** *Small Steps*

Look for context clues in this excerpt from *Small Steps* (pp. 30–31). Underline them as you read.

"We hope the oxygen will keep you breathing on your own," he continued. "If not, a **respirator** will help you."

I looked where he pointed, and a wave of horror poured over me as I realized **respirator** was another name for what was popularly called an **iron lung**.

I had seen pictures of people in iron lungs. The tube-shaped machine completely **enclosed** the patient's body. Only the head stuck out. **Bellows** pumped air in and out, causing the patient's lungs to expand and contract. Small doors and portholes on the sides of the iron lung allowed the nurses to put their hands in to bathe the patients and help with toileting. Portions of the doors were clear plastic so the nurses could see what they were doing.

Some patients stayed in iron lungs for the rest of their lives, never again breathing by themselves. I thought it would be like being put in a coffin while you were still alive.

Now an iron lung stood beside my bed, hoses hanging like **tentacles**—a gray octopus ready to swallow me at any moment.

Think about what you have read. Using the context clues you underlined in the passage, choose the best definition for each of the words printed in bold. Underline the correct answer.

1. respirator
   a. a device to help a person breathe easier
   b. a device to help a person stop snoring
   c. a device to help a person sleep
   d. a device to help a person eat

2. **iron lung**
   a. a device that helps a person lose weight
   b. a device that prevents breathing
   c. a device that forces air in and out of a patient's lungs
   d. a device used in deep-sea diving

3. **enclosed**
   a. dressed
   b. surrounded
   c. hidden
   d. paralyzed

4. **bellows**
   a. an instrument that draws air in and blows air out
   b. an instrument that you play in an orchestra
   c. screaming
   d. a covering for a bell

5. **tentacles**
   a. long arms
   b. tent straps
   c. claws
   d. hoses

READER RESPONSE 5-5 From the prologue to *Small Steps*, what did you learn about polio? List three facts.

Fact 1. _____

Fact 2. _____

Fact 3. _____

SUMMARY

- All readers will find words that they do not understand in some texts.
- **Context clues** are helpful hints in a text that help you work out what unfamiliar words mean.
- Sometimes the clues come before the actual word or phrase you do not know.
- Sometimes you must read ahead and look for clues that might help you understand the meaning of the word and how it relates to the other words in the text.
- Remember, what you already know will help you understand new material.

Types of Context Clues

1. **Definition clues:** The unknown word is defined following its use.
2. **Example clues:** The unknown word is followed by one or more examples that help you understand the meaning of the word.
3. **Antonym clues:** A word that means the opposite of the unknown word is used.
4. **Synonym clues:** A word that means the same as the unknown word is used.
5. **General sense of the passage:** Other words in the sentence or in the sentences before or after the unknown word give you a general sense of what the word means, based on your knowledge and experience.

Cape Mears Lighthouse

MASTERY LEVEL EXERCISES

MASTERY 5-1 Context Clues in Sentences

For each of the following sentences, underline the correct definition of the word in bold type and write the one type of context clue you used to find its meaning. (More than one type of context clue may be correct for any particular sentence.)

Remember:

- Word defined following its usage (definition clue)
- Word followed by examples (example clue)
- Opposite of word (antonym clue)
- Similar to word (synonym clue)
- Sense of word from other words and experiences (general sense of the passage)

1. I can't believe that James acts in such an **infantile** way. When his car broke down, he threw a fit, broke the door handle, and slammed the car door.

   Infantile means:
   a. instant   c. angry
   b. like an infant   d. like an adult

   Type of context clue: _____

2. Her campaign for the senate seat is very **haphazard**. It is poorly organized and has no real goals or plans.

   Haphazard means:
   a. lacks order or planning   c. full of dificulty
   b. organized and logical   d. full of hazards

   Type of context clue: _____

3. When I saw the killer, a **paralysis** came over me. In my mind, I was racing swiftly down the path and leaping over fallen logs, but in reality, I could do nothing.

   Paralysis means:
   a. overwhelming terror   c. inability to move
   b. fear   d. ability to move

   Type of context clue: _____

4. The geometry lesson **concentrated** on angles. Our teacher drew our attention to the difference between right angles and obtuse angles; we focused on angles all afternoon.

   Concentrated means:
   a. talked about   c. thought about
   b. drew on   d. focused on

   Type of context clue: _____

5. Her illness was **temporary**; that is, it lasted only a short time.

   Temporary means:
   a. treatable   c. last a brief time
   b. terminal   d. last a lengthy time

   Type of context clue: _____

MASTERY 5-2   **Context Clues in Sentences**

Use the words in the box to fill in the blanks in the following sentences.

tentacles	enclosed	verify	accurate	temporary

1. It would be an _____ and true statement to say that I was terrified.

2. Now, out of the shadows, a giant creature loomed over me; long _____ with suction cups slowly squeezed the air out of my body.

3. The giant squid _____ me in its grasp as it guided my body toward its black mouth.

4. I can _____ the truth of my experience with the giant squid, because I was able to take a picture before lunging out of its grasp.

5. I was grateful it was only a _____ moment of fear.

Match each word with its definition.

1. temporary   _____ prove the truth of

2. accurate   _____ surrounded

3. enclosed   _____ device that draws air in through a hole and
                             sends it out through a tube

4. bellows   _____ lasting for a short time

5. verify   _____ true or correct

MASTERY 5-3   Context Clues and Comprehension: *Unplanned*

Read the poem and underline the correct definition for each word in bold.
Then answer the questions about the poem.

Unplanned
By Laura Ream

I am not **petite**.
I am a broad shouldered bison.
My pulse flies when I run
Flat footed through the grass.
Calloused feet hard enough to hold out the cold
Naked enough to feel the dew.
I do not fit low-ride jeans.
I do not like the low-ride shirts.
My breast is my chest and
My ribs, like their ribs
Enfold the aching, raging, pounding heart.
I contain every craziness allowed to a man.
I stand as tall.
I am an Amazon Queen
And when my bonds break
With the **resounding** boom that is my freedom—
Me.
I am not petite.

1. **petite:**
   a. large
   b. old
   c. small
   d. gentle

2. **calloused:**
   a. hardened
   b. softened
   c. wrinkled
   d. blistered

3. **enfold:**
   a. give
   b. take
   c. release
   d. surround

4. **resounding:**
   a. loud
   b. quiet
   c. sorrowful
   d. tearful

5. How does the author describe herself?

   _____

6. How is she the same and how is she different from a magazine model?

   _____

   _____

   _____

7. What do you like or dislike about the poem?

   _____

   _____

   _____

   _____

MASTERY 5-4 **Context Clues: *Trapping the Tsetse Fly***

As you read the following passage, underline the context clues that help you understand the words in bold type.

Trapping the Tsetse Fly

1   The bite of the tsetse fly can cause sleeping sickness, a disease often **fatal** to humans and cattle. The tsetse fly thrives in some parts of the African **savanna.** Each year the fly causes more than 20,000 new cases of sleeping sickness among people. The disease also kills thousands of cattle, causing the loss of 3 billion pounds of beef annually. Sometimes, people have had to **abandon** their communities because of the tsetse fly.

2   In the past, people used **drastic** measures against insect populations, such as setting fire to large areas to destroy the insects' breeding grounds. Another method was to use highly **toxic** pesticides. Yet these pesticides killed many other things besides pests.

3   Today, scientists use **techniques** that destroy the tsetse flies without harming the **environment.** One research team invented a simple trap that can catch more than 20,000 tsetse flies in a week. **Constructed** of blue cloth, a few staples, and a plastic bag, the trap uses no poisons at all. Tsetses just cannot **resist** the trap's bait—ox-breath perfume.

Use the context clues you found in the passage to choose the correct meaning of the bold words. Fill in each blank, or circle the correct answer for each multiple-choice question.

Paragraph 1

1. What is a synonym for the word **fatal**? _____

2. The word **savanna** is not defined or explained. You are told, however, that sleeping sickness kills thousands of cattle every year. From the general sense of the paragraph and your personal knowledge of where cattle graze, you can conclude that a **savanna** is made up of:
   a. flood plains   c. rain forests
   b. grasslands   d. desert

3. From the general sense of the passage and your personal knowledge, **abandon** means to:
   a. stay   c. leave
   b. settle   d. tear down

Paragraph 2

4. What is the meaning of the word **drastic**?
   a. extreme   c. bad
   b. small   d. thoughtful

5. What is the meaning of the word **toxic**?
   a. strong   c. scientific
   b. poisonous   d. tested

Paragraph 3

6. What is the meaning of the word **technique**?
   a. poison   c. method
   b. device   d. plan

7. The word **environment** means:
   a. geography and climate
   b. all animals, but not plants
   c. all humans, plants, and animals
   d. all plants, but not humans and animals

8. Which word is *not* a synonym for the word **constructed**?
   a. built   c. performed
   b. made   d. designed

9. The trap for the tsetse fly is _____ in color.

10. **Cannot resist** means the opposite of *resist*. The tsetse fly likes the scent of ox breath. Therefore, the tsetse fly will:
    a. go to the bait   b. not go to the bait

MASTERY 5-5 Prereading: *University Days*

1. Preread the title, author, and source of the following story. What do you predict about this reading?

   _____

   _____

   _____

   _____

MASTERY 5-6   **Comprehension and Context Clues:** *University Days*

Now read Thurber's story, and then answer the following questions.

University Days
By James Thurber

Excerpted and adapted from *My Life and Hard Times* (New York: Harper & Brothers, 1933).

1   I passed all the other courses I took at my university, but I could never pass **botany**. This was because all botany students had to spend several hours a week in a lab looking through a **microscope** at plant cells, and I could never see through a microscope. This made my instructor furious. He walked around the lab to see all the students drawing the structure of flower cells until he came to me. I would just be standing there. "I can't see anything," I would say. He would kindly explain that anybody can see through a microscope, but he would always end up in a fury, saying that I really could see through a microscope but just pretended that I couldn't. "It takes away from the beauty of flowers anyway," I used to tell him. "We don't care about beauty in this course," he would say. "We care only about cells." "Well," I would say, "I can't see anything." "Try it just once again," he would say, and I would put my eye to the microscope and see nothing at all, except now and again some milky-looking stuff. This was caused by the microscope being out of **focus**. You were supposed to see **vivid**, sharply defined plant cells. "I see what looks like a lot of milk," I would tell him. He said this was because I had not adjusted the microscope for my eyes, so he would readjust it for me, or rather for himself. And I would look again and see milk.

2   I finally took a deferred pass, as they called it, and waited a year and tried again. (You had to pass one of the biological sciences or you couldn't graduate.) The professor had come back from vacation all suntanned and eager to explain plant cells again to his classes. "Well," he said to me, cheerfully, when we met in the first lab hours of the semester, "we're going to see the cells this time, aren't we?" "Yes, sir," I said. Students sitting all around me were seeing cells and quietly drawing pictures of them in their notebooks. Of course, I didn't see anything.

3   "We will try it," the professor said to me, "with every adjustment of the microscope known to man. As God is my witness, I will arrange this glass so that you see cells through it or I'll give up teaching. In twenty-two years of botany, I—" He cut off his speech because he was shaking all over, and he very much wanted to hold onto his temper; having me in class had taken a great deal out of him.

4   So we tried every adjustment of the microscope known to man. With only one of them did I see anything but blackness or the milky stuff, and that time I saw, to my pleasure and amazement, a colorful bunch of flecks, specks, and dots. I quickly began to draw. The instructor, seeing that I was so busy, came to my desk smiling hopefully. He looked at my cell drawing. "What's that?" he demanded. "That's what I saw," I said. "You didn't, you didn't, you didn't!" he screamed, losing control of his temper, and he bent over and looked into the microscope. "That's your eye," he shouted. "You've fixed the lens so that it reflects like a mirror! You have drawn your eye!"

5   If I went through hard times in botany, physical education was even worse. I don't even like to think about it. They would not let you play games or do exercises with your glasses on, and I could not see with mine off. I bumped into professors, tripped over balls, and fell over other students. Not being able to see, I could take it, but I couldn't dish it out. Also, in order to pass PE (and you had to pass it to graduate) you had to learn to swim if you didn't know how. I didn't like the swimming pool, I didn't like swimming, and I didn't like the swimming instructor, and after all these years, I still don't. I never swam, but I passed PE anyway by having another student give my ID number and swim across the pool in my place. He was a quiet, friendly guy, and he would have seen through a microscope for me if we could have gotten away with it, but we couldn't get away with it. Another thing I didn't like about PE was that they made you strip the day you registered. It is impossible for me to be happy when I am stripped and being asked a lot of questions. Still, I did better than a tall **agriculture** student who was **cross-examined** just before I was. They asked each student what college he was in—that is, whether Arts, Engineering, Commerce, or Agriculture. "What college are you in?" the instructor demanded of the young man in front of me. "Ohio State University," he said.

WORDNOTES

botany	science of plant life
microscope	an instrument that magnifies
focus	adjustment for clear vision
vivid	lifelike, sharp, intense
agriculture	relating to the science of growing things
cross-examined	questioned closely

1. What information in paragraph 5 does the author give explaining why he had a hard time in PE? Give two or three examples.

   _____

   _____

   _____

Circle the correct answer.

2. This reading is about the author
   a. graduating from college.
   b. learning to swim.
   c. taking college courses.
   d. having poor eyesight.

3. The author didn't pass botany because
   a. he failed the final exam.
   b. he couldn't draw colorful pictures.
   c. he couldn't see through a microscope.
   d. he didn't attend class.

4. In paragraph 2, the author tells how he took botany again because

a. he wanted to study plant life.

b. he liked the professor.

c. he needed the course to graduate.

d. he wanted to be a scientist.

Using context clues, circle the correct definition of the following words:

1. structure (paragraph 1)

a. parts of a diagram

b. parts of a flower

c. organization of parts

d. parts of a microscope

2. defined (paragraph 1)

a. carefully drawn

b. truthful

c. clearly detailed

d. accurate

3. deferred (paragraph 2)

a. took a short vacation

b. put off until later

c. got a free pass

d. got an unearned grade

4. adjustment (paragraph 3)

a. knob

b. setting

c. mirror

d. lens

5. demanded (paragraph 4)

a. asked thoughtfully

b. asked hesitantly

c. asked quietly

d. asked with authority

6. reflects (paragraph 4)

a. gives back an image

b. gives a different picture

c. gives a bigger picture

d. gives another picture

7. **strip** (paragraph 5)
    a. remove hats
    b. remove shoes
    c. remove clothing
    d. remove t-shirts

8. Look up the following words in your dictionary, and write how to pronounce each word.

Example: botany   bŏt'ə nē

    microscope   _____
    focus   _____
    vivid   _____
    agriculture   _____
    cross-examined _____

9. Write six sentences, each using a different word from the WORDNOTES.

    a. _____
    b. _____
    c. _____
    d. _____
    e. _____
    f. _____

10. Find words in the excerpt that contain three syllables. Write each word below, followed by its dictionary definition. Then write a sentence using each word.

Example: botany: the study of plants. I have four herb gardens in the back yard, and I plan to study botany to learn more about plants.

    a. _____
    b. _____
    c. _____
    d. _____
    e. _____

READER RESPONSE 5-6

Write a description of your major course of study. If you have not decided yet, describe a major you are considering or want to learn more about.

_____

_____

_____

Many courses are required to earn a college degree. List two or three courses required for the degree you are working on, or two or three courses you must take in the first two years of college.

_____

_____

LOOKING BACK

LOOKING BACK 5-1 **Word Study**

1. Write the word parts in the word *autobiography*. Then write what each part means (see Chapter 3, pages 84–91).

   _____

   _____

   _____

2. What does the word *autobiography* tell us about the book *Small Steps*?

   _____

3. *Porthole* is a compound word (see Chapter 3) found in the excerpt from *Small Steps*. Write your own definition of this word.

   _____

4. Divide the following words into syllables (check your dictionary if necessary).

   a. **paralysis**

   _____

   b. **verify**

   _____

   c. **respirator**

   _____

   d. **contagious**

   _____

5. Read the following prefixes and their definitions. For each prefix, write a word that contains it.

Example: Circum = around

(circumference) I was looking for the circumference of a circle.

1. con = with

2. dict = speak

3. ex = out

4. inter = between

ONLINE PRACTICE

Go to **MyReadingLab** at www.myreadinglab.com. Click on **Reading Road Trip**, and select your textbook or the **Pioneer Level**.

1. For further practice with **context clues**, take a Road Trip to **San Francisco**.
2. For further practice using the **dictionary**, take a Road Trip to **Historic Boston**.
3. For practice with **active reading strategies**, take a Road Trip to **New Orleans**.
4. For practice using **vocabulary**, take a Road Trip to the **Library of Congress**.

NAME _____ DATE _____

PROGRESS CHART CHAPTER 5

SECTION ONE

Fill out the number of correct answers you have for each item below. Your instructor will tell you how to calculate your percentage score.

PRACTICE 5-1 Number right _____ out of a possible score of 4.   Percentage score _____

PRACTICE 5-2 Number right _____ out of a possible score of 4.   Percentage score _____

PRACTICE 5-3 Number right _____ out of a possible score of 4.   Percentage score _____

PRACTICE 5-4 Number right _____ out of a possible score of 5.   Percentage score _____

PRACTICE 5-5 Number right _____ out of a possible score of 5.   Percentage score _____

PRACTICE 5-6 Number right _____ out of a possible score of 5.   Percentage score _____

PRACTICE 5-7 Number right _____ out of a possible score of 5.   Percentage score _____

MASTERY 5-1 Number right _____ out of a possible score of 5.   Percentage score _____

MASTERY 5-2 Number right _____ out of a possible score of 10.   Percentage score _____

MASTERY 5-3 Number right _____ out of a possible score of 7.   Percentage score _____

MASTERY 5-4 Number right _____ out of a possible score of 10.   Percentage score _____

MASTERY 5-5 Number right _____ out of a possible score of 1.   Percentage score _____

MASTERY 5-6 Number right _____ out of a possible score of 14.   Percentage score _____

LOOKING BACK 5-1 Number right _____ out of a possible score of 4.   Percentage score _____

SECTION TWO

How do you feel? There are no wrong or right answers to how you feel about what you have learned. Circle Yes, Somewhat, or No in response to the following questions.

1. Do you know what context clues are?	Yes	Somewhat	No
2. Can you identify the five types of context clues?	Yes	Somewhat	No
3. Have you increased your vocabulary by completing this chapter?	Yes	Somewhat	No
4. Are you reading ahead to use context clues to help you identify unknown words?	Yes	Somewhat	No

5. Are you using your own experiences and knowledge to connect to new ideas?   Yes   Somewhat   No

6. Have you created your own vocabulary log?   Yes   Somewhat   No

7. Has your reading improved?   Yes   Somewhat   No

8. Has your reading in other classes improved?   Yes   Somewhat   No

9. Are you using new vocabulary in your speaking and writing?   Yes   Somewhat   No

SECTION THREE

Take a minute or two to reflect on your reading development. Write a few sentences or discuss with other students how this chapter has changed your reading habits.

_____

_____

_____

_____

_____

_____

_____

_____

_____

_____

_____

Finding Main Ideas

CHAPTER PREVIEW

In this chapter, you will learn the difference between the main idea of a reading and the details that support the main idea. Understanding this difference will help you to read with purpose and to understand what you read. You will learn to recognize:

- **Topics**
- **Main ideas**
- **Topic sentences**
- **Thesis statements**
- **Details**

MAKING MEANING

As college students, you are expected to read and study with a purpose, but how do you do that? Students come to college for different reasons: to earn a degree, to advance to a higher-paying job, or to earn the credits needed to transfer to a university. Each student knows what his or her purpose is. When you read, you have a purpose as well. It might be to learn a new skill, understand a new idea, complete a homework assignment, or study for a test.

To read with purpose, you should begin by thinking about the author's purpose. What is the author's reason for writing? For example, each chapter in a psychology textbook is about a topic related to psychology. The table of contents might show that the topic of one chapter is the brain. The brain? That may surprise you. Maybe you thought psychology meant figuring out why you sometimes feel sad on a Saturday afternoon or why your older brother made fun of you when you were just learning how to drive. You might ask yourself, what does the brain have to do with the way I feel or how my brother acts? What does the brain have to do with psychology? Those questions lead you to wonder: What does the author want me, the reader, to know about the brain?

When you ask that last question, you are looking for the main idea of the chapter. Reading with purpose begins by looking for the author's main idea—the answer to the question, "What does the author want me to know?"

INTRODUCTION

The **topic** is the general subject of a paragraph. It is a broad idea that can be summed up in a word or brief phrase. A **topic sentence** tells you what a paragraph is going to be about. It contains the **main idea**—the main point the author is making about the topic. The other sentences in a paragraph develop the topic sentence by providing details that explain or illustrate it. **Supporting details** are examples, facts, or other information that support the main idea.

The following paragraph is about the movies based on the three books that make up *The Lord of the Rings*:

The Lord of the Rings, written by J. R. R. Tolkien, has been made into three highly successful movies. Shown all over the world, the movies have earned more than 1.1 billion dollars in ticket sales. The three movies have won an amazing total of 17 Oscars, including 11 for the last movie, *The Return of the King.* A further sign of the popularity of the movies is that the radio station Classic FM has made the soundtrack for the *Lord of the Rings* number one on its "Top 40 Movie Soundtracks" list.

An outline of the paragraph would look like this:

Lord of the Rings (topic, general)

I. Made into three highly successful movies (main idea)
   A. Earned more than $1.1 billion in ticket sales worldwide (detail)
   B. Won total of 17 Oscars (detail)
   C. Number one on Classic FM "Top 40 Movie Soundtracks" list (detail)

The main idea about a topic in longer readings is usually found in the first or last paragraph (sometimes elsewhere in the reading) and is called the **thesis statement.** A thesis statement tells you what a longer reading is about and states the overall idea the writer has about a topic. The paragraphs that follow each contain a main idea that explains or illustrates the thesis statement, and details, such as facts and statistics, that support the main idea.

STRUCTURED INSTRUCTION AND EXERCISES

TOPICS

To understand what you read, it is important to be able to see the difference between broad, general ideas (**topics**) and the more specific ideas (**main ideas**) that provide information about them

EXERCISE 6-A   Each of the following lists contains one general word and three more-specific words. Beside each word, write G (for general) or S (for specific.)

Example: _____ baby toys

_____ rattle

_____ music box

_____ teddy bear

List 1	*List 2*	*List 3*
_____ enchiladas	_____ winter	_____ ants
_____ mexican food	_____ snowstorm	_____ crickets
_____ tacos	_____ icy roads	_____ cockroaches
_____ nachos	_____ low temperatures	_____ bugs

List 4	*List 5*	*List 6*
_____ office supplies	_____ checkbook	_____ backing up
_____ pencil	_____ bank	_____ using brakes
_____ paper	_____ ATM card	_____ turning left
_____ eraser	_____ deposit slip	_____ driving a car

List 7	*List 8*
_____ delete	_____ slice
_____ caps lock	_____ cooking instructions
_____ computer commands	_____ measure
_____ esc	_____ stir

The first thing to look for in a paragraph is the **topic**, the general idea. Ask yourself these questions as you read: What is the paragraph about? What broad topic does it deal with? Sometimes the topic is stated in the title, as in the following paragraph, which gives information about an important time of the year. At other times, you find the topic by reading the entire paragraph and picking out a word or phrase that sums up the general idea of what it is about.

The Equinox

The word **equinox** means "equal night." There are two times during the year when day and night last 12 hours each. One is called the **vernal** or spring equinox and takes place about March 21. It marks the beginning of spring. The second one is the **autumnal** equinox, which begins on September 22 or 23. It signals the beginning of the fall season.

WORDNOTES

equinox	time of year when day and night are equal in length
vernal	belonging to the spring season
autumnal	belonging to the fall season

What is the topic of "The Equinox"? _____

MAIN IDEAS IN PARAGRAPHS

The **main idea** of a paragraph is the main point the author wants to make about the topic. It is less broad in scope than the general idea and is usually stated in the form of a **topic sentence**. Authors often place the main idea of a paragraph in the first sentence, although sometimes the main idea is in a sentence in the middle or at the end of a paragraph. Once you know what the topic of a paragraph is (what the paragraph is about), you can ask yourself what the writer wants you to know about the topic. What about it? The answer to that question is the main idea of the paragraph.

Look for the main idea—topic sentence—that answers the question, "What about the equinox?" in "The Equinox" passage. Write the sentence here.

_____

Now read the next paragraph.

Stormchasers

Stormchasers are people who love stormy weather—the big storms, like tornadoes, hurricanes, cyclones, and twisters. Stormchasers often keep special equipment in their cars so they can report the locations and strengths of storms. They may report the weather on the radio or television, or they may just be interested in watching and following storms. They take pictures that we see on TV or in the newspaper that show what a tornado looks like. Stormchasers' reports can help people avoid dangerous weather areas and get important information about storms.

The topic of the paragraph—what it is about—is stormchasers. (Notice that the topic is also the title of the paragraph.) An author usually answers the "what about it" question in a topic sentence. The topic sentence states the main idea of a paragraph. It lets you know what the paragraph is about. Remember, the topic sentence is usually the first sentence in a paragraph, although it can come in the middle or at the end. In the "Stormchasers" paragraph, the topic sentence is the first sentence: "Stormchasers are people who love stormy weather—the big storms, like tornadoes, hurricanes, cyclones, and twisters." This sentence states the main idea about the topic, stormchasers. The rest of the sentences in the paragraph give specific supporting details, or narrow ideas, about stormchasers. On the lines provided, write four supporting details found in the "Stormchasers" paragraph.

1. _____

_____

2. _____

_____

3. _____

_____

4. _____

_____

MAIN IDEAS IN LONGER READINGS

In a longer reading containing several paragraphs, the first paragraph usually introduces the topic. The main idea of the reading is often in the first or last paragraph. This is called the **thesis statement**. Each of the other paragraphs contains a topic sentence, which provides a main idea, and details that support and explain that main idea. Each paragraph adds to the information you learn from the entire reading about the main idea the writer has about the topic.

The following article from a geography textbook defines and explains the term *ethnic cleansing*. The topic of the reading, ethnic cleansing, is in the title, "What Is Ethnic Cleansing?" Each paragraph includes a topic sentence followed by supporting details. Together, these paragraphs provide information that will help you understand the term *ethnic cleansing*. Sentence 5 is the thesis statement. There are several words in this reading that you may have heard in news reports or read in newspapers and magazines. Some of them are defined in WORDNOTES.

What Is Ethnic Cleansing?

Abridged from James M. Rubenstein, *An Introduction to Human Geography: The Cultural Landscape,* 8th ed. (New York: Pearson Prentice-Hall, 2005), p. 250.

Paragraph 1

(1) Throughout history, **ethnic** groups have been forced to run from other ethnic groups' more powerful armies. (2) The largest level of forced **migration** came during World War II (1939–45). (3) Especially **notorious** was the movement by the German Nazis of millions of Jews, gypsies, and other ethnic groups to the terrible **concentration camps**, where most of them were killed.

Paragraph 2

(4) The many forced migrations during World War II have not been repeated, but in the 1990s a new name—"ethnic cleansing"—was used to describe new practices by ethnic groups against other ethnic groups. (5) Ethnic cleansing happens when a more powerful ethnic group removes a less powerful one by force in order to create an ethnically **homogeneous** area. (6) The point of ethnic cleansing is not simply to defeat an enemy or to control them.

Paragraph 3

(7) Ethnic cleansing is used to rid an area of an entire ethnic group so that the ethnic group left behind will be the only people in the area. (8) Rather than a clash between armies of male soldiers, ethnic cleansing removes every member of the less powerful group—women as well as men, children as well as adults, the **frail** elderly as well as the strong youth. (9) Ethnic cleansing has been seen in portions of the former Yugoslavia, especially Bosnia-Herzegovina and Kosovo.

WORDNOTES

ethnic	referring to a group of people having the same customs, language, religion, and culture
migration	movement to another area or country
notorious	widely and unfavorably known
concentration camps	camps set up for political and ethnic prisoners
homogeneous	made up of the same parts
frail	delicate, weak

Write the thesis statement for the reading.

Thesis statement: _____

_____

_____

The topic sentence of paragraph 1 provides the first idea that helps you to understand the term *ethnic cleansing*. Write this sentence on the lines provided:

First main idea: _____

_____

Now add the main ideas from paragraphs 2 and 3:

Second main idea: _____

_____

_____

Third main idea: _____

_____

Each paragraph contains supporting details that expand and explain the main idea in the topic sentence. Usually a detail that supports the main idea is in a sentence. Within such a sentence you may find minor details as well that further explain the idea in the detail sentence. For each paragraph, first write the number of details you found. Then write the details for each paragraph on the lines provided.

Paragraph 1:

Number of details: _____

Details: _____

_____

_____

_____

Paragraph 2

Number of details: _____

Details: _____

_____

_____

_____

Paragraph 3

Number of details _____

Details: _____

_____

_____

_____

Even though each paragraph has two main supporting details, sentence 8 in paragraph 3 includes several more minor details that explain how ethnic cleansing affects all people within an ethnic group. There is much to learn from details within a longer reading, but it is important to first identify the topic of the writing and then decide how each main idea, and the details that support it, refers to and supports the topic.

EXERCISE 6-B Each of the following groups of words includes one general idea and three specific ideas. Underline the general idea in each group.

Example: boat   <u>transportation</u>   automobile   airplane

1. bed   chair   furniture   table
2. trees   oak   maple   elm
3. hurricanes   tornadoes   typhoons   storms
4. hours   time   minutes   seconds
5. desserts   pie   cakes   cookies

EXERCISE 6-C On the lines provided, write two specific ideas that are covered by each general idea.

Example:

General idea: flowers
Specific ideas: rose   ___daisy___   ___tulip___

1. General idea: planets

Specific ideas: Earth   _____   _____

2. General idea: calendar

   Specific ideas: days   _____   _____

3. General idea: beach

   Specific ideas: sand   _____   _____

4. General idea: shirt

   Specific ideas: collar   _____   _____

5. General idea: candy

   Specific ideas: taffy   _____   _____

EXERCISE 6-D

Are You Sleeping?

About 90 minutes after you fall asleep, an **automatic** response occurs called rapid eye movement (REM). Dreaming begins during REM sleep. Your eyes move rapidly, your heart beats faster, and your brain wave pattern changes. Scientists are not able to explain why humans dream during this **phase** of sleep.

WORDNOTES

automatic   done by habit

phase   a stage

1. What is the topic of the paragraph? _____

2. Write the topic sentence (main idea).

   _____

   _____

3. How many details (major and minor supporting ideas) are there? _____

   Write the detail sentences on the lines provided.

   _____

   _____

   _____

4. What do the initials REM stand for?

   _____

5. When does REM occur?

   _____

EXERCISE 6-E   Read the "Hybrid Cars" paragraph, and then answer the questions that follow.

Hybrid Autos

In the next few years, we will be seeing more and more **hybrid** automobiles on the road. Hybrid cars use two forms of power to make them go: gasoline and electricity. This saves on fuel and keeps the car going for many more miles. They offer the power of gasoline engines for travel on highways and the power of electricity, through the use of rechargeable batteries, for stop-and-go city driving. These cars are kind to our **atmosphere** because hybrids do not **pollute** the air as much as regular cars.

WORDNOTES

hybrid	a blend of two elements
atmosphere	the mass of air surrounding the earth
pollute	to make impure or unclean

1. What is the topic of the paragraph? _____

2. What is the main idea of "Hybrid Cars"?

   _____

   _____

3. How many supporting details are in the paragraph? _____

4. How are hybrid autos powered? _____

5. What is the gasoline power used for? _____

6. What is the battery power (electricity) used for?

_____

7. What is the benefit of hybrid cars?

_____

EXERCISE 6-F   Read the next paragraph, and then complete the sentences that follow. You can use your own words or words from the paragraph.

A Freedom Celebration

Juneteenth is an African-American celebration of the ending of slavery in the United States. Slavery ended when President Abraham Lincoln signed the Emancipation Proclamation during the Civil War. The celebration began in Texas on June 19, 1865, when Major General Gordon of the Union army led his troops into Galveston. He brought news of the slaves' freedom after the signing of the official proclamation.

WORDNOTES

emancipation	the act of being set free
proclamation	a formal public announcement
official	formal

---

1. In "A Freedom Celebration," the topic is _____

2. Write the topic sentence.

_____

_____

3. One interesting detail is _____

_____

4. What group of people began the Juneteenth celebration?

_____

5. When and where did Juneteenth begin?

_____

EXERCISE 6-G   In the following reading (one you might find in a health or psychology text-book), the topic is the title, so you know what the article is about. Because you have probably heard or read about marijuana, you already know some of the information you will be reading about. If you have not made up your mind about whether you believe marijuana is harmless or dangerous, look for information in the article that might help you decide.

Read the complete article. Pay particular attention to the first and last sentences of each paragraph to understand the main ideas the author is discussing. Then answer the questions that follow.

Marijuana

1   There is an argument in our society about the use of marijuana. Some believe smoking marijuana is a harmless way to enjoy life, to kick back and think about something other than daily events, even to find relief from pain. Others believe that smoking marijuana is dangerous and can lead to serious problems in life.

2   Marijuana seems to have its most **adverse** effects on **adolescents**. Young people feel a lot of pressure to try new things, and often friends encourage them to use marijuana. Research shows people in that age group who use marijuana are more likely to commit crimes, rebel against school and family, and have poor relationships with parents. Users may lose the desire to work regularly, do not care about how they look, feel **fatigued**, and perform poorly in school or work. Those who oppose making marijuana legal fear that teenagers will be the ones most tempted to abuse the drug and suffer the most.

3   People who support the use of marijuana for medical purposes claim it is an effective pain reliever for patients with cancer, MS (multiple sclerosis), epilepsy, Parkinson's disease, Huntington's disease, and AIDS (all illnesses that people do not recover from). But various studies of how well marijuana relieves pain in these illnesses have not proven it to be more effective than other known medications.

4   The long-term effects of marijuana smoking include the same dangers as tobacco smoking: breathing problems with frequent coughing and **wheezing**, cell and tissue damage, and damage to **reproductive systems**. Also, women who use marijuana may give birth to children who suffer from developmental delays. Many in the medical field believe that the long-term risks of marijuana may outweigh the **potential** benefits in treating illnesses. Currently, most people agree that the problems caused by its effects are too great for marijuana to be made legal.

WORDNOTES

adverse	harmful
adolescents	people in their teens
fatigued	overly tired
wheezing	breathing with difficulty, usually with a whistling sound
reproductive systems	organs for producing offspring
potential	possible

1. What is the topic of "Marijuana"? _____

2. Where is the thesis statement, the overall main idea of the article, stated?

_____

3. What is the thesis statement?

_____

_____

4. What is the topic sentence of the second paragraph?

_____

5. How many details (major and minor) are in paragraph 2? _____

6. What are the detail sentences from paragraph 2?

_____

_____

_____

_____

_____

7. What is the topic sentence of paragraph 3?

_____

_____

_____

_____

8. What is the topic sentence in paragraph 4?

_____

_____

9. What are the details in paragraph 4?

_____

_____

_____

_____

_____

_____

10. According to the article, what are the most serious effects of using marijuana?

_____

_____

_____

PRACTICING WHAT YOU HAVE LEARNED

PRACTICE 6-1 **General and Specific Ideas**

In each of the following groups of words, one word express a general idea, and the other three words are details covered by the broader idea. Underline the word expressing the general idea in each line.

Example: sweet   baked   <u>potato</u>   mashed

1. apple   grapefruit   fruit   cherries
2. cave   house   shelter   tent
3. lantern   camping   cot   tent
4. fork   knife   spoon   utensils
5. canary   pets   puppy   kitten

PRACTICE 6-2 **General and Specific Ideas**

On the lines provided, write two specific ideas that are covered by each general idea.

Example:

General idea: senses
Specific ideas: hearing   seeing   smelling

1. General idea: languages

   Specific ideas: German   _____   _____

2. General idea: cookware

   Specific ideas: skillet   _____   _____

3. General idea: vegetables

   Specific ideas: corn   _____   _____

4. General idea: foot

   Specific ideas: heel   _____   _____

5. General idea: wedding

   Specific ideas: bride   _____   _____

PRACTICE 6-3 **General and Specific Ideas**

Underline the general-idea word and add two specific-idea words on the lines provided.

Example: bull riding   <u>rodeo</u>   cowboys   clowns

1. driver's license   wallet   _____   _____
2. crib   nursery   _____   _____

3. Atlantic   oceans   _____   _____

4. sports   football   _____   _____

5. weather   sunshine   _____   _____

PRACTICE 6-4   **Alike and Different**

Place an *X* beside the idea that is different from the other ideas in each of the following lists.

Example: _____ TV

_____ computer

_____ textbook

_____ cell phone

_____ pager

In the example, all the items on this list are electronic except *textbook*.

List 1	*List 2*	*List 3*	*List 4*
_____ castles	_____ matches	_____ dolphins	_____ pencil
_____ teepees	_____ logs	_____ sharks	_____ paper
_____ dwellings	_____ grate	_____ horses	_____ eraser
_____ carriage	_____ ashes	_____ whales	_____ software
_____ caves	_____ light bulb	_____ eels	_____ notebook

PRACTICE 6-5   **Topic: *Run for Cover!***

Read the following paragraph about thunderstorms.

> ## Run for Cover!
>
> It is possible to discover just how far away a thunderstorm is from you. When you see a flash of lightning, begin counting until you hear the sound of thunder. Then divide the number of seconds you have counted by 5. This will tell you about how many miles away the lightning has struck. For example, if you count 15 seconds between seeing the lightning and hearing the thunder, the storm is 3 miles away: $15 \div 5 = 3$. If you see the flash and hear the thunder at the same time, the storm is directly overhead. Run for cover!

Underline the topic of "Run for Cover!"

1. definition of thunderstorm   4. definition of lightning

2. how to divide   5. how to know how far away a

3. how many seconds in a minute   thunderstorm is

PRACTICE 6-6 **Topic, Main Idea, Details, and Word Skills:** *Sports in Popular Culture*

Read the following paragraph, and then answer the questions that follows.

Sports in Popular Culture

From James M. Rubenstein, *An Introduction to Human Geography: The Cultural Landscape,* 8th ed., (New York Pearson Prentice-Hall, 2005), p.122

Each country has its own **preferred** sports. Cricket is popular **primarily** in Britain and former British colonies. Ice hockey **prevails** in colder climates, especially in Canada, northern Europe, and Russia. The most popular sports in China are martial arts, known as *wishu,* including archery, fencing, wrestling, and boxing. Baseball, once played only in North America, became popular in Japan after it was **introduced** by American soldiers who occupied the country after World War II.

WORDNOTES

preferred	liked better
primarily	mainly
prevails	is used widely
introduced	brought in for the first time

1. What is the topic of "Sports in Popular Culture"?

   _____

2. Write the main idea or topic sentence of "Sports in Popular Culture."

   _____

3. List all the sports mentioned in the paragraph.

   _____

4. Why is ice hockey the main sport in Canada, northern Europe, and Russia?

   _____

5. List the most popular sports in China.

   _____

6. How was the sport of baseball introduced to Japan?

   _____

7. From context clues in the paragraph, what is the definition of *wishu*?

   _____

8. From your own knowledge and the context clues in the last sentence, what is the meaning of the word *occupied*?

   _____

   _____

   _____

   _____

Using the words from the WORDNOTES, complete the following sentences.

9. Juanita _____ crossword puzzles until her brother _____

   her to Sudoku.

10. I listen _____ to classical music, but jazz _____

    as the favorite of my friends.

READER RESPONSE 6-1   Write a few sentences about a sport you have enjoyed playing or watching.

_____

_____

_____

_____

PRACTICE 6-7   **Organization, Topic, Context Clues, and Word Skills: *Out of the Way!***

In the following paragraph about the sport of soccer, the sentences are not in the proper order. Rewrite the paragraph so the sentences are in order and it is easier to understand. Then answer the questions that follow.

Out of the Way!

During the late thirteenth century, the sport was so popular that London's streets became too crowded for **merchants** to conduct their business. However, even the **threat** of going to prison failed to keep players out of the streets, and the ban did not work. Thus, in the year 1314, the first football ban came into force. The game of organized football (which is called soccer in the United States) **originated** in England.

W O R D N O T E S

merchant	one who buys and sells
originated	began
threat	declaration of intention to harm

1. Rewrite:

_____

_____

_____

_____

_____

2. What does the title tell you about the information in the paragraph?

_____

_____

3. What is the topic of "Out of The Way!"?

   _____

4. Write the topic sentence.

   _____

   _____

5. From the context clues in the paragraph, write your own definition of the word *ban*.

   _____

6. Why did merchants want football to be banned from London streets?

   _____

7. Look up the word *soccer* in the dictionary. Give the pronunciation, part of speech, and definition of the word.

   _____

   _____

Using the words from the WORDNOTES, fill in the blanks in the following sentences.

8. Did you know that soccer _____ in England?

9. The _____ of a hurricane did not scare the community, but it should have!

10. After the _____ opened their stores, the shoppers rushed in.

PRACTICE 6-8 **Organization, Comprehension, Context Clues, and Word Skills: *The Hoover Dam***

In a history or engineering class, you would learn about famous places like the Hoover Dam. Rewrite the following paragraph so the sentences are in order and it is easier to understand. Then answer the questions that follow.

The Hoover Dam

Thousands of men arrived in Black Canyon to **tame** the Colorado River, which had caused serious flooding for years. The Hoover Dam, located in Nevada, was built during the **Great Depression** and was completed in 1935. Now, 70 years later, the Hoover Dam is known as one of America's seven modern civil engineering **wonders**. The dam controlled the river, brought water to the cities, and created Lake Mead **Reservoir**.

WORDNOTES

tame	change from a wild state
Great Depression	decline of business in 1930s
wonders	amazing accomplishments
reservoir	a place where something is stored for future use

1. Rewrite:

   _____

   _____

   _____

   _____

   _____

2. What is the topic of the paragraph?

   _____

3. Write the topic sentence of the paragraph.

   _____

   _____

4. There are _____ details in the paragraph.

5. How did the Hoover Dam help people?

   _____

   _____

6. What river was controlled by the Hoover Dam?

   _____

7. From context clues, write a definition of the term *civil engineering*.

   _____

   _____

Complete the following sentences using words from the WORDNOTES.

8. Christopher's grandmother learned to save money during the hard times of the _____.

9. It takes a lot of patience and gentleness to _____ a wild animal.

10. Since the _____ was completed, the village has had plenty of water.

11. There are many natural _____ to see at Yellowstone National Park.

PRACTICE 6-9   **Thesis, Main Ideas, and Details:** *Special Athletes*

Special Athletes

Paragraph 1

The Special Olympics is an international program that gives learning-disabled young people a chance to become physically fit. It helps local communities and athletes learn to accept and respect each other. The Special Olympics officially began on July 20, 1968, at Soldiers Field, Chicago, Illinois. One thousand athletes from 26 states and Canada competed in that first series of events. Money from the Joseph P. Kennedy, Jr. Foundation made the Special Olympics possible.

Paragraph 2

The Special Olympics provides enjoyable yet challenging activities for athletes with learning disabilities. Each athlete who wishes to compete in the program receives quality training, and activities are age-and ability-appropriate. The program makes it possible for the more talented athletes to move into regular school programs. However, it is always up to the individual to decide whether to remain in the Special Olympics or become involved in regular sports programs.

Paragraph 3

A vital part of the Special Olympics program is the encouragement provided by local volunteers. College-age students and senior citizens work to make this program successful.

Paragraph 4

Everyone who competes in the games is awarded a ribbon, whether they place first or last. Each athlete receives an award in a special ceremony. The Special Olympics enhances the athletes' self-esteem and dignity and provides an opportunity for them to feel equal to other young people.

WORDNOTES

appropriate   suitable, fitting
enhances   improves, adds to

1. What is the topic of "Special Athletes"?

   _____

2. Write the thesis statement from "Special Athletes."

   _____

   _____

   _____

3. a. Where did you find the thesis statement?

   _____

Write the main ideas from paragraphs 2, 3, and 4.

b. **Paragraph 2:** _____

_____

c. **Paragraph 3:** _____

_____

d. **Paragraph 4:** _____

_____

4. How many supporting details are in each paragraph?

Paragraph 1: _____

Paragraph 2: _____

Paragraph 3: _____

Paragraph 4: _____

5. When and where did the Special Olympics begin?

_____

6. Who started the Special Olympics?

_____

7. Who can take part in the Special Olympics?

_____

8. Who are the volunteers who make the Special Olympics possible?

_____

9. How are the athletes in the Special Olympics recognized?

_____

10. How does the Special Olympics competition help the athletes?

_____

_____

SUMMARY

- The **topic** is the general idea of a paragraph, chapter, or essay. It can be summed up in a word or brief phrase. The topic of a reading is often referred to in the title of a paragraph or longer reading.
- The **main idea** is the main point an author makes about a topic.
- The main idea of a paragraph is stated in a **topic sentence**, which is usually found at the beginning or end of a paragraph
- **Details** provide specific information and examples that support the main idea stated in the topic sentence.
- The main idea of a longer reading is stated in a **thesis statement** and is often found in the first or last paragraph (sometimes elsewhere).

MASTERY LEVEL EXERCISES

MASTERY 6-1 **Prereading:** *Stingers*

1. Before reading the following paragraph, write what you know about how bees and wasps are alike. _____

_____

_____

MASTERY 6-2 **Main Idea and Details:** *Stingers*

Stingers

Bees and wasps are alike in many ways; however, there are important differences between the two insects. Wasps have a long, thin body divided by a very narrow waistline. They are typically brown or shiny black, with little or no hair on their bodies or legs. A bee's body is shorter and plumper, with hair on its body and legs. Most bees are light to golden brown, and some are yellow with stripes. Like the wasp, the bee has a narrow waistline dividing its body. Both insects have antennae (feelers) on their heads and a double set of wings. Unlike the stingers in wasps, the bee's stinger is barbed (like a fishhook) and remains in the flesh of its victim. The bee can sting only once, but a wasp can sting several times. Both insects have six legs. Wasps make their nests out of paper and mud, and bees make their nests from wax. Bees feed on flowers and make honey to feed their young. Many wasps are meat eating and feed on spiders, flies, and caterpillars. Although bees and wasps belong to the same family, they have physical qualities that help humans identify them as two separate insects.

1. Underline the topic of "Stingers."
   a. flying insects   d. stinging insects
   b. bees and wasps   e. bright-colored insects
   c. food for insects

2. Write the topic sentence from the paragraph.

_____

_____

3. From the information in the paragraph, write a description of a bee—what it looks like and how it lives.

_____

_____

_____

_____

_____

_____

4. From the information in the paragraph, write a description of a wasp—
what it looks like and how it lives.

_____

_____

_____

_____

_____

READER RESPONSE 6-2   From the information in the paragraph, draw a wasp and a bee.

Bee   **Wasp**

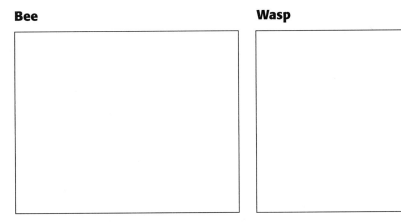

MASTERY 6-3   **Topic, Main Idea, and Details:** *River Drivers—On a Roll!*

River Drivers—On a Roll!

In the past, the heroes of the lumber business were river drivers. These men had the most dangerous job of all the lumberjacks: they moved freshly cut logs downstream from the inner forest to the closest sawmill. Horses and oxen dragged the fallen logs to the river. Once the logs were at the riverbank, the river drivers would put on their caulked boots and grab a piked pole. The river drivers had to balance themselves on the logs while traveling through rapids and often over dams. Many river drivers were killed during the process of logrolling when a logjam would occur. In the act of dislodging the jam, men lost their lives as they lost their footing and fell beneath the pile of logs. These brave men won the respect of the other workers because of their highly developed skills. They were paid the highest wages of all the lumber workers, often as much as seventy-five cents to a dollar an hour! More than a hundred years later, these heroes are still admired by workers in the lumber industry.

WORDNOTES

river driver	lumber workers who moved logs down a river
lumberjacks	worker who cuts logs in the forest and moves them to a sawmill
caulked	spiked
piked pole	pole with a metal pick on one end
logrolling	ability to move logs downriver by balancing on them
logjam	jumble of logs pushed together in a stream

1. What is the topic of "River Drivers—On a Roll!"?

   _____

2. What is the main idea?

   _____

3. What was the most dangerous job in the lumber industry?

   _____

4. How were logs moved from the inner forest to the sawmill?

   _____

   _____

5. What were caulked boots and a piked pole used for?

   _____

6. Why was a river driver's job so dangerous?

   _____

READER RESPONSE 6-3 Have you or someone you know had a dangerous job? Describe why the job was dangerous.

_____

_____

_____

_____

_____

_____

_____

_____

MASTERY 6-4 **Topic, Main Ideas, and Details:** *Cars That Think?*

Cars That Think?

1   Cars are getting smaller and smarter. You may have noticed them on television or the Internet, and many more will appear in the future. How can a car be intelligent? The new "smart" cars have many features that help and protect the people who drive them and make the places where they live safer. Cars can be smart in many ways.

2   Smart Cars, which were first produced in 1998 in Europe, are designed to be easy to drive. They are well suited for people who live in large cities. They are about eight feet long and weigh just over 1,600 pounds. A car that size can hold two passengers with storage behind the seat. They maneuver well in heavy traffic. Two of these little autos can fit into a single parking space designed for the typical American car.

3   There are many benefits to driving Smart Cars. They cost less to operate than larger cars and offer gas mileage of more than 60 miles to the gallon. They are made with a diesel engine, and the engine parts can be recycled. In addition, safety features such as cameras for blind spots and alarms for dangerous highway conditions make the cars even more attractive.

4   But what is appealing to many auto buyers is the unique look of these automobiles. Smart Cars are coming to the United States: we will soon see a "cute car" that also thinks.

WORDNOTES

maneuver	move skillfully
typical	average

Answer the following questions using your own words or words from the article.

1. What is the topic of this article?

_____

2. What is the main idea of this article?

_____

3. What is the main idea of paragraph 2?

_____

_____

4. List the details in paragraph 2.

_____

_____

_____

_____

_____

5. Write the main idea of paragraph 3.

_____

6. What do you learn in paragraph 3?

_____

_____

7. In paragraph 4, why is the auto called a "cute car?"

_____

8. Does the article answer the question in the title? _____

9. How does it answer the question in the title?

_____

_____

10. What do you think is the most interesting information in the article?

_____

_____

_____

MASTERY 6-5   **Topic, Main Ideas, and Details:** *A Modern Plague*

A Modern Plague

Paragraph 1

(1) For as long as the world has been keeping records, there have been diseases that people feared. (2) The worst of these diseases was the bubonic plague, sometimes called the Black Death. (3) In second-century Rome, as many as 5,000 people died every day during one outbreak of the plague. (4) In the 1300s, this illness wiped out one-quarter of the population of Europe and began to spread throughout the known world. (5) Everyone who heard about the plague knew that those who caught it would die. (6) It was very contagious, and people with the disease had to be kept isolated so others would not catch it. (7) Centuries later, antibiotics and then a vaccine were developed and used to treat those who were infected, but without rapid treatment the disease is still fatal.

Paragraph 2

(8) The source of bubonic plague was not discovered until the beginning of the twentieth century. (9) It came from fleas carried by rats. (10) Because of poor sanitary conditions, people caught the disease from the fleas and then passed it to other people. (11) Rats came into countries on ships and infested cities. (12) People learned that preventing the disease began with knowing what caused it. (13) Rigid sanitation efforts and quarantining incoming ships finally controlled the spread of the plague. (14) Today, all countries in the world advise each other about possible outbreaks of plague and cooperate to control it.

Paragraph 3

(15) A modern plague that spreads illness and death is affecting people today—HIV/AIDS. (16) Every six seconds, someone becomes infected with this disease, and it is expected to spread to 40 million more people across the world in the next year. (17) The countries most affected are Africa and India. (18) HIV/AIDS

was identified in 1981. (19) People become infected through sexual intercourse with a person who has the disease or by using intravenous drugs and sharing needles. (20) Pregnant mothers can pass it on to their babies. (21) Younger and younger people are being affected by HIV/AIDS because of intravenous drug use. (22) Several successful anti-HIV drugs have been developed, although they can sometimes cause severe side effects. (23) People taking these drugs can live longer, healthier lives than they would have been able to do a few years ago. (24) The disease is always fatal if not treated.

Paragraph 4

(25) People can prevent HIV/AIDS by taking part in a faithful sexual relationship with one partner, **abstaining** from sexual intercourse with someone who has the disease, and avoiding the use of **intravenous** drugs. (26) Knowing the cause of bubonic plague taught people how to prevent it, and knowing the cause of HIV/AIDS could conquer this modern plague as well.

WORD NOTES

bubonic plague	disease that is caused by Yersinia Pesta bacteria and spreads quickly
contagious	"catching," spread by contact
isolated	set apart from others
infected	spread from one to another
infested	overrun in numbers large enough to be harmful
quarantining	enforcing isolation to prevent spread of disease
abstaining	doing without
intravenous	injected into a vein

1. What is the topic of the article?

   _____

2. Where is the thesis sentence of the article written?

   _____

   Write the thesis sentence.

   _____

   _____

3. Write the main ideas of the first three paragraphs. Use your own words or copy sentences from the article.

   Paragraph 1: _____

   _____

   Paragraph 2: _____

   _____

   Paragraph 3: _____

   _____

4. How many supporting details are in each paragraph?

   Paragraph 1:_____

   Paragraph 2:_____

   Paragraph 3:_____

   Paragraph 4:_____

5. Why did people fear the bubonic plague?

   _____

6. What caused the plague?

   _____ _____

7. How did the plague spread over so many countries?

   _____

   _____

8. How is HIV/AIDS similar to the bubonic plague?

   _____

9. What countries are most affected by HIV/AIDS?

   _____

10. What three ways do people become infected with HIV/AIDS?

    _____

    _____

11. Can HIV/AIDS be prevented? How?

    _____

    _____

    _____

LOOKING BACK

LOOKING BACK 6-1   **Topic and Context Clues:** *It's Not Funny!*

It's Not Funny!

Your funny bone is not a bone; it is a nerve. If you hit the inside of your elbow in just the right spot, you will feel a tingling or prickly kind of pain. The nerve that has been hit is the *ulnar nerve*, which then bumps against the *humerus bone*. This long bone runs from the elbow up to the shoulder. The resulting "funny feeling" led to the nickname of "funny bone" because the tingling feeling was felt in the humerus bone.

1. Underline the topic of "It's Not Funny!"
   a. nerve
   b. the humerus bone
   c. the lunar nerve
   d. nickname
   e. the funny bone

2. Write the topic sentence of the paragraph.

   _____

3. Using the context clues in the paragraph, write the definition of *tingling*.

   _____

4. Using context clues, write a definition of *humerus bone*.

   _____

5. Using context clues, write the definition of *nickname*.

   _____

   _____

   _____

LOOKING BACK 6-2   **Prereading: *Dream Catcher***

1. Preread the following passage, and then list three things you discovered from doing so. Answers will vary. Possible answers are:

   a. _____

   b. _____

   c. _____

LOOKING BACK 6-3   **Comprehension and Word Skills: *Dream Catcher***

Dream Catcher

(1) Dream catchers are fascinating objects of art. (2) American Indian women have been making them for many generations. (3) The Native American Ojibwe tribe (some call this group the Chippewa) originally created the dream catcher, although they have been observed in many tribes. (4) The making of dream catchers started with a folktale about the Spider Woman and her web. (5) The original Spider Woman wove webs to bring the sun to the tribe's people. (6) When the tribe dispersed, Native American women began weaving dream catchers, based on Spider Woman's web. The dream catchers let good dreams slide down the weaving to their babies and trapped bad dreams, which shriveled up in the light of day. (7) This special woven web was hung on the cradles of children to ensure that only good thoughts and dreams would influence them.

(8) In the first designs, a feather was used to represent breath or air. (9) The feather of the owl represented wisdom, and the eagle feather represented

courage. (10) Today, owls and eagles are protected, so their feathers are no longer used. (11) In **souvenir** shops across America, dream catchers are **plentiful** and popular. (12) Many contain four gemstones now instead of feathers to represent the four directions: north, south, east, and west. (13) The folktale of Spider Woman and her web still fascinates all who hear it.

W O R D N O T E S

fascinating	enchanting
generations	groups of people born around the same time (children, parents, grandparents represent three generations)
dispersed	broken up, scattered
shriveled	shrunk, withered
ensure	make sure
influence	power to affect others
souvenir	a keepsake
plentiful	large supply of

1. What is "Dream Catcher" about?

   _____

   _____

2. A dream catcher is patterned after _____.

3. Why did Native Americans hang dream catchers on babies' cradles?

   _____

   _____

4. Why are gemstones used to make dream catchers today?

   _____

5. From context clues in "Dream Catcher," what is the definition of *folktale?*

   _____

6. In sentence 2, find a four-syllable word. _____

7. In sentence 1, which word has a long e sound? _____

8. Write two words from sentence 6 that have suffixes. _____

   _____

9. Which two words from sentence 12 have prefixes? _____

   _____

10. Write the three words in sentence 12 that have the digraph *th.*

    _____

LOOKING BACK 6-4   **Prereading and Predicting:** *American Monument*

1. From the title "American Monument," what can you predict about the following article?

_____

_____

2. Preread the article by looking at the title and the first sentence of each paragraph. What did you learn?

_____

_____

LOOKING BACK 6-5   **Comprehension:** *American Monument*

American Monument

In the Black Hills of South Dakota, there is a monument to America's democracy called the Mount Rushmore National Memorial. It displays the faces of four presidents: George Washington, Thomas Jefferson, Theodore Roosevelt, and Abraham Lincoln. These faces represent the first 150 years of American history. The four men were chosen for their contributions as American leaders. George Washington was chosen because he was the father of our country and the first president; Thomas Jefferson was selected because he was the author of the Declaration of Independence. Theodore (Teddy) Roosevelt was the third selection because he completed the Panama Canal linking the Atlantic and Pacific Oceans. Abraham Lincoln was chosen because he preserved freedom and equality for all races during the Civil War.

The creator of Mount Rushmore was John Gutzon Borglum. Between 1927 and 1941, he and 400 workers sculpted the 60-foot busts of the four presidents. It cost 1 million dollars. Each head is as tall as a six-story building, and during the carving, more than 800 million pounds of stone were removed from the mountain. Among the most highly skilled workers were those using dynamite to blast rock from the mountain. Each face has a nose that is 20 feet long, a mouth 18 feet wide, and eyes 11 feet across. The workers had to climb 506 steps daily to get to the top of Mount Rushmore. Amazingly, there were no deaths and only a couple of injuries during the 15-year period of carving and sculpting at Mount Rushmore.

President and Mrs. Calvin Coolidge dedicated the monument on August 10, 1927. President Coolidge was the first person to call Mount Rushmore a "national shrine," and he pledged federal support for the project. The memorial of the four chosen presidents was a tribute to the American ideals and goals they helped shape.

WORD NOTES

monument	something set up to keep alive the memory of one or more persons or an event
contributions	the act of giving something
sculpted	carved or shaped
bust	the likeness of a person's head and shoulders
dedicated	to set apart for a special purpose
shrine	a place that is sacred because of its associations
tribute	a statement of gratitude, respect, honor, or praise

Mount Rushmore National Memorial, South Dakota
Photo provided by South Dakota Tourism and State Development

3. Where is Mount Rushmore? _____

4. Whose faces are on the monument?

_____

5. Why is Thomas Jefferson's face on the monument?

_____

6. Who created the Mount Rushmore National Memorial?

_____

7. How long did it take to carve the monument? _____

8. What is the size of each face?

_____

9. Who described Mount Rushmore as a "national shrine?"

_____

10. Why is Mount Rushmore important to America?

_____

LOOKING BACK 6-6 **Prereading and Predicting: _Gardner Rules!_**

1. From prereading the title and the boldfaced headings and looking at the picture, write three or four questions you predict will be answered in the following article.

_____

_____

_____

LOOKING BACK 6-7 **Comprehension, Main Idea, and Word Skills: _Gardner Rules!_**

Gardner Rules!

Excerpted and adapted from Rulon Gardner's official website, http://www.rulongardner.com.

Meet Rulon Gardner

1 Born August 16, 1971 in Afton, Wyoming, Rulon Gardner is the youngest of nine children born to Reed and Virginia Gardner. Raised on a dairy farm, where they grew crops, milked cows twice a day, and always had plenty of work to do, Gardner was taught to work hard at a young age.

2 School did not come easy for Gardner. Most school nights found him after 10 p.m. lying on his mom's bed while she read his books to him and then helped him with his assignments. He struggled with reading speed and comprehension, but with the help and support of his family, Gardner was able to complete his schoolwork. With a great deal of frustration, he successfully completed high school and won a wrestling scholarship to Ricks College in Idaho. From Ricks College, he received a Division I scholarship to wrestle for the University of Nebraska.

3 Gardner says this about his college years:

In 1995 while wrestling at the University of Nebraska, I set a goal to become part of the United States Olympic Team. I was not expected to make the 2000 Olympic Team; however, after I defeated the 1996 silver medallist, people began to believe in my abilities. I continued to work hard, I never gave up, I stuck with my dreams, and I was successful in my quest to represent the United States in the Sydney 2000 games.

Rulon Gardner Defeats Legendary Alexander Karelin

4 In the 2000 Sydney Olympics, Rulon Gardner beat the unbeatable in a match that came to be called "The Miracle on the Mat" because no one thought he could win. With no major title to his name, Gardner ended Russian Alexander Karelin's record of three Olympic gold medals and a 13-year unbeaten streak. Until that day, Karelin had never lost in international competition and had not given up a point in 10 years. Gardner celebrated his 1-0 victory with a cartwheel and a somersault.

Rulon Survives Snowmobile Mishap

5   A snowmobile accident on Valentine's Day, 2002, left Olympic gold medallist Gardner trapped in a Wyoming forest in sopping wet clothes as temperatures dropped to 25 below zero. In addition to dragging his 600-pound sled across thigh-deep water several times (something that would later take four male rescuers to do) and dropping off the edge of a 150-foot cliff, Gardner proved his strength by surviving nearly 18 hours in the cold. When rescuers finally reached him, Gardner's body temperature was 80 degrees. A person usually becomes unconscious at 82 degrees. Although doctors told him he would lose his feet and never walk again, much less wrestle, Gardner began the road to recovery. As an athlete concerned about drug addiction, Gardner refused painkillers. In the end, only one toe was amputated, and the others were attached to his foot with pins. One year later, he was training again for the Athens Olympics.

Gardner Leaves Shoes on the Mat in Athens

6   After one last Greco-Roman battle at the birthplace of the sport at the 2004 Athens Olympics, an emotional Rulon Gardner left his wrestling shoes at the center of the mat in a farewell to his sport. "To leave them on the mat meant I left everything on the mat as a wrestler," said Gardner, who also blew kisses to the fans and waved a U.S. flag after his victory in the bronze medal match.

7   Today Gardner is a sports commentator and motivational speaker. He also tells his story in his book *Never Stop Pushing*. Gardner travels and speaks to young people and businesses about how he followed his goals and overcame his challenges. He shares the "important lessons" he learned in his life:

Respect God's creations. We have been given a beautiful earth, and it is our responsibility to treat it with respect.

Recognize the significance of the family unit. How much better would society be if more people put the family first?

Work hard. Success is never accomplished without sacrifice.

Never give up. We each will have difficult times; never break that grip.

Stick with your dreams. Even though the odds may be stacked against you, always believe in yourself.

For Rulon Gardner, these lessons describe the way he lives.

2. What kind of work did Gardner do at home while growing up?

_____

3. Why was reading difficult for Gardner?

_____

4. What goal did he set for himself while at the University of Nebraska?

_____

5. How did he reach his goal?

_____

_____

6. What is the main idea of paragraph 2?

_____

7. How many specific details are in paragraph 4? _____. Write the details that are in paragraph 4.

a. _____

b. _____

c. _____

d. _____

e. _____

f. _____

g. _____

h. _____

8. Write five compound words from the article, and use hyphens to show how they should be separated into syllables.

_____

_____

9. Write a word from the article that contains each of the following prefixes.

un _____

re _____

de _____

10. Write a word from the article that contains each of the following suffixes.

s _____

ed _____

ing _____

ly _____

READER RESPONSE 6-4

1. Write the answers to the questions you predicted in Looking Back 6-6.

_____

_____

_____

_____

2. What do you believe is Rulon Gardner's greatest victory? Why?

_____

_____

_____

_____

3. Go to http://www.rulongardner.com for more information about this courageous athlete. List 3 facts you learned on the website.

_____

_____

_____

_____

ONLINE PRACTICE

Go to **MyReadingLab** at www.myreadinglab.com. Click on **Reading Road Trip** and select your textbook or the **Pioneer Level**.

1. For further practice in **finding main ideas**, take a Road Trip to the **Maine Coast**.
2. For the further practice in identifying **supporting details**, take a Road Trip to the **St. Louis Arch**.

PROGRESS CHART   CHAPTER 6

SECTION ONE

Fill out the number of correct answers you have for each item below. Your instructor will tell you how to calculate your percentage score.

PRACTICE 6-1   Number right _____ out of a possible score of 5.   Percentage score _____

PRACTICE 6-2   Number right _____ out of a possible score of 5   Percentage score _____

PRACTICE 6-3   Number right _____ out of a possible score of 5   Percentage score _____

PRACTICE 6-4   Number right _____ out of a possible score of 4.   Percentage score _____

PRACTICE 6-5   Number right _____ out of a possible score of 1.   Percentage score _____

PRACTICE 6-6   Number right _____ out of a possible score of 10.   Percentage score _____

PRACTICE 6-7   Number right _____ out of a possible score of 10.   Percentage score _____

PRACTICE 6-8   Number right _____ out of a possible score of 11.   Percentage score _____

PRACTICE 6-9   Number right _____ out of a possible score of 10.   Percentage score _____

MASTERY 6-1   Number right _____ out of a possible score of 1.   Percentage score _____

MASTERY 6-2   Number right _____ out of a possible score of 4.   Percentage score _____

MASTERY 6-3   Number right _____ out of a possible score of 6.   Percentage score _____

MASTERY 6-4   Number right _____ out of a possible score of 10.   Percentage score _____

MASTERY 6-5   Number right _____ out of a possible score of 11.   Percentage score _____

LOOKING BACK 6-1   Number right _____ out of a possible score of 5.   Percentage score _____

LOOKING BACK 6-2   Number right _____ out of a possible score of 3.   Percentage score _____

LOOKING BACK 6-3   Number right _____ out of a possible score of 10.   Percentage score _____

LOOKING BACK 6-4   Number right _____ out of a possible score of 2.   Percentage score _____

LOOKING BACK 6-5   Number right _____ out of a possible score of 8.   Percentage score _____

LOOKING BACK 6-6   Number right _____ out of a possible score of 1.   Percentage score _____

LOOKING BACK 6-7   Number right _____ out of a possible score of 10.   Percentage score _____

SECTION TWO

How do you feel? There are no wrong or right answers to how you feel about what you have learned. Circle Yes, Somewhat, or No in response to the following questions.

1. Do you understand the advantage of reading each paragraph to locate its main idea?   Yes   Somewhat   No

2. Once you locate the main idea of a reading, does it improve your comprehension?   Yes   Somewhat   No

3. Does reading with purpose now help you to focus on the author's reason for writing the material?   Yes   Somewhat   No

4. Has this chapter on finding main ideas helped you improve your personal vocabulary?   Yes   Somewhat   No

5. Has this powerful skill of finding the main idea helped your reading comprehension in other classes?   Yes   Somewhat   No

6. As you write paragraphs and essays, does this chapter on main idea help you in your writing?   Yes   Somewhat   No

7. Could you explain "main idea" to a fellow classmate?   Yes   Somewhat   No

SECTION THREE

Take a minute or two to reflect on your reading development. Write a few sentences or discuss with other students how this chapter has changed your reading habits.

_____

_____

_____

_____

_____

_____

_____

_____

_____

_____

Identifying Supporting Details

CHAPTER PREVIEW

In this chapter, you will learn about supporting details. **Supporting details** define, describe, explain and illustrate the main ideas in a reading by providing specific information such as:

- **Facts or statistics**
- **Examples**
- **Incidents or descriptions**
- **Visual explanations of ideas through charts and graphs**

You will also learn about **transitional words** or phrases. These are words or phrases that writers use to link ideas together and help readers follow their ideas.

 MAKING MEANING

A kitten is just a kitten until you add the supporting details. What color is she? How big? Does she bite, sleep in your lap, chase you through the living room, or climb the curtains? Does she purr like a motorboat and like to be scratched behind the ears?

Details complete the picture, because a kitten is never just a kitten.

▌INTRODUCTION

A **topic sentence** tells you the **main idea** of a paragraph. Although a paragraph is usually about a specific subject, the topic sentence makes a fairly general or broad statement about it. Topic sentences are usually placed at the beginning of a paragraph but can sometimes be found in the middle or at the end. **Supporting details** are used to define and describe the main idea. They are narrower ideas and provide facts, examples, incidents, and graphics that explain and illustrate the main point of a paragraph. Knowing which is the main idea and which are the supporting details in a paragraph helps you make sense of what you read.

There are four types of supporting details.

1. **Facts and statistics:** If the topic sentence of a paragraph is "Don't fall for these common shopping scams," the reader can expect the rest of the paragraph to present some facts about the scams. **Facts** are knowledge or information about things known to exist or events known to have happened. The other sentences in the paragraph should tell which particular shopping scams the writer has in mind and how to avoid them. **Statistics** are numerical data. "This tactic increases sales between 30 percent and 105 percent" is a statistic that supports the topic sentence about not falling for shopping scams.

2. **Examples: Examples** are used to illustrate the point of a topic sentence. If the topic sentence of a paragraph is "Anyone who baby-sits for my nephew Todd should receive combat pay," then the following sentences will provide specific examples of his out-of-control behavior.

3. **Incidents or descriptions:** Sometimes a brief story of a distinct occurrence, also called an **incident,** is used to illustrate the point of the broad topic sentence. An incident could be considered a long, sustained supporting detail. For example, if the topic sentence of a selected reading is "In the rural East Texas community where I grew up, the woods behind our house were definitely haunted by a sad lady; I'll never forget one night in particular," the reader can expect the rest of the reading to tell exactly what happened on that particular night.

4. **Charts, diagrams, and graphs:** A **chart, diagram,** or **graph** is a picture of a main idea and its supporting details. For example, a graph can compare the yearly profits for several competing companies: if the main idea is that different companies make different amounts of money, the supporting details in the graph will show exactly how much each company makes and how it compares with the others.

Often the sentence at the end of a paragraph summarizes or comments on the information that has been presented. This is the called the **concluding sentence.** A concluding sentence is a sort of topic sentence in reverse. Think about a sandwich. A sandwich is made with two slices of bread; in between the bread slices are ham, lettuce, and tomato. The two slices of bread are like the topic and concluding sentences, and the ham, lettuce, and tomato are like the supporting details. The topic sentence and the concluding sentence hold the supporting detail sentences, just as the two slices of bread hold the ham, lettuce, and tomato.

Not every paragraph contains a concluding sentence, especially if the paragraph is very short. Sometimes you have to use your prior knowledge and experience to **infer** (reach a conclusion) based on the information presented. Sometimes you can infer several conclusions from the information presented.

Transitional words or phrases are used to link ideas together and to help a reader understand and follow the connections between ideas. Common transitional words include *however, therefore, such as, first, second, third, next,* and *finally.*

STRUCTURED INSTRUCTION AND EXERCISES

PARAGRAPH ORGANIZATION AND SUPPORTING DETAILS

A typical paragraph is organized like this:

  I. Topic sentence (main idea)

    A. Supporting detail 1

    B. Supporting detail 2

    C. Supporting detail 3

  II. Concluding (or summary) sentence

(A paragraph can have more than or less than three supporting details.)

Read this paragraph, noticing the main idea and the details.

Easy Gardening

With a little thought and planning, gardening can be made easier and more enjoyable. Use a small wagon to haul your tools around the garden. You don't have one? Check yard sales for good deals on used wagons or even just used wagon wheels. Make a comfortable little kneeling pad. Take a two- or three-inch thick piece of foam rubber that is wide enough for both knees. Wrap it in plastic or put it in a large resealable bag, and you're ready to go. Wear latex gloves, rather than cloth ones, because they are easier to clean. You can just rinse them under the hose and let them air dry, and they don't stiffen up like cloth gloves do. Apply hand cream before putting on gardening gloves. The cream makes dirt and

grime easier to remove later as well as keeping your hands soft and smooth. Your garden will look better because you will spend more time working in it when you try these easy, no-fuss ideas.

Now look at how the details in this paragraph are organized into an outline, starting with a topic sentence and ending with a concluding sentence.

I. **Topic sentence**: With a little thought and planning, gardening can be made easier and more enjoyable.

   A. **Supporting detail 1**: Buy a small wagon.

   B. **Supporting detail 2**: Make a little kneeling pad.

   C. **Supporting detail 3**: Wear latex gloves.

   D. **Supporting detail 4**: Use hand cream.

II. **Concluding sentence**: Your garden will look better because you will spend more time working in it when you try these easy, no-fuss ideas.

EXERCISE 7-A Read this paragraph, underline the supporting details, and then list them in the order they appear in the outline that follows.

Easy Traveling

Few traveling experiences are worse than spending hours, or even an entire night, in a back-breaking airport chair! Here are few tips to avoid airline delays in the first place as well as pointers on what to do if you get stuck at the airport. If possible, use smaller airports. Smaller airports have fewer flights; therefore, they have fewer delays. Begin your trip early in the day. That way, if something goes wrong, there is probably another flight. Fly nonstop to your destination if you can. Remember, in the strange world of "airlinespeak," the word *direct* does not mean "nonstop." If a flight is canceled, don't stand in line with everyone else. Get to a phone and call the airline to book another flight. Paper tickets can be transferred to another airline faster than electronic tickets. In the time it takes the e-ticket holders to go through the transfer process, you will have snagged a good seat! Sometimes avoiding the frustrations of flight just isn't possible, but these tips will increase your chances for a stress-free vacation.

I. **Topic sentence:** Here are a few tips to avoid airline delays in the first place as well as pointers on what to do if you get stuck at the airport.

    A. **Supporting detail 1:**

_____

    B. **Supporting detail 2:**

_____

    C. **Supporting detail 3:**

_____

    D. **Supporting detail 4:**

_____

    E. **Supporting detail 5:**

_____

II. **Concluding sentence:**

_____

_____

Each of the details in the preceding paragraph expands on, or gives more information about, the main idea: how to avoid airline delays. These details—for instance, using smaller airports, flying nonstop, and using paper tickets—make up the paragraph's development. They provide information that directly relates to the main idea and supports it. Understanding the difference between main ideas and supporting details helps you see where an author is going. Knowing which are the main ideas and which are the supporting details in a passage helps you to recognize the most important ideas or points an author is making and to make sense of what you read.

EXERCISE 7-B   Put the following groups of sentences in the correct order. Each group includes a topic sentence and three sentences containing supporting details. When choosing the order of the details, put the most general one (the topic sentence) first, followed by the more specific ones.

Example: Birds of Prey

They eat rats, insects, and other pests that destroy crops.

Some birds are called birds of prey.

These birds help the environment.

They clear away dead animals that can spread disease.

Topic sentence: <u>Some birds are called birds of prey.</u>

Supporting detail: <u>These birds help the environment.</u>

Supporting detail: <u>They eat rats, insects, and other pests that destroy crops.</u>

Supporting detail: <u>They clear away dead animals that can spread disease.</u>

1. **Sound and Pitch**

A grown man's voice is usually at a low pitch.

The pitch of a sound is how high or low that sound is.

Many birds make sounds that are at a high pitch.

A cat's meow is usually at a medium pitch.

Topic sentence: _____

Supporting detail: _____

Supporting detail: _____

Supporting detail: _____

2. **Animal Homes**

Chipmunks dig underground burrows to live in.

Bears often make their dens in caves.

Animals may build or find homes.

Birds build nests.

Topic sentence: _____

Supporting detail: _____

Supporting detail: _____

Supporting detail: _____

3. **Fish and Their Scales**

They overlap each other like shingles on a roof.

Fish have scales that cover their bodies.

These scales are part of the fish's skin.

Scales protect the fish from disease and from other animals.

Topic sentence: _____

Supporting detail: _____

Supporting detail: _____

Supporting detail: _____

4. Vines

Sometimes vines wrap themselves around other things.

Vines need something to hang on if they are going to stand up.

A vine is a plant that usually has a soft stem.

Some vines creep along the ground.

Topic sentence: _____

Supporting detail: _____

Supporting detail: _____

Supporting detail: _____

5. Fishing Rods

The axle is the part that the fishing line is wound around.

The wheel is the handle you turn.

The wheel and axle make it easier for people to bring in their fish.

A fishing rod is a machine that uses a wheel and axle.

Topic sentence: _____

Supporting detail: _____

Supporting detail: _____

Supporting detail: _____

VISUAL SUPPORTING DETAILS

A main idea and supporting details can often be presented in a chart, diagram, or graph format. Look at the pie graph in Figure 7-1. The title, "Nina's Day (24 hours)," gives the main idea of what the pie graph is about. Now look at the supporting details. The details consist of how Nina spends her day. She has time for sleeping, eating, working, and visiting friends. Pie graphs, or other graphs and charts, are visual aids that provide lots of information. Where is the concluding sentence in a pie graph? Often the reader has to infer the conclusion (or conclusions) by trying to answer the question, What is the pie graph telling me?

Figure 7-1 Nina's Day (24 hours)

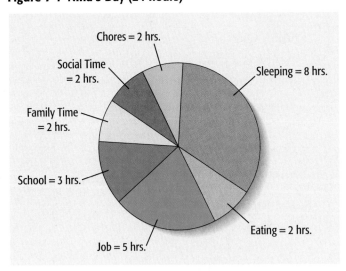

EXERCISE 7-C I. **Main idea:** The main idea of the pie graph is how Nina spends her day, for example, she sleeps for 8 hours and works for 5 hours a day. Fill in the missing details in the outline below.

    A. **Supporting Detail #1:** Nina sleeps 8 hours a day.

    B. **Supporting Detail #2:** _____

    C. **Supporting Detail #3:** Nina works 5 hours a day.

    D. **Supporting Detail #4:** _____

    E. **Supporting Detail #5:** _____

    F. **Supporting Detail #6:** _____

    G. **Supporting Detail #7:** Nina does chores for 2 hours a day.

  II. **Conclusions:** Two conclusions you can reach from reading this pie chart are that Nina has a part-time job, and she gets 8 hours of sleep at night. What other conclusions can you draw?

_____

_____

_____

EXERCISE 7-D Create a pie graph that describes a typical weekday (24 hours) in your life, using the chart in Figure 7-2 which has been divided into 12 two-hour blocks. Color and label the number of two-hour blocks you need for sleeping, eating, entertainment, child care, and so forth in a 24-hour period. Use the bulleted outline to label your activities. Once you have completed the pie graph, fill in the outline that follows, using sentences or phrases, and write one or more conclusions.

Note: If you sleep 8 hours each night, write "sleeping" on four of the lines on the right side of the graph, because each line represents a 2-hour block of time. If you spend only 1 hour eating, then you will need to divide a two-hour block in half.

Figure 7-2 My Weekday (24 hours)

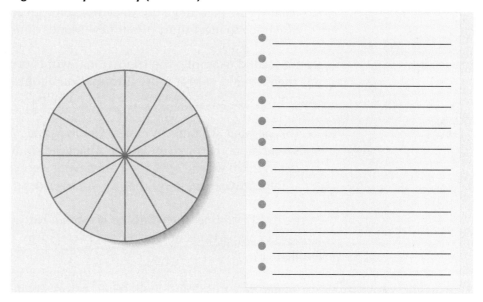

I. **Main idea** _____

   A. **Supporting detail 1:**_____

   B. **Supporting detail 2:**_____

   C. **Supporting detail 3:**_____

   D. **Supporting detail 4:**_____

   E. **Supporting detail 5:**_____

   F. **Supporting detail 6:**_____

   G. **Supporting detail 7:**_____

   H. **Supporting detail 8** _____

II. **Conclusion(s):** _____

_____

TRANSITIONAL WORDS AND PHRASES

The English language contains **transitional words and phrases** that are used to link ideas together and tell readers what to expect as they are reading. For example, the following paragraph contains three **transitional words**:

> *First*, Louis and I will buy our tickets online. *Next*, we will drive to the theater. *Finally*, we will watch the movie.

The words *first*, *next*, and *finally* tell the reader that there is a specific order or sequence to the way events will happen. Now, look at the next example:

Besides going to the movie, Louis and I plan to do some shopping. *In addition*, we plan to go out to eat for some great Chinese food. We *also* hope to meet some of our new friends during the evening.

In the second example, the transitional words *besides*, *in addition*, and *also* tell the reader to expect more information about the topic. Here is another example:

On one hand, we hope to have a fabulous time, *but* the plan is not to spend more than we can afford. *Although* it is difficult to keep a budget in mind when Louis and I are having a good time with friends, it is imperative (necessary) that we not overspend.

In the third example, the words *on one hand*, *but*, and *although* tell the reader to expect comparisons or contrasts between ideas. Now consider a fourth example:

To illustrate this point, I will relate a story about the last time Louis and I went out together. The movie cost us $16 and dinner was $40. I bought an outfit on sale for $54 *and* Louis bought a great-looking shirt for $27. By the time we got home, we had spent well over $100. These expenses *certainly* seemed necessary at the time, *particularly* the clothing. *Consequently*, we both had gone over our budgets for the month. *Therefore*, our plan is to stay within our budgets the next time we go out together.

In the fourth example, the transitional words tell the reader to expect several things:

To illustrate: indicates that an example will follow.

and: indicates that more information will follow.

certainly and particularly: show certain ideas are important or being emphasized.

Consequently and Therefore: indicate that a result or outcome will follow.

College textbooks are full of transitional words that tell the reader what to expect. Transitional words are cues that lead the reader into the next piece of information. They also help writers to present information more effectively. Read the following list of transitional words, and look for them as you read books and magazines. Not all transitional words have been listed. What words can you add? Use the lines provided to write other examples of transitional words and phrases.

- Addition:

furthermore, in addition to, besides

- Emphasis or importance:

  really, again, furthermore, certainly, definitely, obviously

  _____

- Sequence (order), time:

  first, second, third fourth (etc.), next, soon, finally, then, previously, immediately, to begin with

  _____

- Comparison (how things are alike) or contrast (how things are different):

  on the other hand, however, but, although, in contrast

  _____

- Repetition or reiteration:

  as I have said, as I have noted, in essence

  _____

- Generalization:

  usually, generally, for the most part

  _____

- Example or illustration

  in other words, to illustrate, for example

  _____

- Summary, conclusion, or consequence

  in conclusion, thus, as a result, hence, therefore, for that reason, in this case

  _____

EXERCISE 7-E   Complete each of the following sentences using appropriate transitional words.

1. Yesterday, the car broke down and our cell phone was dead. _____, we were stranded on the side of the road.

2. Miguel is planning to make good grades this year; _____, he is also trying to work a full-time job.

3. Kim's herb garden was wrecked by the hailstorm that hit last week; _____ she is planning on buying new plants at the farmer's market on Saturday.

4. All my magazine subscriptions have expired, _____ I'm going online to subscribe to new magazines this afternoon.

5. My children are running all over the house. Their toys are left on the stairs and in the yard. _____, it is chaos at my house today.

EXERCISE 7-F   Complete the following paragraph using appropriate transitional words.

Operating the Pontoon Boat

_____, remove the cover of the boat and place the sandbags on the dock. _____, put the cover inside the boathouse where it will be out of the way. _____, remove the ignition key from the locker. _____, we keep the key in the locker by the main boathouse door. _____, insert the key into the ignition. _____, lower the motor.

PRACTICING WHAT YOU HAVE LEARNED

PRACTICE 7-1   **Supporting Details**

After each topic sentence, write three supporting details, using complete sentences.

Example: Topic: Good Losers

Topic sentence: Good losers display three important behaviors.

Supporting detail: Good losers praise the winners of the competitions they are in.

Supporting detail: They learn from their mistakes.

Supporting detail: They resolve to win the next time.

1. **Topic:** Favorite TV Show

   Topic sentence: My favorite TV show is popular for several reasons.

   Supporting detail: _____

   Supporting detail: _____

   Supporting detail: _____

2. **Topic:** Football

   Topic sentence: Professional football is very different from college football.

   Supporting detail: _____

   Supporting detail: _____

   Supporting detail: _____

3. **Topic:** Favorite Store

   Topic sentence: _____ (fill in the name of a store) is my favorite store.

   Supporting detail: _____

   Supporting detail: _____

   Supporting detail: _____

4. **Topic:** A Great American

   Topic sentence: _____ (fill in a name) is a great American.

   Supporting detail: _____

   Supporting detail: _____

   Supporting detail: _____

5. **Topic:** Education

   Topic sentence: A good education is an asset for several reasons.

   Supporting detail: _____

   Supporting detail: _____

   Supporting detail: _____

PRACTICE 7-2 **Supporting Details and Concluding Sentence:** *Scamming the Shopper*

Read the following paragraph. On the lines following the paragraph, write three supporting details and the concluding sentence.

Scamming the Shopper

Don't fall for these common shopping **scams**. The shortage scam is the latest version of "Hurry while supplies last!" This scam lists a high limit on a sale item. ("No more than 10 per customer.") This **tactic** increases sales between 30 and 105 percent. The package deal is another scam you've undoubtedly experienced. When you buy a movie ticket, you are handed a coupon for a free soft drink with the purchase of a large popcorn. So you pay out money for munchies, even though you are not hungry, thinking you are actually *saving* money. The mini shopping cart is also very **sly**. Kid-size shopping carts are very cute, but they give children a place to **stash** the candy and other goodies they grab from eye-level shelves. Don't be a shopping sap!

WORDNOTES

scams	swindles, cons, hoaxes
tactic	a particular approach to a problem
sly	sneaky, cunning, shrewd
stash	to put away or hide

   I. **Topic sentence:** Don't fall for these common shopping scams.

   A. **Supporting detail 1:** _____

   B. **Supporting detail 2:** _____

   C. **Supporting detail 3:** _____

   II. **Concluding sentence:** _____

PRACTICE 7-3   **Main Ideas and Supporting Details: *Storms***

Many people feel very strongly about storms. They either love them or are afraid of them. Look at the photograph, and then fill in the **graphic organizer** (a diagram showing groups of ideas) that follows, using what you know and how you feel about storms. This graphic organizer identifies the topic (storms) and three main ideas (kinds of storms, how you feel about storms, and things that have happened to you in storms). For each main idea, add details from your own experience that supports it.

Figure 7-3 Storms

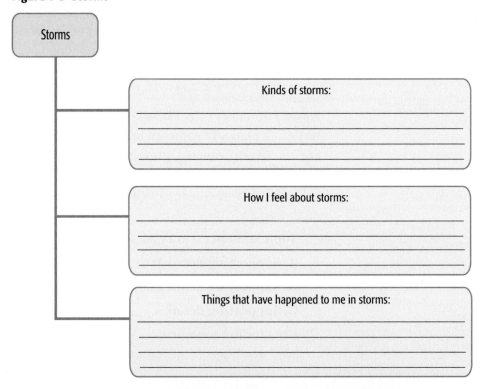

READER RESPONSE 7-1 Use the graphic organizer you completed in Practice 7-3 to write a paragraph about how you feel about storms and why. Be sure to add a concluding sentence to your paragraph.

_____

_____

_____

_____

_____

_____

_____

_____

_____

_____

_____

PRACTICE 7-4 **Topic, Main Idea, Supporting Details, and Conclusions:** _What Goes Down_

The following paragraphs make up a short story, also called an incident. Remember that a story can be used to illustrate a main idea. No matter how long the story, it should be clearly related to the main idea, and the action of the story is moved along through the use of supporting details. The conclusion of a story is not always stated in a concluding sentence. As with graphs and charts (visual explanations), sometimes you need to infer a conclusion, or conclusions, by using the information in the story and your own knowledge and experience. Read the following story and complete the outline that follows.

What Goes Down

By Don K. Scott

Last summer my family drove to the Grand Canyon. For those who don't know, the Grand Canyon is a very, very big gap in the ground. When I peered down into the canyon, I could see a long, winding trail. Even though I knew people were on it, we were so high up that we couldn't even see them! I decided right then that it was something I wanted to do. When it was time for the rest of my family to go hiking, I told them that I was hiking down the trail we had seen. My parents looked at each other, grinned and said, "Okay, but remember, What goes down, must come up!"

The trail was not too steep, and there were several rest stops, but it was extremely hot! I was very relieved that I had taken lots of water and trail mix to keep me going. Whenever I felt too tired, I rested on the side of the trail to catch my breath. I knew that I shouldn't keep going if I felt weak. I might trip and hurt others or myself. It was vital to me to reach the bottom, but I knew that I had to do it safely!

I was almost to the Colorado River when I remembered what my parents had said, "What goes down must come up!" So far, the trail had been downhill, and I didn't like the prospect of hiking back up, but I knew that I was going to have to do it or be rescued by a helicopter! One of the rangers had explained that helicopter rescues were expensive, so I decided to grit my teeth and bear it. I kept on walking toward the end of the trail, ready to turn around when I needed to.

How amazing! I finally made it to the spot where the trail ended. I looked up and could see the canyon above and around me. I could even see where my family had first stopped to look down, and it was so far up! I felt really proud that I had made it all the way. The Colorado River flowed below me, and I watched it for a while, thinking about how cold it must be. I was trying to do anything not to think about walking back up again!

After watching the river, gazing at the cliffs, and taking a lot of digital photographs, I had to begin the second part of my journey. Slowly, I put one foot in front of the other and started my hike. It was getting late in the day, but the heat still baked the landscape. As I was walking, a couple asked if I would take a picture of them with their camera. I did, and we began talking about the Grand Canyon. I said, "What goes down. . ."

"Must come up!" they finished. My two new friends and I decided to walk together, and we became so busy talking that before we knew it, we were halfway up the side of the canyon! I realized that good company could make any trip seem short. I pulled out my water and took a few big gulps and kept on walking with my friends to the top of the Grand Canyon.

I. Topic: _____

   Main idea: _____

     _____

   A. Supporting detail 1: _____

   B. Supporting detail 2: _____

     _____

   C. Supporting detail 3: _____

   D. Supporting detail 4: _____

   E. Supporting detail 5: _____

     _____

II. Your conclusion(s): _____

PRACTICE 7-5   **Main Idea, Supporting Details, and Conclusions: *Travel Destinations***

You will find charts and graphs in many college textbooks. These visual materials explain important information in graphic form. Understanding charts and graphs can help you understand the main ideas and the narrower supporting details in a text. Read the following bar graph, and then fill in the outline that follows.

Figure 7-4 Travel Destinations by Distance from Oklahoma City

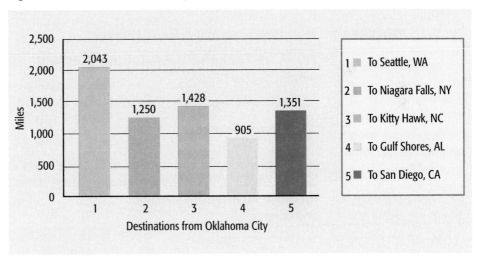

I. Main idea: _____

     _____

   A. Supporting detail 1: _____

   B. Supporting detail 2: _____

   C. Supporting detail 3: _____

   D. Supporting detail 4: _____

   E. Supporting detail 5: _____

II. Your conclusion(s): _____

_____

_____

_____

PRACTICE 7-6 **Main Idea and Supporting Details**

Use the Internet or an atlas to collect data about five places in the United States that you would like to visit. Create a chart like the one in Practice 7-5, ranking travel destinations by distance from where you live to those places. Then use the chart to fill in the outline that follows.

   I. **Topic:** _____

   Main idea: _____

   A. **Supporting detail 1:** _____

   B. **Supporting detail 2:** _____

   C. **Supporting detail 3:** _____

   D. **Supporting detail 4:** _____

   E. **Supporting detail 5:** _____

   II. **Your conclusion(s):** _____

PRACTICE 7-7 **Transitional Words: *Friends Forever***

Fill in the blanks in the following story with the appropriate transitional words.

Friends Forever

My friend Marla and I are alike in some ways and different in other ways. _____ of us are female, we are about the same age, and we grew up within 40 miles of each other. _____, we both enjoy traveling and writing.

_____, we are quite different. Marla can speak Spanish, _____ I can only speak English. _____ she now lives in Texas, I enjoy living in Chicago. _____ difference is that I love to swim, but she is _____ afraid of the water.

_____ our differences, we are still close friends. After all, we both love chocolate!

PRACTICE 7-8   **Transitional Words**

Write a paragraph comparing yourself with a friend or family member. Use at least five transitional words.

_____

_____

_____

_____

_____

_____

SUMMARY

- A **topic sentence** states the **main idea** of a paragraph and is usually found at the beginning of a paragraph, although it is sometimes placed in the middle or at the end.

- **Supporting details** define, describe, explain, and illustrate main ideas. The focus of supporting details is narrower than that of main ideas. Supporting details provide important information about main ideas in several ways:

  - **They offer facts and statistics.** For example:

    The black widow spider is considered the most deadly spider in North America (main idea). Her venom is 15 times more toxic than that of a prairie rattlesnake (fact). Her body is about 1.5 inches long (statistic).

  - **They provide examples.** For instance:

    I hate getting up in the morning (main idea). I throw things at my alarm clock (example). I put my pillow over my head (example). I grind my teeth (example).

  - **They present incidents or descriptions.** For example:

    I never thought we'd make it back safely (main idea). The gust of wind slammed into our small sailboat and knocked it into the water (incident). We had stupidly not worn life-jackets (incident).

  - **They can be conveyed through visual materials, like charts, diagrams, and graphs.** For example:

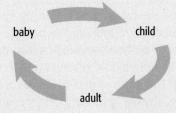

- **Transitional words or phrases** link ideas and act as cues that tell the reader what to expect next in the text.

MASTERY LEVEL EXERCISES

MASTERY 7-1   **Supporting Details and Conclusions:** *Miami, Here We Come*

Most plays are written in **dialogue** form. However, many books that discuss career and interview situations also use dialogues as examples of what to do or what not to do in certain situations. You may find examples of dialogues in English, psychology, criminology, and career textbooks. Understanding the main idea and supporting details expressed in dialogues will help you make meaning from texts. Read the following transcript of a phone conversation, and then fill in the outline that follows.

Miami, Here We Come

RITA: Von, we need to plan our trip to Miami. What about the hotel? I want a balcony overlooking the beach.

VON: That's probably too expensive. Besides, I can't book the hotel until you make the airline reservations. I need to know which day we will arrive.

RITA: OK Did you say you could get a discount on a rental car?

VON: Yes, my car insurance offers rental car discounts. But I might try to get a package deal on a hotel and rental car.

RITA: Sounds good. I'll get the airline reservations taken care of. You check the Internet for package deals and call me back with the details.

VON: No problem. Now all we have to worry about is the weather!

RITA: That's one detail we have no control over! But I'll check the weather for Miami on the Internet. I don't want to end up in the middle of a hurricane.

VON: Miami, here we come!

I. **Topic sentence (main idea):** Von, we need to get our trip to Miami planned.

    A. **Supporting detail 1:** _____

    B. **Supporting detail 2:** _____

    C. **Supporting detail 3:** _____

    D. **Supporting detail 4:** _____

    _____

II. **Your conclusion(s):** _____

    _____

MASTERY 7-2   **Topic, Main Idea, Supporting Details, and Conclusions:** *Lady of the Woods*

After reading the following short story, write the topic, the sentence that states the main idea, three supporting details (use complete sentences, either from the story or in your own words), and the conclusion(s).

Lady of the Woods

In the **rural** East Texas community where I grew up, the woods behind our house were definitely haunted by a sad lady; I'll never forget one night in particular. About dusk, my best friend Jebbie and I were returning from a walk to town. My Aunt Ruby was standing in the front yard with her hands on her hips. "You kids didn't fasten the gate on the pen. Sadie is gone. If Joey Bill gets back and finds her gone, you two are in *big* trouble." Sadie was my uncle's bird dog. There was nothing to do but go look for her. We were more than a little **hesitant** to enter the dark woods. The entire 12 years of my life I had heard stories about the Lady of the Woods. I repeated some of them to Ruby: her form was **transparent** and gaslike; she cried out for help to the passing traveler; she carried an old-fashioned yellow lantern. Ruby said, "Fiddlesticks. Go find that dog," and went back into the house.

We grabbed a flashlight, a leash, and a whistle and entered the woods at the southeast corner of the pasture. At first, nothing happened. It was just any warm, summer evening sinking from the long twilight to total darkness. However, after about 10 minutes walking, I noticed the air seemed cool. It felt wonderful. East Texas in July is hot and humid, and nighttime is very little, if any, cooler than daytime. But why was it getting cooler now? I glanced up through the trees to a patch of sky. The stars were out by now. No clouds covered them, so no front was moving in. The further we walked the cooler the woods became. I looked at Jebbie. Uh-oh. What might happen next?

We had been calling for Sadie every other breath, but we got quiet when we saw a speck of light in the distance. It was yellow, like an old lantern, not the white light of a flashlight. We grabbed each other and practically stopped breathing. Then we heard something. At first we thought it was sobbing and moaning, but soon we could make out a high-pitched dog howl. Unfortunately, the howl was coming from the same direction as the light. What should we do?

I thought about how much Joey Bill loved Sadie. I thought about how much Sadie cost. I thought about what Joey Bill would say to me. He wouldn't whip me, but I would be punished. Also, my uncle would be very disappointed in me. Compared to that, a ghostly light or even a ghostly lady seemed to be something I could handle. I turned to Jebbie. "Come on, let's follow that howl."

Oddly, the light retreated in front of us, almost like it was leading us to Sadie. Soon, though, I forgot about the light. Sadie was lying down, pinned under a huge, rotten tree. She must have been chasing something, maybe a squirrel. Sometimes old trees become rotten, and the least little thing will topple them. They don't seem all that heavy to us, but they are heavy to a 35-pound dog. Sadie wasn't crushed, but she was trapped. She whimpered pitifully. We freed her and knelt down to examine and pet her. Then a sudden breeze sprang up. We looked up and saw a beautiful, but see-through, lady dressed in old-fashioned clothes, holding a lantern. She wasn't sobbing or moaning. She was smiling. She nodded at us, looked at Sadie with pity, and turned and walked away, swinging her lantern.

Jebbie and I took turns carrying Sadie. We were silent most of the way home. As we neared the pasture, I looked at Jebbie and spoke. "What did we just see?" "We saw a ghost, a nice ghost. We saw the Lady of the Woods," Jebbie replied. We decided that we would not tell anyone what had happened to us. We weren't hallucinating. It was real, but no one, especially grownups, would believe us. We really didn't even talk about it very much more between ourselves. We were almost teenagers, and soon other interests crowded out ghost stories. We grew up, went to college, married, and moved away from our rural community. I haven't talked to Jebbie in about three years now, but I don't think he'd mind if I told this story about the Lady of the Woods for the first time to you.

WORDNOTES

rural	relating to the country or country life
hesitant	holding back in doubt
transparent	sheer enough to be seen through
retreated	withdrew
whimpered	whined, cried

I. Topic: _____

II. Main idea: _____

_____

   A. Supporting Detail 1: _____

   B. Supporting Detail 2: _____

   C. Supporting Detail 3: _____

   D. Supporting Detail 4: _____

III. Your conclusion: _____

_____

MASTERY 7-3 **Supporting Details and Conclusions:** *Babysitting Terrible Todd*

Read the following paragraph and then complete the outline that follows.

Babysitting Terrible Todd

Anyone who babysits for my nephew Todd should receive combat pay. This adorable looking 4-year-old defines the term "high maintenance." For example, Todd loves to sneak up behind me and scream as loud as he can. For a little twist on the screaming act, he will go upstairs and let out a hair-raising scream. Of course, I think he has cut off his fingers, at the very least, so I rush madly upstairs, my legs and heart pumping, only to see him sitting on his bed, grinning his charming grin. His effect on animals is also noteworthy. My sister's dog is a cranky 10-year-old poodle that has started gnawing off his own right paw since Todd's birth. Buddy used to be a fairly well adjusted dog, but now he growls and snaps at anyone who gets near him. This increases the danger of being in Todd's home. Todd's latest episode was to lock himself in the hall bathroom, run the sink full of water, and place the iron in the sink of water. He only opened the door because he wanted me to get the footstool from the utility room so he could reach the outlet and plug in the iron. My sister called me a few minutes ago. I told her that from now on the going rate for Todd-sitting is $25 an hour, but I'm not sure that even that is enough.

WORDNOTES

maintenance	preservation, upkeep, support
noteworthy	worthy of attention
gnawing	biting or wearing away with the teeth
episode	a happening

I. I. **Topic sentence:** Anyone who babysits for my nephew Todd should receive combat pay.

    A. **Supporting detail 1:** _____

    B. **Supporting detail 2:** _____

    C. **Supporting detail 3:** _____

II. **Conclusion:** _____

_____

MASTERY 7-4 **Supporting Details**

Read the following topic sentences (main ideas) and write three supporting details for each. Write each detail as a complete sentence.

1. Topic sentence: When a friend asks you to, it is important to keep a secret.

    Supporting detail: _____

    Supporting detail: _____

    Supporting detail: _____

2. Topic sentence: The three activities I like to do most in my free time help me relax.

    Supporting detail: _____

    Supporting detail: _____

    Supporting detail: _____

3. Topic sentence: It is very important to make a good impression during a job interview.

    Supporting detail: _____

    Supporting detail: _____

    Supporting detail: _____

4. Topic sentence: Everyone has favorite foods.

    Supporting detail: _____

    Supporting detail: _____

    Supporting detail: _____

5. Topic sentence: _____ (fill in a name) is the person I admire the most.

    Supporting detail: _____

    Supporting detail: _____

    Supporting detail: _____

MASTERY 7-5 **Main Idea, Supporting Details, and Conclusions: *Travel Destinations***

Look at the map in Figure 7-5. Do you see some information that you were working with earlier in the chapter? Information can be presented in many ways. This map includes both the distances to various cities and the driving times. The bar graph on page 239 had only the distances from Oklahoma City. This map also shows the location of the different cities. Study the map carefully, and then complete the outline that follows.

Figure 7-5 Travel Destinations by Distance and Driving Time from Oklahoma City

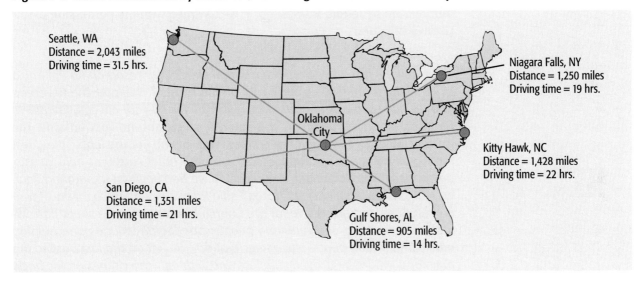

I. **Main idea:** _____

_____

A. **Supporting detail 1:** _____

_____

B. **Supporting detail 2:** _____

_____

C. **Supporting detail 3:** _____

_____

D. **Supporting detail 4:** _____

_____

E. **Supporting detail 5:** _____

_____

II. **Your conclusion(s):** _____

_____

_____

_____

MASTERY 7-6 **Supporting Details:** *Of Horrors and Heroes*

Read this eyewitness account of the earthquake and tsunami (tidal wave) that happened in the Indian Ocean on December 26, 2004. The Reverend Charles Ramsden, an Episcopal priest in the Diocese of California, recounts the wash of waters and emotions the fateful day the tsunami struck Thailand.

Of Horrors and Heroes

From *Episcopal Life* 15, no. 2 (2005). Written by Charles Ramsden with Introduction by Jerrold Hames. pp. 1, 6–7. Printed with the permission of Charles Ramsden and *Episcopal Life.*

When the first wave from the tsunami struck their resort on Ko Phi Phi, a small island formed by volcanic rock off the coast of Thailand, the Reverend Charles Ramsden was enjoying breakfast with his 30-year-old son, Charlie, of Bangkok, and his Thai daughter-in-law, Ae, on the second-floor balcony. The walls of water tore through the ground floor, wiping out the lobby, the guest rooms, all personal belongings and even the hotel safe that held guests' passports, airline tickets and valuables. "If we had been on the ground floor, we would have been washed to sea," said Ramsden, an Episcopal priest who is West Coast representative for the Church Insurance Co. He spent harrowing hours rescuing and reuniting people, bandaging wounds and helping others into rescue boats. Much later that day, he left on the last boat to the mainland, where he arrived shoeless and with only the clothes on his back. This is an excerpt of his account of the tragedy, written for friends and family on Dec. 29, 2004, in the Bangkok airport, waiting for his flight home.

It was all so innocent, and all such a disaster. If we had made different choices at almost any point, I probably wouldn't be writing this.

On this trip, I decided to see a little more of Thailand than the urban congested city of Bangkok. On Christmas Day, we boarded a ferry to Ko Phi Phi, a small island that is, or was, quite a tourist destination. Charlie and Ae had spent their honeymoon there.

The only reservation available was at the most expensive resort on the island. I was a little miffed, but we had a swim, a nice dinner, talked about plans for our few days. We met in the restaurant about 9:30 the next morning and talked about what we were going to do that day. Charlie and Ae were going to snorkel, and I was going to sit by the pool and take in the sights.

About 10, we noticed staff running away from the beach as if something was chasing them. Then we saw the water rising. It wasn't as much a wave as a very rapid swell. The water rose 15 feet in as many seconds.

We were dry on the second-floor restaurant balcony. We rushed to the rail. Charlie saw a young woman clinging to a tree and the water and floating furniture pounding her with terrible force. He started tying tablecloths together to make a rope. When the flow ebbed for a second, he waded out and brought the woman to the steps up to the balcony. I grabbed her. She was shaking so hard that I could hardly hold on. Then Charlie brought up an injured man, and the triage center opened right there in the restaurant.

The water flowed over the island with enough force to destroy almost everything in its path. The building we were in was spared because it was built on reinforced concrete posts and open to the second floor. After the first surge, everything on the central part of the island was gone.

When the water came back over the island in the opposite direction, it washed into the sea everything that had been knocked down the first time.

I started to walk around the deck to see what I might do to help. At the top of a stairway, I found a little boy about three shaking like he was freezing cold and screaming, "My papa!" He was bleeding and had a pretty big lump over one eye. I picked him up and tried to console him. He was Japanese and couldn't tell me what happened, so I carried him around asking if anyone spoke Japanese. No luck.

The crowd started to get hysterical, fearing the next wave would be even bigger. People started climbing on tables to get onto the roof. I handed the little boy to a Thai man and continued to look for a Japanese-speaking person.

The wounded continued to arrive. One young man, a fireman or paramedic of some sort, took charge of the first-aid center. He and other volunteers cleaned wounds with whiskey, hotel towels and restaurant linen. Charlie and others rounded up chaise-lounge cushions. Pretty soon, we had 15 to 20 patients in various stages of disrepair. It was just awful. We had nothing to work with. The whole island was absolutely unprepared. I can't tell you how helpless I felt.

If we had stayed in the hotel we first tried to reserve—the place Charlie and Ae stayed on their honeymoon—we would have been washed away in the first wave. If we had gone to breakfast half an hour earlier, we probably would have been down on the ground when the swell hit the island and been washed into the sea. Our rooms were on the second floor. After the big surge, there were fish in the hallway of the second floor. The lobby and all of the first floor were demolished.

My son moved into a leadership role. He was taking care of people, digging out folks stuck under debris piles and breaking down doors to get folks in and out. By 3 o'clock, Charlie and the manager were consulting about what to do next, and Charlie (who speaks pretty good Thai) was making announcements in English.

Early in the afternoon, they brought a small boat up to the shore, a diving boat that held 25 or so. Charlie and his crew loaded the seriously injured into the boat—doors were the stretchers of choice—and the boat headed for the mainland about two hours away.

A military helicopter flew over the island to survey the damage and pulled up two of the injured. Thai police arrived with a couple of choppers and evacuated some of the seriously injured folks.

We stayed in the triage center to help those who couldn't walk. Then we spotted a ferryboat waiting out beyond the cluttered harbor. Thai "long tail" boats were carrying the injured from the pier to the ferry. We started taking the rest of the injured down to the pier to put them on the little boats.

As the last injured person from our group was loaded, it was getting dark. We got on the boat ourselves and went out to the waiting ferry. We felt a little guilty to be leaving while hundreds of others, some in worse shape than we were, were waiting up on the hillside, but it didn't seem to make any sense to let the boat go with empty seats. We knew that the ferry would have to leave before dark because without lights there was no way to avoid the tons of debris in the sea. Three hours later, in Krabi, we got the injured off the boat, found a hotel, had a little fried rice and said our prayers! At that point it seemed that we were going to survive.

On the third day we reached Hua Hin by car. I finally was able to use a computer and get a message out that we had survived. I called the U.S. Embassy and told them that I had lost my passport. They told me to come that evening, and they would issue a temporary passport. I called United Airlines and told them that my ticket was gone, and they told me to come to the airport at 5 a.m. and they would get me on a plane.

Now it is about 4 a.m., time for me to go get in line with the hope that I'll be on my way home in a few hours. There are a few details to add.... First, the story of the little Japanese boy ended happily. In about two hours, the child's mother arrived with the boy's sister. She found her husband in the triage center, injured but alive, and her son still in the arms of the Thai man on the roof.

Rarely do we see the power of nature. No words can adequately describe what we experienced, and it leaves me feeling pretty helpless and powerless. Never again will I travel without a flashlight. I will buy travel insurance. I will never stay right on the beach, and I will have my will brought up-to-date within a week. I never again will feel the earth move without feeling panic, and I'll never hear the word "tsunami" without feeling fear.

About justice: In a natural disaster, there is none. I could give you a hundred reasons why I should be the one missing. The German man who was able to get his two small children to safety before he was swept away and the Israeli man who had his infant and toddler swept from his arms as he tried to escape the torrent come to mind. I am older. My children are adults. You know what I mean.

And about my hero: God, the things you learn in a natural disaster. Watching my son spring into action, address real life and death human needs and be of considerable assistance in addressing emergencies and maintaining order was enough to bring tears to my eyes. There is something in that man...a sense of confidence, a great deal of ability to relate to people that reassures and calms.

All I can say is that if either you or I are ever again in a situation of great peril, I hope Charlie or someone like him is there with us.

And one last note. The day I arrived in Bangkok, Charlie and Ae discovered that sometime this summer they will have a baby in their household (and guess who will be a grandfather)!

1. On a separate sheet of paper, create a timeline of the events of the day the tsunami hit Ko Phi Phi, a small island formed by volcanic rock off the coast of Thailand. The heading of your timeline will be the main idea of the reading. The events on your timeline will be the supporting details for the main idea of the reading.

2. Use the following charts to add more supporting details from the text:

Figure 7-6 Of Horrors and Heroes

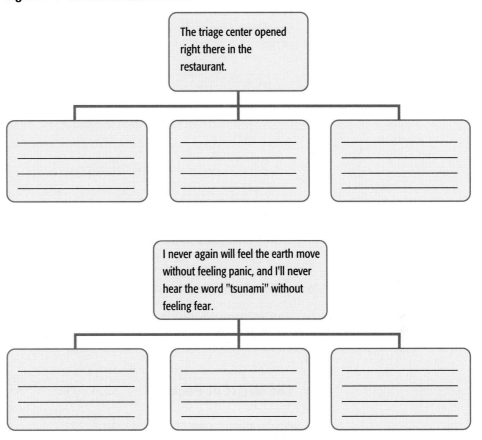

3. Look up the word *tsunami* on the Internet using a search engine like Yahoo or Google. Write five factual sentences on the lines below about the tsunami that hit on December 26, 2004. Information could include times, locations, numbers of people lost, rescue efforts, volunteer efforts, assistance from various countries, and changes that have occurred since the disaster.

a. _____

_____

b. _____

_____

c. _____

_____

d. _____

_____

e. _____

_____

4. From the information that you have gathered, write a paragraph that includes a topic sentence (main idea), supporting details, and a concluding sentence. Use at least three transitional words to link your ideas to each other.

_____

_____

_____

_____

_____

_____

_____

_____

MASTERY 7-7 **Transitional Words:** *The Magic of Poetry*

The following paragraphs on poetry might be found in an English literature textbook. Fill in the blanks with appropriate transitional words.

The Magic of Poetry

Poetry makes use of crisp, musical, _____ highly emotional language. _____, poetry can be magical, meaningful, entertaining, or sad. Poetry can emphasize a point or tell a story. _____, poetry can share a feeling, ask for help, or communicate ideas. _____, poetry can change people.

Poetry uses the literary devices of alliteration _____ onomatopoeia (on" o mat" o poe'). Alliteration is the repetition of sound. An _____ of alliteration is "Somewhere silent stars are searching, searching for my sweetheart." _____, the repetition of sound may not always occur in the beginning of the word. To _____ this point, look at the following _____: "Rarely do leaves linger in the air, but they dance quickly and quietly through the falling light." _____, the repetition of the "*l*" sound came at the beginning, middle, or end of several words.

The _____ literary device, onomatopoeia, is the use of words that imitate sounds. *Whoosh*, *buzz*, *whisper*, and *ping-pong* are _____ of onomatopoeia. _____, *crack* and *spit* are good examples of onomatopoeia. Onomatopoeia makes poetry fun to read out loud.

_____, poetry is a creative use of language that can make a difference to those who read and write it.

MASTERY 7-8 **Main Idea, Supporting Details, Concluding Sentence, and Transitional Words: *Write About a Photograph***

Look back over the photographs in this chapter. Choose one that you like, and write a paragraph about it that includes a topic sentence, several supporting details, and a concluding sentence. Make use of transitional words to link your ideas together.

_____

_____

_____

_____

_____

_____

_____

_____

LOOKING BACK

LOOKING BACK 7-1 **Topic Sentences**

Read the topic sentences listed here. For each of the following groups of supporting details, write the correct topic sentence (main idea) from the list.

- A baby is expensive.
- You can make your home's entrance more interesting.
- It is easy to spot an e-mail hoax.
- You can help your child ace the next standardized test.
- It is easy to develop your "sixth sense."
- Give affectionate signals to your spouse.
- Ask your bank questions.
- Think in images.
- Listen when your body talks.
- Write without editing yourself.

1. Topic sentence: _____

   The price for formula and bottles are very high.

   Diapers cost a fortune.

   Only shop at designer baby-clothing stores when they are having a sale.

2. Topic sentence: _____

   Greet each other at the door every evening.

   Create a child-free space for just you and your spouse.

   Show sincere, but tasteful, physical affection in front of others, such as holding hands.

3. Topic sentence: _____

You haven't heard about the subject on the six o'clock news.

It mentions conspiracy.

You are told to "pass this on to everyone you know."

4. Topic sentence: _____

What is the cost of online bill paying?

Is overdraft protection available?

Is there a charge for banking by phone?

5. Topic sentence: _____

Educate yourself about the test your child will be taking.

Teach your child ways to handle test stress.

Offer some test-taking tips.

6. Topic sentence: _____

Add bright paint, wreaths, or colorful plants on or around your door.

Clear away overgrown shrubs that block your entrance.

Add a bench or chair to give your entryway a welcoming feel.

LOOKING BACK 7-2 **Context Clues and Charts:** *Jenny's Science Project*

You are helping your third-grade daughter with her science project, which consists of a homemade chart. After weighing her pets, herself, and you, she made lists of the items she weighed, the weights she estimated, and the actual weights. But she mixed up the figures in her lists. Using context clues and your knowledge about charts, help your daughter fill in her chart. Keep in mind your daughter's age and the commonsense weights of each item. After you have filled in the chart, record the differences between the estimated weights and the actual weights.

- My gerbil, my dog, my cat, me, my mom
- Estimated weights: 140 pounds, 14 ounces, 10 pounds, 70 pounds, 35 pounds
- Actual weights: 7 ounces, 38 pounds, 147 pounds, 8 pounds, 65 pounds

Figure 7-7 Jenny's Science Project

Item	Estimated Weight	Actual Weight	Difference
dog	35 lbs.	38 lbs.	3 lbs.

LOOKING BACK 7-3 **Prereading and Charts**

Look at the pie graph in Figure 7-8, including the title and subheading. After studying the information on various kinds of living arrangements for college students, write a paragraph on the topic. Start with a topic sentence, include several supporting details, and end with a concluding sentence.

Figure 7-8 College Students' Living Arrangements

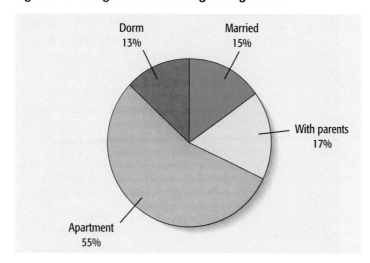

Most Students Live Off-Campus in Apartments

_____

_____

_____

_____

_____

_____

LOOKING BACK 7-4 **Consonant Blends, Main Idea, and Supporting Details: *Spring***

Read the poem and write down each word that contains a consonant blend (consonants that create connected but separate sounds). Then write a paragraph about the poem that starts with a topic sentence, includes several supporting details, and ends with one or more conclusions.

Spring
By William Blake

Sound the flute!
None are mute;
Birds delight
Day and night;
Nightingale

In the dale,
Lark in the sky-
Merrily,
Merrily, merrily to welcome in the year.

Little boy,
Full of joy;
Little girl, sweet and small;
Cock does crow
So do you,
Merry voice,
Infant noise;
Merrily, merrily to welcome in the year.

Little lamb,
Here I am;
Come and lick
My white neck;
Let me pull
Your soft wool;
Let me kiss
Your soft face;
Merrily, merrily, we welcome in the year.

Ten words that contain blends:

1. _____   5. _____   8. _____
2. _____   6. _____   9. _____
3. _____   7. _____   10. _____
4. _____

_____

_____

_____

_____

_____

_____

_____

ONLINE PRACTICE

For further practice identifying **supporting details**, go to **MyReadingLab** at www.myreadinglab.com. Click on **Reading Road Trip,** and select your textbook or the **Pioneer Level.** Take a Road Trip to the **St. Louis Arch.**

PROGRESS CHART

CHAPTER **7**

SECTION ONE

Fill out the number of correct answers you have for each item below. Your instructor will tell you how to calculate your percentage score.

PRACTICE 7-1   Number right _____ out of a possible score of 5.   Percentage score _____

PRACTICE 7-2   Number right _____ out of a possible score of 4.   Percentage score _____

PRACTICE 7-3   Number right _____ out of a possible score of 3.   Percentage score _____

PRACTICE 7-4   Number right _____ out of a possible score of 8.   Percentage score _____

PRACTICE 7-5   Number right _____ out of a possible score of 7.   Percentage score _____

PRACTICE 7-6   Number right _____ out of a possible score of 8.   Percentage score _____

PRACTICE 7-7   Number right _____ out of a possible score of 8.   Percentage score _____

PRACTICE 7-8   Number right _____ out of a possible score of 5.   Percentage score _____

MASTERY 7-1   Number right _____ out of a possible score of 5.   Percentage score _____

MASTERY 7-2   Number right _____ out of a possible score of 7.   Percentage score _____

MASTERY 7-3   Number right _____ out of a possible score of 4.   Percentage score _____

MASTERY 7-4   Number right _____ out of a possible score of 15.   Percentage score _____

MASTERY 7-5   Number right _____ out of a possible score of 7.   Percentage score _____

MASTERY 7-6   Number right _____ out of a possible score of 4.   Percentage score _____

MASTERY 7-7   Number right _____ out of a possible score of 14.   Percentage score _____

MASTERY 7-8   Number right _____ out of a possible score of 5.   Percentage score _____

LOOKING BACK 7-1   Number right _____ out of a possible score of 6.   Percentage score _____

LOOKING BACK 7-2   Number right _____ out of a possible score of 16.   Percentage score _____

LOOKING BACK 7-3   Number right _____ out of a possible score of 5.   Percentage score _____

LOOKING BACK 7-4   Number right _____ out of a possible score of 15.   Percentage score _____

How do you feel? There are no wrong or right answers to how you feel about what you have learned. Circle Yes, Somewhat, or No in response to the following questions.

1. Do you understand the purpose of supporting details?	Yes	Somewhat	No
2. Has understanding supporting details helped improve your reading comprehension?	Yes	Somewhat	No
3. By recognizing supporting details, has your reading outside the classroom improved?	Yes	Somewhat	No
4. Do you understand how transitional words and phrases connect ideas?	Yes	Somewhat	No
5. Could you understand the main idea of a paragraph just as easily without adding supporting details?	Yes	Somewhat	No
6. Have you added to your personal vocabulary log while studying supporting details?	Yes	Somewhat	No
7. Can you infer a conclusion from a chart or reading?	Yes	Somewhat	No

SECTION THREE

Take a minute or two to reflect on your reading development. Write a few sentences or discuss with other students how this chapter has changed your reading habits.

_____

_____

_____

_____

_____

_____

_____

_____

_____

_____

Additional Readings

CHAPTER PREVIEW

In this chapter, you will practice the reading strategies presented in the first seven chapters of the book to develop your own method of successful reading. Each reading selection provides review and reinforcement activities for the following:

- **Prereading or previewing a text**
- **Recognizing consonants and vowels**
- **Recognizing word parts and using syllables**
- **Using a dictionary**
- **Discovering context clues**
- **Finding main ideas**
- **Finding supporting details**

MAKING MEANING

If you have done many jigsaw puzzles, you know how good it feels when you put in the last piece and the picture is finally complete. Everyone has a method of putting puzzles together. Some people start with all the outside pieces—the ones with the straight sides—and put a frame in place. Others gather all pieces of the same color or pattern or object and create small groups of images that are complete in themselves and then work to the outside edges. Both methods have one thing in common: they demonstrate a plan that results in a completed project and brings a sense of satisfaction and success.

Reading is similar to making the pieces of a puzzle into a complete picture. Just like putting the puzzle together, satisfying, successful reading results from having an effective plan. The earlier chapters of this book presented strategies to help you improve your reading. This final chapter presents various reading selections for you to practice using these strategies. There are short articles, newspaper reports, stories, poems, and visual materials, all with

activities that review the reading strategies from the first seven chapters. You may have found two or three methods that work especially well for you. Your plan of reading is probably different from that of other students, but that really doesn't matter. The important thing is that you now have reading strategies that work for you and will give you confidence in the reading you will be required to do in your college courses and career.

READINGS

READING 8-1

Omaha's First Water Company
By Harold Whipple

1   I grew up in Omaha, Illinois, during the 1930s. To get water, you had to haul it from a town water pump. My brother, Gene, and I made some of our spending money hauling water for other people. I was 9 years old, and Gene was 6 years old. We got a nickel for each full can we delivered. We went to the water pump

and filled cans. We put the cans in our little wagon and started our deliveries. Gene and I would take turns pulling or pushing the wagon.

2   It was hot, and we wore pants made from grain sacks. Many times, we struggled up the hills only to have the chain on the wagon cart break. We felt helpless as we stood and watched the water run down the hill from the tipped cans. Gene and I would just have to go back to the water pump and start again.

3   I am 75 now. I wish that I had a count of how many cans we filled and hauled away from that pump. Omaha did build a water tower, but Gene and I started the first Omaha Water Company.

Comprehension and Skills Exercises

1. How old were Gene and his brother when they hauled water to make spending money?

   _____

2. What was the procedure for hauling water?

   _____

   _____

3. Other than the date, what words and phrases in the story tell you that the story happened a long time ago?

   _____

4. From the following list of transitional words, choose appropriate ones to rewrite the three sentences that follow.

   first, finally, next, but, in addition, then, therefore, although

   We went to the water pump and filled cans. We put the cans in our little wagon and started our deliveries. Gene and I would take turns pulling or pushing the wagon.

   _____

   _____

   _____

5. Write every word in paragraph 2 that has a suffix added.

   a. _____   f. _____

   b. _____   g. _____

   c. _____   h. _____

   d. _____   i. _____

   e. _____

READING 8-2

Sawmill Revenge
By Harold Whipple

1 My brother, Gene, and I earned all our spending money when we were little. Once we were hired to work in a sawmill. The mill was set up in some woods south of town. A long belt that ran a wheel on a steam engine turned the saw blade. Logs were put on a wheeled platform that ran on tracks. As the platform moved back and forth past the saw blade, boards were cut.

2 Gene and I stacked the boards. We worked there for one week. It was hot, sweaty work. We got plenty of splinters and cuts. At the end of the week, we did not get paid, and Gene and I decided to get revenge. After Sunday school and fried chicken, we visited the closed sawmill and showed them what you got when you stole Whipple boys' sweat.

3 There was a lot of grease around the mill. Gene and I put a good thick coat of it on every lever, valve, and wheel on the engine. We greased both log platform tracks from one end to the other. We walked home and told mom we had been playing in the woods. It was two days before they could saw logs again.

Comprehension and Skills Exercises

1. What did Gene and his brother do to earn money at the sawmill?

   _____

2. Why did Gene and his brother want to get revenge?

   _____

3. What did Gene and his brother do to get revenge?

   _____

   _____

4. Match the words in the following list with their correct vowel sound. (Short *o*, stop; short *i*, pill; long *e*, eel; long *a*, stay; long *i*, high; short *e*, step.)

   mill   wheel   not   paid   fried   get

   a. long e _____   d. long a _____

   b. long i _____   e. short i _____

   c. short e _____   f. short o _____

5. The following words from the story are misspelled. Rewrite them correctly on the line next to each word.

   a. steem _____   d. greese _____

   b. fryed _____   e. levver _____

   c. whealed _____   f. engun _____

READING 8-3   **Preview the Visual**

1. Look carefully at the following map. Make a list of what you see, starting with the first thing you notice.

Social Studies Problem Solving and Data Interpretation

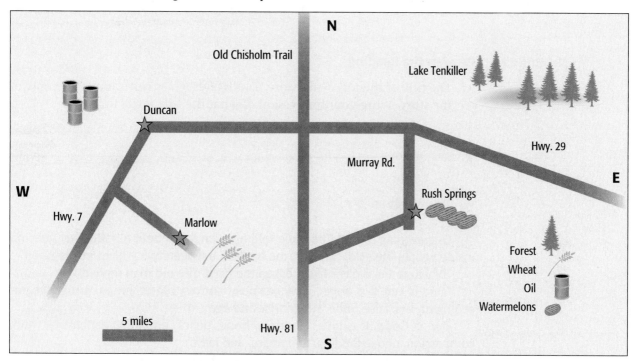

Comprehension and Skills Exercises

Answer the following social studies questions using information from the map.

2. Every map indicates compass directions. Which direction is always at the top? _____ the bottom? _____, on the left? _____, and on the right? _____

3. Annie and her mother live in Duncan. They want to buy watermelons in Rush Springs. Underline how many miles it is from Duncan to Rush Springs.

a. 25

b. 52

c. 5

d. 9

4. Joey's dad is looking for a job. He decided to try to find a job in Duncan. Underline the product that Duncan is known for.

a. forest products

b. watermelons

c. wheat

d. oil

5. Between 1870 and 1890, cattle were driven up the Old Chisholm Trail. Underline what the Old Chisholm Trail is now known as.

a. Highway 29

b. Highway 7

c. Highway 81

d. Murray Rd.

READING 8-4 **Preview the Reading**

1. The title of the following story, *Two Wolves*, gives clues about the topic of the story. Write your impression of what the title refers to.

_____

_____

Two Wolves

One evening an old Cherokee told his grandson about a battle that goes on inside people. He said, "My son, the battle is between two wolves inside us all."

"What are the wolves like?" asked the child. The old man replied,

"One is Evil. It is anger, envy, jealousy, sorrow, regret, greed, arrogance, resentment, lies, false pride, superiority, and ego.

One is Good. It is love, kindness, hope, peace, empathy, generosity, truth, compassion, understanding, happiness, and faith."

The grandson thought about this story for a few minutes and then turned to his grandfather and asked, "Which wolf wins?"

The old Cherokee simply replied, "The one you feed."

Comprehension and Skills Exercises

2. What might the old Cherokee mean when he speaks about "a battle that goes on inside people?"

_____

_____

3. Why do wolves provide an effective image of battling animals in the story?

_____

_____

4. What other words would you add to the definitions of good and evil in the story?

_____

_____

5. We know it is impossible for two wolves to be inside a person. From the context of the reading, what do the wolves represent?

    _____

6. Use your dictionary to find the definition of *arrogance*.

    _____

7. List four compound words used in the story.

    a. _____

    b. _____

    c. _____

    d. _____

8. Name the first vowel sound you hear in the following words from the first sentence in *Two Wolves*. (Short *a*, hat; short *e*, men; short *i*, big; short *o*, hog; short *u*, cup; long *a*, ape; long *e*, eel; long *i*, iodine; long *o*, moan; long *u*, mule.)

    a. evening   _____

    b. an   _____

    c. old   _____

    d. his   _____

    e. people   _____

9. Write three digraphs (consonants that work together to create one sound) from the following sentence on the lines provided:

    "What are the wolves like?"asked the child.

    a. _____

    b. _____

    c. _____

10. Record the number of syllables you hear when you pronounce the following words.

    a. evening   _____

    b. wolves   _____

    c. jealousy   _____

    d. happiness   _____

    e. turned   _____

    f. Cherokee   _____

READER RESPONSE 8-1 How would you "feed" either the evil or the good "wolf" inside you?

_____

_____

_____

_____

READING 8-5 **Preview the Reading**

1. From the title and your knowledge of Santa Claus, what do you expect the story to be about?

_____

_____

_____

_____

_____

Santa Claus Did Visit
By Christina Page

One year my parents took us to Grandma's house for Christmas. My brother, sister, and I did not want to go. We told our parents that Santa would not know where to take our toys. Mom and Dad told us that Santa would not forget us. We packed our bags and loaded into the car. Dad and Mom had to go back into the house to find the cat and let him out.

We drove two days from Massachusetts to Illinois. All our cousins were there. On Christmas day, we got up, and Santa Claus had not left us toys under the tree. We had presents from Mom and Dad, but no toys. We were all sad, and I cried. Mom and Dad were wrong. Santa Claus could not find us.

When we got back to Massachusetts, we helped Mom get the suitcases while Dad unlocked the house. We stepped into the living room and saw toys, candy canes, and presents under the brightly lighted Christmas tree. There were three dolls, a train set, and action toys. Mom and Dad were right. Santa Claus had not forgotten us.

Comprehension and Skills Exercises

2. Why didn't the children want to go to Grandma's house for Christmas?

_____

_____

3. Write words that describe how the children felt at different times in the story.

_____

_____

4. Use your dictionary and look up the definition of the word *suitcase.* Then, create an original sentence, at least eight words in length, that contains the word.

_____

_____

_____

5. Identify the part of speech (noun, pronoun, verb, adverb, adjective, preposition, conjunction, or interjection) of each of the underlined words in this sentence.

When <u>we</u> got <u>back</u> to <u>Massachusetts</u>, we <u>helped</u> <u>Mom</u> <u>get</u> the suitcases while Dad <u>unlocked</u> the <u>house</u>.

Word	*Part of Speech*
a. we	_____
b. Massachusetts	_____
c. helped	_____
d. Mom	_____
e. get	_____
f. back	_____
g. unlocked	_____
h. house	_____

READING 8-6   **Preview the Reading**

1. Based on your experience, what images come to mind when you read the title of the following poem?

_____

_____

_____

_____

Symbols of Christmas
By Alice Doray

May children today have knowledge and faith   1
In the birth of Christ our King.
May they know the meaning of Christmas joy
And the happy carols we sing.
Let them help to acclaim this event of yore   5
With symbols of truth and glee,
With a circular wreath for a "World without end,"
And "life everlasting" with an evergreen tree.

Houses and holly ablaze with bright lights
Means the "Light of the world" did appear. 10
Angels and carolers, tolling of bells
Proclaim this famed birth each year.

Jolly old Santa, our white-bearded friend
Is the symbol of loving and care.
His spirit endures, for the giving of gifts 15
Is an age-old custom we share.

He'll always be with us at Christmas time
To remind us that happiness caught
By loving spirit and tender heart
Was a lesson the Christ child taught. 20

May Christmas for children be festive and bright,
A celebration unrivaled on earth.
May they know decorations and exchanging of gifts
Honor Christ and His glorious birth.

WORDNOTES

yore	time past, usually long past
unrivaled	cannot be beaten

Comprehension and Skills Exercises

2. What is the meaning of each of the following symbols according to the poem?

   a. Circular wreath: _____

   b. Evergreen tree: _____

   c. Bright lights: _____

   d. Tolling of bells: _____

   e. Santa: _____

3. Add three rhyming words to each of the following words.

   a. king, sing, _____

   b. glee, tree, _____

   c. care, share, _____

   d. caught, taught, _____

   e. earth, birth, _____

4. Using context clues in the poem, write a definition of the word *carolers*

   _____

5. Write the number of syllables that you hear in each of the following words. Use hyphens to separate the syllables.

Words	Number of Syllables	Separation into Syllables Syllables
Example: acclaim	2	ac-claim
a. everlasting		
b. carolers		
c. happiness		
d. forgotten		
e. cousins		

READER RESPONSE 8-2 Describe a holiday tradition in your family.

_____

_____

_____

_____

_____

READING 8-7 **Preview the Reading**

1. As you preview this reading, notice the title in bold print and the last sentence printed in italics. Write your prediction of what you will read about in the article. Use your dictionary to find the meaning of any words you do not understand.

_____

_____

_____

Mars!

1 The red planet was spectacular in July and August 2005. During those months, Earth caught up with Mars in the closest approach between the two planets in recorded history. Perhaps Mars will come that close to Earth again in 2287. But because of the way Jupiter's gravity tugs on Mars and disturbs its orbit, astronomers can only be certain that Mars has not come that close to Earth in the last 5,000 years, and it will most likely be 60,000 years before it happens again.

2 The encounter peaked on August 27, when Mars was within 34,649,589 miles of Earth and was the brightest object in the night sky (except for the moon). At a modest 75-power magnification, Mars looked as large as the full moon to the naked eye. The red planet was thus very easy to spot. At the beginning of August, it rose in the east at 10:00 PM and reached its zenith at about 3:00 AM. At the end

of August, when the two planets were the closest, Mars rose at nightfall and reached its highest point in the sky at 12:30 AM.

3   It was amazing to see something that no human being had seen in recorded history! Many people watched Mars during the month of August 2005—a sight that *no one alive today will ever see again.*

Comprehension and Skills Exercises

2. Underline the sentence that states why the night sky was brighter in July and August 2005.

   a. There were no clouds, wind, or rain.

   b. the moon was full and the stars glowed in the sky.

   c. Mars came closer to Earth than ever before in recorded history.

   d. Jupiter flew out of its orbit.

3. Why was Mars so easy to see in the sky?

   _____

   _____

4. When can we see this happen again?

   _____

   _____

5. What context clues tell you that the red planet is Mars?

   _____

6. Give three supporting details from paragraph 2.

   a. _____

   b. _____

   _____

   c. _____

7. The first paragraph of the reading contains the following sentence:

   During <u>those</u> months, Earth <u>caught</u> up with <u>Mars</u> in the closest <u>approach</u> between the <u>two</u> planets in recorded <u>history</u>.

   Write the part of speech for each of the underlined words.

   Example: those   _____adjective_____

   a. caught   _____

   b. Mars   _____

   c. approach   _____

   d. two   _____

   e. history   _____

8. How many syllables do you hear in the word *spectacular*. _____.

   Write a definition of the word *spectacular*: _____

9. Find the definition of the word *zenith* in your dictionary and write it on the line provided.

   _____

   _____

10. Use two of the following three words from the reading to fill in the blanks in the sentence.

    spectacular   magnification   zenith

    While performing an experiment in the biology lab, Joseph saw a

    _____ sight due to the _____ of the new microscope.

READING 8-8   Preview the Reading

1. From reading the title of the following poem and looking at the photograph on the next page, describe what the couple might be talking about.

   _____

   _____

   _____

An old tradition says a bride should have something old, something new, something borrowed, something blue for her wedding ceremony. Here is a poem that expresses the joy of a young couple's wedding day. (Line numbers are printed to the right of every five lines.)

Wedding Charm
By Deborah Cummings Doray

The oldest thing was the earth beneath.   1
A firemist cooled beneath our feet.
And massive—turning slowly through
Eternal words in ancient beat.

The newest thing was the bond we formed,   5
Fresh and tender, newly born
Unequal, yet, to hopes we weighed
Upon the strengths of this new join.

The borrowed thing was the words we used,
Handed down, some changed, abused.   10
But precious still, as said by all
Who came before, their lives to fuse.

And the bluest things were your two eyes
A little scared, perhaps surprised
At finding us here—this place, this time,
And promising worlds and loves and lives.

15

Comprehension and Skills Exercises

2. Write the first four words of the first line of each stanza on the lines provided and complete the sentences as if you were writing your own wedding poem.

_____

_____

_____

_____

3. Look up the following words and write the meaning or meanings that fit in the context of the poem.

charm _____

_____

beat _____

_____

bond _____

_____

fuse _____

_____

4. a. Sometimes words in poems do not rhyme exactly, but poets use similar sounds or words (that would be incorrect in a sentence) to give the poem a good sound and make its meaning clearer. In your opinion, which stanza has the best rhyme?

_____

b. List the rhyming words.

_____

_____

5. Write the root word for each of the following words.

formed _____   newly _____

weighed _____   landed _____

READING 8-9   Preview the Reading

1. Using your prior knowledge, describe your image of a buffalo. How does this image compare to the image in the title of the poem?

_____

_____

_____

The Flower-Fed Buffaloes
By Vachel Lindsay

The Flower-fed buffaloes of the spring
In the days of long ago,
Ranged where the locomotives sing
And the prairie flowers lie low:
The tossing, blooming, perfumed grass   5

Is swept away by the wheat,
Wheels and wheels and wheels spin by
In the spring that still is sweet.
But the flower-fed buffaloes of the spring
Left us, long ago.   10

They gore no more, they bellow no more,
They trundle around the hills no more:
With the Blackfeet, lying low.
With the Pawnee, lying low,
Lying low.   15

Comprehension and Skills Exercises

1. Find three examples of pairs of rhyming words in the poem.

   a. _____

   b. _____

   c. _____

2. Write three definitions of the word *gore* taken from your dictionary.

   a. _____

   b. _____

   c. _____

3. Find the origin of the word *gore* in your dictionary. Underline where all three meanings for the word come from.

   a. Old French

   b. Old English

   c. Old Scots

5. a. Define the word *lying*. (Look in dictionary under *lie*.)

   _____

   b. Explain how more than one meaning of the word *lying* fits in the poem.

   _____

   _____

   _____

6. Who and what are lying low?

   _____

7. Prairie flowers are small and delicate. Buffaloes are big and strong. Yet they both were victims of changing times. The prairie flowers were replaced by _____. Buffaloes were replaced by _____.

8. Some of the words in the poem have suffixes and prefixes. In the first five lines of the poem, find words that fit in the two categories and list them here. Underline the prefix or suffix in the words you have written.

Prefix	*Suffix*
_____	_____
_____	_____
_____	_____
_____	_____
_____	_____
_____	_____
_____	_____

9. List every noun and verb from the last stanza (lines 11 through 15) in the correct column. If a noun or verb is repeated within these five lines, list it only once.

Noun	*Verb*
_____	_____
_____	_____
_____	_____

10. Separate each of the following words into syllables by rewriting them and using a hyphen to show how they are separated.

Word	*Separated into Syllables*
ago	_____
perfumed	_____
Blackfeet	_____
gore	_____
lying	_____

READER RESPONSE 8-3

The Pawnee and the Blackfoot Indians hunted the buffalo by finding a herd and being quiet before they attacked on horseback, using arrows and later, guns. Before the arrival of horses, the Indians sneaked up on the buffalo and stampeded them off a cliff. In both cases, the Indians were lying low before an attack. But the poet has a double meaning by using the words *lying low*. He says the buffaloes are no more, and the flowers and the Indians are lying low. Explain what the poet is saying about lost prairie flowers, buffaloes, and Indians (Look back at questions 5 and 6 in the previous exercises.)

_____

_____

_____

_____

READING 8-10 **Preview the Reading**

1. From the title of the following reading, what do you expect to learn about Laura?

_____

_____

_____

From the Online College Journal of Laura Eskridge, August 31, 2004

A waffle and a smoothie made my morning groovy,
And now I've got to get movie (ing) to class.
My head is so full; I've studied too long,
But I can't stop now because my chem. problems are wrong.
I don't understand multiple **conversions**   5
The more I try—the more I want a diversion.
There are Pre-Lecture Explorations and After-Class Applications,
And we're thinking of forming a nation out of the people with lost expectations.
I'm supposed to be with my friends all day—
Playing, and straying into the fray!   10
Instead, I'm inside learning the properties of **bromine**
Then moving on to study **adenine** **and** **guanine**.
At this rate I'm going to burn out fast!
Please leave a suggestion to help my brain last!
Well, I'm off to botany where plants are the star;   15
I wish we could lower the academic bar.
But thanks for reading, and please pray for me
Later, dream squirrels—stay happy and free.

WORDNOTES

conversion	a change into another form
bromine	a chemical element; usually, a reddish-brown corrosive liquid
adenine and guanine	two of the building blocks of DNA

Comprehension and Skills Exercises

2. Define the term _prior experience_ (refer to Chapter 1 if necessary).

_____

3. How did your prior experience help you make sense of this online college journal entry?

_____

_____

4. What problems does the author mention she is having in the entry?

_____

_____

_____

5. Give three reasons the author had for writing this journal entry.

a. Reason 1. _____

b. Reason 2. _____

c. Reason 3. _____

6. The author's online journal entry allows others to respond to her entry by adding comments and ratings. What would you write to the author regarding her journal entry?

_____

_____

_____

_____

_____

READER RESPONSE 8-4

Create your own journal entry for your first week in college. What did you learn?

_____

_____

_____

_____

_____

READING 8-11 **Preview the Reading**

1. After reading the first sentences of paragraphs 1 and 2 on the next page, write your prediction of what the story will be about.

_____

_____

_____

_____

This is an excerpt from John Grisham's novel *A Painted House*. The time is the mid-1950s. Young John is about to see a major league game on television for the first time.

From *A Painted House*
By John Grisham

1 My heart froze; my mouth dropped open. I was too stunned to move. Three feet away was a small screen with lines dancing across it. It was in the center of a dark, wooden cabinet with the word Motorola scripted in chrome just under a row of knobs. Pop turned one of the knobs, and suddenly we heard the scratchy voice of an announcer describing a ground ball to the shortstop. Then Pop turned two knobs at once, and the picture became clear.

2 It was a baseball game. Live from Yankee Stadium, and we were watching it in Black Oak, Arkansas.

3 Ed Lopat was pitching for the Yankees, Preacher Roe for the Dodgers. Mickey Mantle, Yogi Berra, Phil Rizzuto, Hank Bauer, Billy Martin with the Yankees, and Pee Wee Reese, Duke Snider, Roy Campanella, Jackie Robinson, and Gil Hodges with the Dodgers. They were all there in Pop and Pearl's living room, playing before sixty thousand fans in the Yankee Stadium. I was mesmerized to the point of being mute. I simply stared at the television, watching but not believing.

4 The game was broadcast into our world by Channel 5 out of Memphis, an **affiliate** of the National Broadcasting Company, whatever that meant. There were commercials for Lucky Strike cigarettes, Cadillac, Coca-Cola, and Texaco. Between innings the game would vanish and there would be a commercial, and when it was over, the screen would change again, and we'd be back in Yankee Stadium. It was a dizzying experience, one that **captivated** me completely. For an hour I was transported to another world.

5 Yogi Berra hit a home run, and as I watched him circle the bases in front of sixty thousand fanatics, I knew I would never again be able to properly hate the Yankees. They were legends, the greatest players on the greatest team the game had known. I softened up considerably but vowed to keep my feelings to myself. Pappy would not allow Yankee **sympathizers** in his house.

WORDNOTES

affiliate	a branch organization
captivated	fascinated
sympathizer	someone with compassionate feelings for a certain person or group

Comprehension and Skills Exercises

2. Describe what the storyteller and his family saw on television.

_____

3. What do you learn about the young storyteller in this selection?

_____

_____

_____

4. Besides getting to see television for the first time, what was so exciting about the baseball game?

_____

5. From context clues, write a definition of the word *stunned.*

_____

6. a. Write two dictionary definitions for the word *fan.*

   _____

   _____

   b. What is the definition of *fanatic*?

   _____

   c. What is the language of origin for both words? _____

7. According to the dictionary, what is a synonym for the word *mesmerized*?

_____

8. Write a definition of the word *captivate.*

_____

9. List the part of speech for each underlined word in the following sentence.

   It was in the center of a dark, wooden cabinet with the word Motorola scripted in chrome just under a row of knobs.

   a. It _____   d. scripted _____

   b. center _____   e. chrome _____

   c. dark _____

10. How many syllables do you hear in the word: *sympathizer*? _____.
    Write a definition of the word.

    _____

11. Write your own sentence using the word *sympathizer*. Make certain your sentence contains at least 10 words.

    _____

    _____

    _____

    _____

12 Divide the following words into syllables; put a hyphen between syllables.

   a. Pappy _____

   b. allow _____

   c. Yankee _____

   d. house _____

13. On the lines provided, write words from the following sentence that contain the indicated vowel sounds. Short *a*, cat; short *e*, pet; short *i*, pin; short *o*, pop; short *u*, cut; long *e*, be; long *a* stay.

    Then Pop turned two knobs at once, and the picture became clear.

    a. short *e* _____

    b. short *a* _____

    c. short *i* _____

    d. short *o* _____ and _____

    e. long *e* and long *a* in the same word _____

    f. long *e* _____

14. a. Write all the words from paragraph 1 of this reading that contain suffixes. If the same word is repeated, write it each time it is used.

    _____

    _____

    b. How many are there? (Count every word, even if it is used more than once.) _____

15. Write four compound words from the reading.

    a. _____

    b. _____

    c. _____

    d. _____

16. Each of the following words has a prefix, a suffix or both. Write the prefix and/or suffix on the lines provided.

	Prefix	*Suffix*
Example: mesmerized	_____	ed
a. greatest	_____	_____
b. watching	_____	_____
c. commercials	_____	_____
d. dropped	_____	_____
e. away	_____	_____
f. suddenly	_____	_____
g. describing	_____	_____

17. For each of the following words, write *C* in the "Correct" column if the word is spelled correctly. If it is spelled wrong, rewrite the word, spelled correctly, in the "Corrected" column.

	Correct	*Corrected*
Example: nobs		knobs
a. meant		
b. describeing		
c. commercial		
d. cabanet		
e. sixtey		
f. woodin		
g. cigarettes		

18. Write the word from paragraph 2 that contains a digraph (consonants that work together to create one sound) _____

19. List each word from the following sentence that contains a consonant blend (consonants that work together to create separate but connected sounds).

Yogi Berra hit a home run, and as I watched him circle the bases in front of sixty thousand fanatics, I knew I would never again be able to properly hate the Yankees.

a. _____   e. _____

b. _____   f. _____

c. _____   g. _____

d. _____

20. What would be an experience for a young boy today comparable to seeing a baseball game on television for the first time?

_____

_____

_____

_____

_____

READING 8-12   Preview the Reading

1. What comes to mind when you see the word *language*, in the title of the following poem?

_____

_____

_____

Language—A Code to Sail Dreams
By Debby Dobbs

A thin girl with long, wispy red hair
crossed her legs as she sat in a chair
fixed on the red clay in Oklahoma
dreaming of a new place to transform her

Reading love tales on an afternoon   5
from the green forests of *Lorna Doone*
Where the flatlands rolled into bogs and pines
Her dreams were ships to castles so fine.

She found the ticket entry to her ship
A code of letters that is called French   10
She loved the class from the very first day
The words were her sail to sweep her away

The games, the sounds, we chanted, we moved
Singing *"Savez-vous planter les choux"*
The rising wave of a foreign culture   15
From stern to bow, it propelled her

While others played, she read *Candide*
She used her French to sail her bright dream
She wrote her verbs, others doodled pictures
In the red clay sea, she was just fixture   20

The sails were filled as she added a code
Spanish is her passage to the land of gold
Her ship first docks in ancient Mexico
Tenochtitlan, Merida, Progresso
Chichen Itza, Cozumel, Saltillo   25

She no longer needs her dreams to sail the sea
To France, England, Holland and Germany
The codes she learned captured the wave
to land on ground wherever she stays.

Remembering forests and mountains she climbed   30
The flatlands roll up, she opens her mind
An older lady with short reddish hair
Embraces new earth as if transplanted there

WORDNOTES

Lorna Doone	a romance novel by R. D. Blackmore
"Savez-vous planter les choux"	a traditional French folk song often used to teach French
Candide	a book by the French writer Voltaire about life in the 1750s
Tenochtitlan	ancient Aztec site in Mexico
Merida	a Spanish city founded in 1542
Progresso	a Mexican fishing village
Chichen Itza	ancient ruins of Mexico's Yucatan Peninsula
Cozumel	the largest island of the Mexican Caribbean
Saltillo	a Mexican town more than 400 years old

Comprehension and Skills Exercises

2. Describe the central character of the poem. What does she look like? What does she like to do?

   _____

   _____

   _____

3. How does the girl in the poem travel to foreign lands?

   _____

4. Define the word *code*. _____

   _____

5. What does the definition of the word *code* tell you about the poem?

   _____

   _____

6. Who is the "older lady with short reddish hair" in the last stanza?

   _____

7. In line 26, the author writes, "She no longer needs her dreams to sail the sea." What does she use instead?

   _____

   _____

8. The title of the poem uses the image of a ship sailing to faraway lands. The ship is really the new language the girl in the poem is learning. What words does she use that describe ships and sailing?

   _____

9. Name the vowel sound you hear in the following words. (Long *e*, bean; short *u*, putt; short *i*, pit; long *a*, ape; long *o*, pole; long *i*, ice; short *e*, hen.)

	Word	*Vowel Sound*
Example:	tales	long *a*

a. rolled   _____

b. fine   _____

c. French   _____

d. sail   _____

e. bright   _____

f. green   _____

g. just   _____

10. a. Look up the word *language* in your dictionary. Write the definition here.

_____

_____

_____

b. Does the above definition match the way the word *language* is used in the poem? _____

11. Lines 11 and 12 end in a rhyming sound. Write the two rhyming words and the vowel sound.

a. words   _____

b. vowel sound   _____

READER RESPONSE 8-5

What is another image that could represent language in a poem you might compose? What words could you use to create your image?

_____

_____

_____

READING 8-13

A Vacation with Ghosts
By Ruth Ozeki
New York Times, August 11, 2004

1   My first six summers growing up in America were filled with the familiar thrills of Slip 'N Slides and sprinklers, the smell of gasoline lawnmowers and the tickle of grass blades sticking to my skin. Then, the summer I was 7, my mother took me to Japan to visit my grandmother. It was my first trip outside the United States. My grandmother was very old. She lived by herself in a tiny house, made of paper and wood, on the side of a mountain. A bamboo forest surrounded it, tall and towering, like some kind of monster lawn grown out of control. The days were **humid** and hot, and the heat made everything, including time, stand still. It was an Asian kind of heat, made of far more than just temperature: strange

sound and scent; the constant whine of cicadas; the moist forest moss; the hot breeze rattling the bamboo's bladelike leaves; the faint odor of sewage drifting up the mountainside from town.

2   I was drawn to the forest but scared of it as well, and so I would stand at the edge, looking in. The forest floor was shadowy, but a bright green sunlight filtered through the **canopy**. There were trees other than bamboo: stout trees, cryptomeria and camphor, with huge wisteria vines looped around their branches that the local children swung from.

3   I was curious about these Japanese children. While my **features** showed that I was half-Japanese, in my heart, I was all American, and where I came from—Connecticut—no one else looked like me. Now, here were children whose faces looked like mine, but who were still not at all like me. Their tongues made high short sounds that my ears could not understand. I recall one little boy calling out to me—taah-zan! taah-zan!—as he swung from his vine. When he landed on the ground, he thumped his chest and howled. I ran back into the house.

4   My mother tried to get me to play with the children, but I didn't exactly trust her. In Japan, she showed hidden sides of herself, that I'd never before expected. She and I had spoken only English. Now, as I watched her talk to my grandmother in Japanese, switching easily from one language to the other, I saw that in this strange new tongue she was a different person—possibly not my mother at all. It made me dizzy, all this switching, but maybe it was the heat.

5   The heat never ended, even at night. After dinner we would put on light cotton kimonos (robes) called *yukata* and walk to the public baths, where it was even hotter. Inside the tiled rooms, steam rose from the surface of the large soaking tubs. Pink-skinned ladies of all sizes and shapes submerged themselves, then slowly rose again from the scalding water. I had never, in all my seven years of living, imagined there could be so many shapes of ladies.

6   After we came out of the bath, my grandmother would buy me a soda in a thick green **refillable** bottle that looked as if it was made of sea glass. The stopper was a heavy marble, held in place by a rubber ring, which popped when you pushed it back inside the bottle. After the scalding heat of the baths, that cold soda was the most delicious thing on earth, and even the warm wind felt cool on my skin as we walked home through swarms of fireflies that lighted the darkness.

7   In the morning my grandmother would make tea; she always offered a cup to the photo of my dead grandfather that sat on the altar, talking to him as though he were alive. He had moved to America in 1896, when he was just 16, to build himself a life, but during World War II, he was **interned**, and my grandmother, who had followed him there, was left alone in Hawaii. By the time the United States government released him, at the age of 65, they had lost everything. Discouraged, he and my grandmother moved back to Japan and he died a few years later. Of course, I didn't know any of this then. I just thought it was strange that my grandmother talked to a dead man. But she wasn't the only one. For three days in August, my grandmother told me, during Obon the spirits of the dead walked among us and the living raised red lanterns to guide them, first safely back to earth, then home again to their spirit world. Obon, the festival of the dead, has been celebrated in Japan since the seventh century. In my grandmother's town, in 1964, a bamboo tower was raised in the schoolyard for the festival and the townspeople danced around it. There were fireworks, and it was fun, but I still found it strange to hang out with ghosts.

8 And then there were the soldiers. Like living ghosts, they wore green military uniforms under ragged white robes, and begged for **alms** on busy street corners. They leaned on dirty crutches. Many were wounded or disfigured—missing arms or legs or parts of their faces. The legless, resting on small scooters, were my height exactly, and I could look into their eyes. What I saw terrified me, and I couldn't help but stare. My mother pulled me away. When I demanded more information, she told me the soldiers were veterans of World War II. She seemed embarrassed. Japan had fought America and lost, she said, as though this explained everything.

9 Years later, when I went back to Japan as a foreign exchange student, I asked people about the crippled soldiers begging on the street corners, but no one seemed to remember them or be willing to talk about them. Confused, I wrote to my mother, but she said I must have made it up. She said that while there may have been soldiers begging shortly after the war, they would certainly have been gone by the time she and I went to Japan. She didn't actually say I was lying, but since I'd always been a storyteller, she usually believed my overactive imagination was at work. But I still see the image of the soldiers. How could I have made it up? I was only 7, a postwar child who knew nothing of war's destructions. I remember the hard red shine of their scars, the brownish bandages. But when I went back to Japan in 1975, it was as if the clocks had been rewound, and the soldiers had been erased from history.

10 Now in midsummer, there are days when the air becomes heavy, and time stands still. Of course, in New York there are no forest mosses, no bamboo or eucalyptus trees looped with vines, but in my neighborhood, there are children swinging in the parks and playgrounds. Watching them, I remember how a lightbulb went off in my head, when I ran back from the forest to my grandmother's house, and my mother translated the little boy's strange words. Taah-zan, she explained, was Japanese for Tarzan.

11 I was delighted! I knew all about Tarzan. It was an American film, after all, and, when I was 7, knowing that these Japanese kids also knew my country's story was hugely comforting to me. So I ran back into the forest. Pushing the little boy out of the way, I grabbed hold of a stout vine, pounded my chest and swung.

WORDNOTES

humid	damp, moist
canopy	roof, cover
features	parts of the face (eyes, mouth, nose)
refillable	able to be filled again
interned	detained or confined during a war
alms	money, food, or clothing given to poor people

1. What is Obon? _____

2. What else grew in the forest besides bamboo?

_____

3. Why did the little girl say she "didn't exactly trust" her mother?

   _____

   _____

4. How was the little girl like Japanese children?

   _____

5. How was she different?

   _____

6. What happened that made her feel closer to the Japanese children?

   _____

   _____

7. Why did the mother believe her daughter had made up the story of "crippled soldiers begging on the street corners" in Japan?

   _____

   _____

8. What does the storyteller mean when she says, "a lightbulb went off in my head?"

   _____

9. Find ten examples of compound words from the story.

   _____

   _____

   _____

10. Underline the context clues that help you understand the meaning of the italicized word in each of the following sentences. Then write the dictionary definition of each word on the lines provided.

    a. The forest floor was *shadowy*, but a bright green sunlight filtered

       through the canopy. _____

       _____

    b. After dinner we would put on light cotton *kimonos* (robes) called

       yukata and walk to the public baths, where it was even hotter. _____

       _____

    c. Pink-skinned ladies of all sizes and shapes *submerged* themselves,

       then slowly rose again from the scalding water. _____

       _____

    d. After the *scalding* heat of the baths, that cold soda was the most delicious thing on earth. _____

       _____

    e. Many were wounded or *disfigured*—missing arms or legs or parts of

       their faces. _____

       _____

READER RESPONSE 8-6   Describe a time when you visited someplace with your family and felt that you didn't belong.

_____

_____

_____

_____

_____

Describe something you learned as an adult that you did not understand when you were a child.

_____

_____

_____

_____

_____

READING 8-14   **Preview the Reading**

1. After reading the first lines of paragraphs 1 and 2 in the following reading, what comes to your mind regarding Hurricane Katrina, which occurred in August 2005?

_____

_____

_____

_____

_____

Hurricane Katrina

1   The horrors of Hurricane Katrina mounted day after day. The **devastation**; the **evacuation**; the victims of crime, hunger, and thirst in the Superdome; the death and **destruction**—all of it was beyond imagination.

2   Katrina first made landfall as a category 1 hurricane just north of Miami, Florida, on August 25, 2005, and then again on August 29 along the central Gulf Coast near New Orleans, Louisiana, as a category 4 storm. Katrina resulted in breaches of the **levee** system that protected New Orleans from Lake Pontchartrain, and most of New Orleans was flooded by the lake's waters. This and other major damage to the coastal regions of Louisiana, Mississippi, and Alabama made Katrina the most destructive, most expensive disaster in the history of the United States. Over a million people were displaced because of Katrina—a human crisis unseen in the United States since the Great Depression. Who could even imagine such a disaster?

3   Oddly enough, the United States pays people to think thoughts that are beyond imagination and then often ignores their recommendations. Early in 2001, experts with the Federal Emergency Management Agency (FEMA) set out to rank the catastrophic disasters most likely to happen in the United States. Reporting on the conference, the *Houston Chronicle* listed the worst disasters that could happen in the United States. Those disasters were a terrorist attack in New York, an earthquake in San Francisco, and a major hurricane in New Orleans. The date of this conference was September 10, 2001. Unfortunately, the United States has now suffered two out of three of these "beyond imagination" disasters.

4   After the terrorist attacks in New York, Washington, and Pennsylvania on September 11, 2001, our government decided to create the Department of Homeland Security to coordinate disaster work. A national emergency plan was devised to manage recovery from catastrophic disasters. On Wednesday, August 31, 2005, two days after Katrina devastated the central Gulf Coast, President Bush enacted the emergency plan for the first time.

5   The emergency plan for New Orleans did not work well. Perhaps no disaster plan could cope with what happened in New Orleans—an entire city under water. New Orleans citizens were left with no homes or jobs to return to. They faced years of rebuilding. No plan envisioned loading hundreds of thousands of refugees onto buses or planes and driving or flying them to live months, perhaps years, maybe forever, at locations all over the United States.

6   However, the thinkers of the unthinkable thought for years that New Orleans' levee system was inadequate and dangerous. In 2001, the Army Corps of Engineers in the New Orleans district spent $147 million on various construction and repair projects. In 2005, the corps spent $82 million in the district, 44 percent less than in 2001.

7   Another Gulf Coast project was underfunded. The Coast 2050 project aimed to restore the wetlands of the Mississippi Delta. The marshes and swamps buffer New Orleans from the Gulf of Mexico. Levees built many years ago on the Mississippi River force the sediment of the river into the gulf instead of spreading it across the marshes south of New Orleans. The delta is disappearing at the rate of the area of one football field every 15 minutes. Without a good buffer, the next time a hurricane hits the city, New Orleans could become Atlantis. And the experts say that there will be a next time. We can plan on it.

WORDNOTES

devastation	complete ruin, waste
evacuation	withdrawal from
destruction	a scene of ruin
breaches	breaks or separations
recommendations	favorable proposals or advice
catastrophic	great, sudden, ruinous
coordinate	bring into harmony or proper relation
enacted	made into a law, accomplished
envisioned	imagined
levee	a dam or dike to hold back water

delta	a triangular deposit of silt at the mouth of a river split into branches
buffer	anything that serves to deaden the shock of striking forces
sediment	matter that settles to the bottom of a liquid
Atlantis	a mythical sunken continent in the Atlantic Ocean

Comprehension and Skills Exercises

2. Based on context clues, how would you define the phrase "beyond imagination" in paragraph 1?

_____

_____

_____

3. What is FEMA?

_____

_____

_____

4. What four disasters are mentioned in the article?

_____

_____

_____

5. What government organization was assigned to manage recovery of Hurricane Katrina?

_____

6. Write the sentence that contains the main idea of paragraph 5.

_____

7. What is the purpose of the second sentence in paragraph 5, "Perhaps no disaster plan could cope with what happened in New Orleans—an entire city under water"?

_____

_____

8. Review the story and list the words you find that contain the following suffixes listed.

Suffix	*Word(s)*
a. tion	_____
	_____
b. ing	_____
	_____

c. ed _____
  _____
  _____

d. able _____
  _____

e. ly _____
  _____

9. Use your dictionary to look up the word *disaster* and write its definition.

  _____
  _____

10. Write the number of syllables contained in each of the following words.

Word	*Number of Syllables*
a. recommendations	_____
b. conference	_____
c. another	_____
d. million	_____
e. security	_____
f. sediment	_____

11. Write the part of speech (pronoun, noun, verb, adverb, adjective, preposition, interjection, or conjunction) for each underlined word in the following sentence.

Oddly enough, the United States pays people to think thoughts that are beyond imagination, then often ignores their recommendations.

Word	*Part of Speech*
a. Oddly	_____
b. their	_____
c. pays	_____
d. thoughts	_____
e. imagination	_____
f. ignores	_____

12. The following words contain consonant blends (consonants that work together to create separate but connected sounds) and/or digraphs (consonants that work together to produce one sound) or neither. For each word, write the blend and/or digraph under the correct column, or put a check mark under "Neither." Note the following example:

Word	*Blend*	*Digraph*	*Neither*
Example: beyond	nd	_____	_____
a. breaches	_____	_____	_____
b. Katrina	_____	_____	_____

c. flooded _____ _____ _____

d. marshes _____ _____ _____

e. catastrophic _____ _____ _____

f. coastal _____ _____ _____

g. attack _____ _____ _____

h. emergency _____ _____ _____

13. Create an original sentence using the following words.

   breaches   **catastrophic**

   _____

   _____

14. Write two words from paragraph 1 that have the schwa sound. (Check your dictionary or Chapter 4 for an explanation of the schwa sound.)

   _____

15. Write the prefix and its meaning for each of the following words. (Check your dictionary on Chapter 3 for a list of prefixes.)

Word	*Prefix*	*Meaning of Prefix*
a. inadequate	_____	_____
b. cooperate	_____	_____
c. displaced	_____	_____
d. unseen	_____	_____

16. Use your dictionary to locate the original language for the following words.

Word	*Original Language*
a. terrorist (use terror)	_____
b. flood	_____

17. Match words from the left column with the vowel sounds in the right column.

	Word	*Matching Vowel Sound*
_____	day	a. long **o**
_____	happen	b. short **i**
_____	Gulf	c. long **a**
_____	time	d. long **i**
_____	system	e. short **i** and short **e**
_____	cope	f. short **a** and short **e**
_____	victim	g. short **u**

18. For each of the following words, write *C* in the "Correct" column if the word is spelled correctly. If it is wrong, rewrite the word, spelled correctly, in the "Corrected" column.

Note the example below.

Word	*Correct*	*Corrected*
Example: terrorest	_____	terrorist
a. regions	_____	_____
b. conferance	_____	_____
c. refuges	_____	_____
d. disasters	_____	_____
e. recomendation	_____	_____
f. cordinate	_____	_____

19. In paragraph 6, identify the transitional word and write it here. (See Chapter 7 for an explanation of transitional words.) _____

Underline the type of information you would expect to follow this transitional word.

a. a comparison or contrast

b. addition

c. example

20. What transitional word could begin paragraph 5?

_____

_____

READING 8-15   **Preview the Reading**

1. After reading the first sentence of each of the first three paragraphs, write your prediction of what the reading will be about.

_____

_____

_____

_____

As Town for Deaf Takes Shape, Debate on Isolation Re-emerges
By Monica Davey
New York Times, March 21, 2005

1   Salem, S.D.—Standing in an empty field along a windy highway, Marvin T. Miller, who is deaf, imagines the town he wants to create: a place built around American Sign Language, where teachers in the new school will **sign**, the town council will hold its debates in sign language, and restaurant workers will be required to know how to sign orders.

2   Nearly 100 families—with people who are deaf, hard of hearing, or who can hear but want to communicate in sign language—have already publicly declared

their intention to live in Mr. Miller's village, to be called Laurent after Laurent Clerc, a French educator of the deaf from the 1800s. Planners, architects, and future residents from various states and other countries are laying out detailed blueprints for the town, which could accommodate at least 2,500 people. Mr. Miller, who has been imagining this for years, intends to break ground by fall. "Society isn't doing that great a job of, quote-unquote, integrating us," Mr. Miller, 33, said through an interpreter. "My children don't see role models in their lives: mayors, factory managers, postal workers, business owners. So we're setting up a place to show our unique culture, our unique society."

3   While deaf communities, like the one that existed in Martha's Vineyard decades ago, have cropped up throughout the nation, this would be the first town expressly created for people who sign. Even the location, in sparsely populated South Dakota, was selected with the intent of rapidly building political strength for the nation's millions of deaf and hard-of-hearing people, a group that has won few elected offices around the country.

4   But in the unique political world of deaf culture, Laurent is an increasingly contentious idea. For some, like Mr. Miller, his wife, Jennifer, who is also deaf, and their four deaf children, it seems the simplest of wishes: to live in a place where they are fully engaged in day-to-day life. Others, however, particularly those who support technologies that help deaf people use spoken language, wonder whether such a town would isolate and exclude the deaf more than ever. "We think there is a greater benefit for people to be part of the whole world," said Todd Houston, executive director of the Alexander Graham Bell Association for the Deaf and Hard of Hearing in Washington. "I understand the desire to be around people like ourselves, and I don't have a problem with that, but I don't think it's very wise. This is a little bit of circling-the-wagons mentality, if you ask me." Over the past 15 years, he said, it has become easier for the deaf and hard of hearing to grow up using spoken language because of a steady rise in the use of cochlear implants, more early diagnoses and therapies for deaf children, and efforts to place some deaf children in mainstream schools. That fact has set off intense political debate over what it means to be deaf and what type of communication—signing or talking—the deaf should focus on.

5   Those who want to live in Laurent say their intent is not exclusivity at all but the inclusion of all kinds of people, especially those who do not have the luxury of communicating with speech. "We are not building a town for deaf people," said M. E. Barwacz, Mr. Miller's mother-in-law and his business partner. "We are building a town for sign language users. And one of the biggest groups we expect to have here is hearing parents with deaf children."

6   Ms. Barwacz, who intends to live in Laurent, is not deaf. She has two daughters, one deaf and one not, and eight grandchildren, four of them deaf. Nationally, experts report that some 90 percent of deaf children are born to hearing parents, setting up a quandary, in some cases, about what language to use in a single household.

7   As early as the 1800s, deaf leaders debated the possibility of a "deaf state," said Gerard Buckley, an official at the National Technical Institute for the Deaf in Rochester. But the notion came and went. Elsewhere, because of nearness to schools and businesses tied to the deaf, large groups of deaf people have gathered in cities like Rochester, Wash.; Olathe, Kan.; Frederick, Md.; and Sioux Falls, S.D.

8   The difference in Laurent, say some among the 92 families who have reserved spaces in the town from as far away as London and Australia, is that every part of it would be designed with them in mind. The homes and businesses, they say, would incorporate glass and open space to easily see across wide distances. Fire and

police services would be designed with more lights and fewer sirens. High-speed Internet connections would be available all over town since the Internet and Video Relay Service have become **vital** forms of communication for deaf people. And any shops, businesses, or restaurants would be required to be sign-language friendly.

9   In Salem, a dusty 125-year-old farming town of 1,300, three miles from the proposed site of Laurent, people seem unsure of what to make of the idea. "No one has ever come along and tried to start a town," said Joseph Kolbeck, the local barber. Along the quiet main street, Mr. Miller and Ms. Barwacz, who are originally from Michigan, recently opened an office in the old King Koin Laundromat to create and promote Laurent. They moved to Salem not long ago, choosing the area after looking over nearly the entire country at factors like population, climate, and cost of land. Some people here wonder how the proposed town of 2,500 would **mesh** with McCook County's 6,000 residents and its economy of corn, cows, and pigs. Others say they doubt Laurent will ever become reality.

10   Mr. Miller and Ms. Barwacz have revealed little about the costs and their plans for financing Laurent. They say they are using family money as well as some from a group of "angel investors" led by a man with a deaf daughter who wishes to remain unnamed. First Dakota National Bank is helping to secure financing, and the two have **optioned** 275 acres so far. They say they are spending about $300,000 for the planning work. Those who have reserved spaces in Laurent will be expected to put down $1,000 deposits for condominiums and home lots.

11   For many of those people—from states like California, Florida and New York— a move to prairie land in South Dakota (population 760,000) would seem to be a huge culture shock. But they plan to start businesses like shops and restaurants, gas stations and hotels, and the benefits, many of them say, outweigh any concerns they have about the location. Lawrence J. Brick, a retired school administrator from Philadelphia, said Laurent held attractions that most hearing people would not understand: no longer having to shy away from the neighbors, fearing he could not communicate; no longer having to guess what a store clerk is saying about a price; no longer having to apologize for being deaf.

12   Although some people argue that Laurent might isolate deaf people, Dirksen L. Bauman, who directs the master's program in deaf studies at Gallaudet University, said the plans actually marked an important **collaboration** between the deaf and the hearing as more hearing people are learning American Sign Language, now the fifth most-studied language on college campuses. Not everyone, Marvin Miller said, is eligible for or would even want to receive technologies like cochlear implants. "I do not want one for myself," he said. "I am very happy being deaf. To me, this is like asking a black or Asian person if he/she would take a pill to turn into a white person."

WORDNOTES

sign	communicate using hand movements instead of speech, especially used by the deaf
decades	ten-year periods
sparsely	spread thinly
intent	plan
contentious	argumentative
cochlear implants	prosthetic devices surgically set in place in the internal ear to restore partial hearing to the deaf

exclusivity	shutting out all others
quandary	difficult choice
vital	essential; critically important
mesh	to fit together
optioned	purchased a right to buy later
collaboration	a group working together

Comprehension and Skills Exercises

2. Where does the name Laurent come from?

   _____

   _____

3. Where is Laurent to be located?

   _____

   _____

4. How many people will live in Laurent? _____

5. Who will live in the town of Laurent?

   _____

   _____

   _____

6. How is Laurent being financed?

   _____

   _____

   _____

7. Why does Marvin T. Miller want to develop Laurent?

   _____

   _____

   _____

   _____

8. Why does Todd Houston believe it would not be wise to create a town like Laurent?

   _____

   _____

   _____

   _____

   _____

9. Why doesn't Marvin Miller want a cochlear implant?

_____

_____

10. What is the main idea of paragraph 10?

_____

_____

11. List three supporting details in paragraph 12.

a. _____

_____

_____

b. _____

c. _____

_____

12. List as many transitions as you can find in the reading (at least 4), and write the meaning of each.

_____

_____

_____

13. In the reading, find all the words that contain the following prefixes and write them on the lines provided.

a. **in** _____

b. **ex** _____

c. **de** _____

d. **a** _____

e. **re** _____

14. Write the number of syllables you hear in each of the following words.

Word	*Syllables*
a. families	_____
b. imagining	_____
c. restaurant	_____
d. accommodate	_____
e. political	_____
f. communicating	_____
g. deaf	_____
h. businesses	_____
i. particularly	_____
j. distances	_____

15. For each of the following words, write *C* in the "Correct" column if the word is spelled correctly. If it is wrong, rewrite the word, spelled correctly, in the "Corrected" column.

Word	*Correct*	*Corrected*
a. resadents	_____	_____
b. various	_____	_____
c. inclusion	_____	_____
d. simplist	_____	_____
e. designed	_____	_____
f. diagneses	_____	_____
g. spokin	_____	_____
h. beggest	_____	_____

Choose words from the WORDNOTES to complete the following sentences.

16. LaShonda was in a _____ about whether to live at home or on campus her freshman year of college.

17. It is _____ for Tran to work with a tutor to understand and complete his chemistry homework.

18. Our study group worked in _____ to prepare for the final exam.

19. After a _____ Sterline was able to hear her little girl speak.

20. Even though her mother could hear her speak, the toddler continued to _____ when asking for a cookie.

READER RESPONSE 8-7

Are you, a family member, friend, or acquaintance deaf? Describe how you communicate—sign language, lip reading, writing. What do you think of a community like Laurent?

_____

_____

_____

_____

_____

READING 8-16   **Preview the Reading**

1. The following article was printed in the *New York Times* on July 18, 2004. What does that tell you about the information you will read in the article?

_____

_____

_____

_____

Next to the Express Checkout, Express Medical Care

By Michelle Andrews

New York Times, July 18, 2004

1   When Jodi West woke up one Friday in May with a teary, crusty right eye, she rinsed her face and hoped that it would clear up on its own. By the next morning, the infection had spread to both eyes, and she realized that she would have to see someone about it. But she knew that she would have to be quick: her 7-year-old daughter was dancing in two programs that day. So they got in the car and drove off, not to a hospital emergency room, but to the Target store in Shoreview, Minn., about 15 minutes from their home in Centerville. There, at a clinic in the store, they went to a **kiosk** and signed the register. After about five minutes, a nurse practitioner took Ms. West, 37, into a tiny examining room. She asked a few questions, looked at her eyes, wrote a prescription and sent them on their way. "It took only 20 minutes," Ms. West said. "I wish these clinics had been around when my son was young and getting ear infections all the time."

2   The clinics, called MinuteClinics, can be found in Target and Cub Foods stores in the Minneapolis—St. Paul area. Now in 10 stores, the MinuteClinics **diagnose** and treat about a dozen common ailments—like strep throat, sinus and ear infections and allergies—in about 15 minutes. They also provide **vaccinations** and offer tests for cholesterol and blood pressure problems. Because waiting times can last for hours at doctors' offices, **urgent**-care clinics and emergency rooms, the clinics' **slogan**, "You're sick, we're quick," has a powerful appeal. The idea is catching on in other cities. Since last fall, clinics with names like FastCare, Quick Care and MEDspot have opened in cities like Milwaukee, Louisville, Ky., and Fort Wayne, Ind. Though the services vary and only some accept insurance, they share a common purpose: "It's all about saving people time," said Linda Hall Whitman, the chief executive of MinuteClinic.

3   The clinics are staffed by nurse practitioners, who usually have a four-year degree and a two-year master's degree in nursing. All clinics have a doctor available by phone during business hours. But some doctors warn that quick clinics, though handy, should not take the place of regular visits to a primary care doctor. At a quick clinic, "you're depending on the patient to know what they have before they get there," said Dr. J. Brian Hancock, president of the American College of Emergency Physicians, who works as an emergency physician at St. Mary's Hospital in Saginaw, Mich. Often, he said, patients come to emergency rooms **complaining** of minor ailments that turn out to be more serious. A patient who thinks she has strep throat, he said, may have an **abscess**, while a supposed cold sore could be a sign of a sexually transmitted disease.

4   Sometimes, if patients need a "quick fix," Dr. Hancock said, a walk-in clinic will do just fine. But that should not take the place of a continuing relationship with a doctor. Infants should never be treated at a quick clinic, he said, because "they may have something that's more serious that's harder to pick up." **Recurring** problems need to be seen by a physician, said Michael O. Fleming, a family doctor in Shreveport, La., who is president of the American Academy of Family Physicians. For example, Dr. Fleming said, recurring bladder infections may **indicate** kidney stones or a tumor.

5   "Physicians have much more training, and that training is to look for early signs of complications," he said. But Jan Towers, director of health policy for the American Academy of Nurse Practitioners, said nurse practitioners are "certainly qualified" for dealing with conditions presented at a quick clinic. They are trained to diagnose different diseases, she said, and to know what to prescribe for them. At MinuteClinic, the computer system identifies patients who come back often with the same ailment, so they can be referred to a doctor, said Catherine L. Wisner, director of national operations. Indeed, when Wendy Haroldson of Lakeville, Minn., brought her 5-year-old son to the MinuteClinic at the Cub Foods in Apple Valley for his fourth strep test last winter, the nurse practitioner recommended taking him to his regular doctor or a specialist. Upon the recommendation of the boy's ear, nose and throat doctor, his tonsils were removed in June. Both MinuteClinic and Aurora Quick Care, part of Aurora Health Care, a network of hospitals and clinics, say they have clear rules, called protocols, that nurse practitioners must follow. The protocols at Aurora, based in Milwaukee, are consistent with care at any of the system's clinics or hospitals, said Sue Ela, senior clinical vice president for the network.

6   MinuteClinic says it invested $15 million in software for nurse practitioners to use in diagnosing and treating patients. The software includes clinical guidelines set up by medical journals and professional academies, Ms. Whitman said. The protocols do not let the nurse practitioner prescribe antibiotics, for example, without a positive test result. Other clinics also follow clinical guidelines but allow nurses more autonomy. All clinics carry liability insurance that protects them from claims like those of medical malpractice. The clinics are popular because they are fast—and relatively cheap. At MinuteClinic, a visit to test for strep throat costs $44, compared with an average of $109 at a doctor's office or $328 in an emergency room, according to the Minnesota Council of Health Plans, a trade group.

7   The morning after Sandra Gadbaw, 53, came down with a urinary tract infection, she drove to the MinuteClinic at the Cub Foods in Maple Grove, Minn. When she arrived, the nurse practitioner was seeing another patient, so Ms. Gadbaw picked up one of the clinic's beepers and did her grocery shopping while waiting to be paged. A half-hour later, she was in a room with the nurse practitioner, who asked questions, took a urine sample and wrote a prescription. The total cost to Ms. Gadbaw, who does not have insurance, was $45. Insured patients, who make up 90 percent of MinuteClinics' patients, pay even less. Most insurance plans cover a MinuteClinic visit, requiring only a co-payment, usually $15 or $20. But MinuteClinics' costs are so low that some self-insured companies, like U.S. Bank in Minneapolis, have cut employee co-payments to as little as $5 if they use the clinic.

8   MinuteClinic can keep prices down partly because of its limited equipment. Each has a computer, a printer and diagnostic tests and vaccines; exam rooms have two chairs but no examining table. "You wouldn't want to use this pattern for everything," said Scott Anthony, a partner at Innosight, a company that has followed MinuteClinic. "But for simple, rules-based problems, why should people have to wait for hours when they can go somewhere else and get it fixed in 15 minutes?" In 2002, the average time spent in an emergency room was 3.2 hours, according to the Centers for Disease Control and Prevention.

9   Steve Pontius, a **founder** of MinuteClinic, said he and his two partners came up with the idea for it in 1999 while talking about the trouble of taking children to a doctor for simple ailments. Once, Mr. Pontius said, he was sure that his son, then 5, had an ear infection. "When it's your fourth child, you just know," he said. After they waited three hours at an urgent-care clinic, a doctor examined him. In three minutes, he gave the expected diagnosis. "We thought if we could find a way to provide the service quickly and easily, that people would be willing to pay for that," Mr. Pontius said.

10   More than 142,000 patient visits later, it looks as if they were right. In August, MinuteClinic will open three new clinics at Targets in Minnesota. And with plans to open in other states, MinuteClinic or one of its **rivals** may soon be in a super-market or discount store near you.

WORDNOTES

kiosk	small open structure
diagnose	recognize and identify a disease or problem
vaccination	injection to prevent disease
urgent	needed at once
slogan	catchy phrase used in advertising
complaining	expressing pain or displeasure
abscess	swollen area of the body containing pus
recurring	occurring again and again
indicate	to point out, to show
autonomy	independence, the right to be self-directed
urinary tract	organs that make and store urine, one of the body's liquid waste products
founder	one who sets up, brings into being
rivals	competitors, people who try to be as good as or better than one another

Comprehension and Skills Exercises

2. According to the article, where are MinuteClinics located?

_____

3. What are some of the names for new clinics providing walk-in medical care?

_____

4. List three services provided by quick clinics.

_____

_____

5. What is the slogan for MinuteClinics?

_____

6. Explain in your own words how the idea for MinuteClinics came about.

   _____

   _____

   _____

   _____

7. Who should not be treated in a quick clinic?

   _____

8. What is the main idea of paragraph 8?

   _____

9. Give three supporting details from paragraph 6.

   a. _____

   _____

   _____

   b. _____

   _____

   _____

   c. _____

   _____

   _____

10. Write a definition of the title *nurse practitioner* based on context clues in the article.

    _____

    _____

11. Write a definition of the word *protocols* based on context clues in the article.

    _____

    _____

12. Write two words for each of the long vowel sounds listed below:

    a. $\bar{a}$ _____

    b. $\bar{e}$ _____

    c. $\bar{i}$ _____

    d. $\bar{o}$ _____

13. List five words with four syllables:

    _____

    _____

14. List two words from the reading for each of the following prefixes:

a. in _____

b. pre _____

c. pro _____

d. re _____

15. From the vocabulary in the box, select the correct words to complete the following paragraph.

kiosk	complaining	diagnose	abscess
recurring	autonomy	indicate	urinary tract
vaccination	founder	slogan	rivals

When Maria took her baby Miguel to the clinic, at first the doctor could not _____ the baby's illness because he was crying so much. The doctor asked Maria if Miguel was up to date with his _____, and she said he was. After several lab tests, the doctor told Maria Miguel had a _____ infection and that was the reason he was crying so much. The doctor gave Maria medication for the infection and also for an _____ he found in the baby's mouth. When Maria left, the doctor told her to bring Miguel back if the infection became a _____ problem.

16. Identify the part of speech (pronoun, noun, verb, adverb, adjective, conjunction, preposition, interjection) of the following words from this sentence:

Often, he said, patients come to emergency rooms complaining of minor ailments that turn out to be more serious.

Word	Part of Speech
a. Often	_____
b. he	_____
c. said	_____
d. patients	_____
e. complaining	_____
f. ailments	_____
g. serious	_____

17. Locate the words from the following sentence that contain blends (consonants that work together to create separate but connected sounds) and digraphs (consonants that work together to produce one sound). Write each word in the first column, and write the digraph(s) or blend(s) it contains in the correct column.

    "Physicians have much more training, and that training is to look for early signs of complications," he said.

	Word	Digraph	Blend
Example:	_____	____ph____	_____
a.	_____	_____	_____
b.	_____	_____	_____
c.	_____	_____	_____
d.	_____	_____	_____
e.	_____	_____	_____

18. Use your dictionary to find the meaning of the word *malpractice*.

    _____

    _____

19. Find the following words in your dictionary and write their languages of origin.

    a. antibiotics   _____

    b. practitioner   _____

    c. infection   _____

    d. physician   _____

20. From your experience and using the information in the reading, what are the advantages of seeking medical care from a quick clinic?

    _____

    _____

    _____

    _____

    _____

READER RESPONSE 8-8   Have you ever visited a quick clinic? Which one? Describe your experience. Would you recommend it to someone else or go back again?

_____

_____

_____

_____

_____

_____

READING 8-17 **Preview the Reading**

1. From your prereading of the title and the first sentences of paragraphs 1 through 3, what do you predict about the story?

_____

_____

_____

_____

The author of the following story is Guy de Maupassant (pronounced Gē də Mō-pə-sân′), whom many people call the greatest short story writer in the French language. De Maupassant was born in 1850 and died in 1893. His stories are often printed in books used for college reading and writing classes. "Was It a Dream?" is one of his many stories about people and events that are not always what they seem. Because this story was written so long ago, the words may seem difficult or different from what you are used to. Be sure to take the time to refer to the WORDNOTES and look up any words that are new to you. Doing so will help you understand the story better and improve your vocabulary.

Was It a Dream?
By Guy de Maupassant

1   I had loved her madly!

2   Why does one love? Why does one love? How queer it is to see only one being in the world, to have only one thought in one's mind, only one desire in the heart, and only one name on the lips—a name which comes up again and again, rising, like the water in a spring, from the depths of the soul to the lips, a name which one repeats over and over again, which one whispers **ceaselessly**, everywhere, like a prayer.

3   I am going to tell you our story, for love only has one story, which is always the same. I met her and loved her; that is all. And for a whole year I have lived on her tenderness, on her caresses, in her arms, on her words, so completely wrapped up in everything which came from her, that I no longer cared whether it was day or night, or whether I was dead or alive, on this old earth of ours.

4   And then she died. How? I do not know; I no longer know anything. But one evening she came home wet, for it was raining heavily, and the next day she coughed, and she coughed for about a week, and took to her bed. What happened I do not remember now, but doctors came, wrote, and went away. Medicines were brought, and some women made her drink them. Her hands were hot, her forehead was burning, and her eyes bright and sad. When I spoke to her, she answered me, but I do not remember what we said. I have forgotten everything, everything, everything! She died, and I very well remember her slight, feeble sigh. The nurse said: "Ah!" and I understood, I understood!

5   I knew nothing more, nothing. I saw a priest, who said: "Your mistress?" and it seemed to me as if he were insulting her. As she was dead, nobody had the

right to say that any longer, and I turned him out. Another came who was very kind and tender, and I shed tears when he spoke to me about her.

6   They asked me about the funeral, but I do not remember anything that they said, though I remembered the coffin, and the sound of the hammer when they nailed her down in it. Oh! God, God!

7   She was buried! Buried! She! In that hole! Some people came—female friends. I made my escape and ran away. I ran, and then walked through the streets, went home, and the next day started on a journey.

8   Yesterday I returned to Paris, and when I saw my room again—our room, our bed, our furniture, everything that remains of the life of a human being after death—I was **seized** by such a violent attack of fresh grief, that I felt like opening the window and throwing myself out into the street. I could not remain any longer among these things, between these walls which had enclosed and protected her, which held a thousand memories of her, of her skin and of her breath, in every room. I took up my hat to make my escape, and just as I reached the door, I passed the large mirror in the hall, which she had put there so that she might look at herself every day from head to foot as she went out, to see if she looked well, and was correct and pretty, from her little boots to her bonnet.

9   I stopped short in front of that looking glass in which she had so often been reflected—so often, that it must have kept her reflection. I was standing there, trembling, with my eyes fixed on the glass—on that flat, empty glass—which had contained her entirely, and had possessed her as much as I, as my passionate looks had. I felt as if I loved that glass. I touched it; it was cold. Oh! the memory! Sorrowful mirror, burning mirror, horrible mirror, to make men suffer such **torments**! Happy is the man whose heart forgets everything, everything that has passed before it, everything that has looked at itself in it, or has been reflected in its affection, in its love! How I suffer!

10   I went out without knowing it, without wishing it, and toward the cemetery. I found her simple grave, a white marble cross, with these few words:

    She loved, was loved, and died.

11   She is there, below, decayed! How horrible! I sobbed with my forehead on the ground, and I stopped there for a long time, a long time. Then I saw that it was getting dark, and a strange, mad wish, the wish of a **despairing** lover, seized me. I wished to pass the night, the last night, in weeping on her grave. But I should be seen and driven out. How was I to manage? I was **cunning**, and got up and began to roam about in that city of the dead. I walked and walked. How small this city is compared with the other, the city in which we live. And yet, how many more the dead are than the living. We want high houses, wide streets, and much room for the four generations who see the daylight at the same time, drink water from the spring, and wine from the vines, and eat bread from the plains.

12   And for all the generations of the dead, for all that ladder of humanity that has descended down to us, there is scarcely anything, scarcely anything, scarcely anything! The earth takes them back, and they are forgotten. **Adieu**!

13   At the end of the cemetery, I suddenly realized that I was in its oldest part, where those who had been dead a long time are mingling with the soil, where the crosses themselves are decayed, where possibly newcomers will be put to-morrow. It is full of untended roses, of strong and dark cypress-trees, a sad and beautiful garden, fed on human flesh.

14   I was alone, perfectly alone. So I crouched in a green tree and hid myself there completely amid the thick and **somber** branches. I waited, clinging to the stem, just as a shipwrecked man does to a plank.

15   When it was quite dark, I left my **refuge** and began to walk softly, slowly, silently, through that ground full of dead people. I wandered about for a long time, but could not find her tomb again. I went on with extended arms, knocking against the tombs with my hands, my feet, my knees, my chest, even with my head, without being able to find her. I groped about like a blind man finding his way. I felt the stones, the crosses, the iron railings, the metal wreaths, and the wreaths of faded flowers. I read the names with my fingers, by passing them over the letters. What a night! I could not find her again!

16   There was no moon! What a night! I was frightened, horribly frightened in these narrow paths, between two rows of graves. Graves! graves! graves! nothing but graves! On my right, on my left, in front of me, around me, everywhere there were graves! I sat down on one of them, for I could not walk any longer, my knees were so weak. I could hear my heart beat! And I heard something else as well. What? A confused, nameless noise. Was the noise in my head, in the dark night, or beneath the mysterious earth, the earth **sown** with human corpses? I looked all around me, but I cannot say how long I remained there; I was paralyzed with terror, cold with fright, ready to shout out, ready to die.

17   Suddenly, it seemed to me that the slab of marble on which I was sitting, was moving. Certainly it was moving, as if it were being raised. I jumped on to the next tomb, and I saw, yes, I clearly saw the stone which I had just sat on rise upright. Then the dead person appeared, a naked skeleton, pushing the stone back with its bent back. I saw it quite clearly, although the night was so dark. On the cross I could read:

> Here lies Jacques Olivant, who died at the age of fifty-one. He loved his family, was kind and honorable, and died in the grace of the Lord.

18   The dead man also read what was inscribed on his tombstone; then he picked up a little, pointed stone, and began to scrape the letters carefully. He slowly marked them out, and with the hollows of his eyes he looked at the places where they had been engraved. Then with the tip of the bone that had been his forefinger, he wrote in **luminous** letters, like those lines which boys trace on walls with the tip of a match:

> Here reposes Jacques Olivant, who died at the age of fifty-one. He hastened his father's death by his unkindness, as he wished to inherit his fortune, he tortured his wife, tormented his children, **deceived** his neighbors, robbed everyone he could, and died wretched.

19   When he had finished writing, the dead man stood motionless, looking at his work. On turning round I saw that all the graves were open, that all the dead bodies had come out of them, and that all had erased the lies inscribed on the gravestones by their relations, substituting the truth instead. And I saw that all had been the tormentors of their neighbors—malicious, dishonest, hypocrites, liars, rogues, slanderers, envious; that they had stolen, deceived, performed every disgraceful, every sinful action, these good fathers, these faithful wives, these devoted sons, these pure daughters, these honest tradesmen, these men and

women who were called honorable and good. They were all writing at the same time, on the doorstep of their eternal home, the truth, the terrible and the holy truth of which everybody was **ignorant**, or pretended to be ignorant, while they were alive.

20 I thought that *she* must also have written something on her tombstone, and now running without any fear among the half-open coffins, among the corpses and skeletons, I went toward her, sure that I should find her immediately. I recognized her at once, without seeing her face, which was covered by the winding-sheet, and on the marble cross, where shortly before I had read:

She loved, was loved, and died.

I now saw:

Having gone out in the rain one day, in order to deceive her lover, she caught cold and died.

21 It appears that they found me at daybreak, lying on the grave unconscious.

WORDNOTES

ceaselessly	constantly, never ending
seized	took hold of, grabbed
torments	miseries, pain
despairing	giving up all hope
cunning	clever, tricky, sly
adieu	farewell (French)
somber	dark, gloomy
refuge	shelter, safe place
sown	planted
luminous	glowing
deceived	betrayed
ignorant	unaware, uneducated

Comprehension and Skills Exercises

2. Why did the storyteller's mistress die?

_____

_____

3. Why did the storyteller go on a journey?

_____

4. The storyteller could not find his lover's grave.

True _____   False _____

5. The storyteller died in the cemetery.

True _____   False _____

6. What did the storyteller see in the cemetery?

_____

7. Does the story answer the question in the title? Why or why not?

_____

8. As we read this story, we wonder what will happen to the storyteller. The events in the story become more and more exciting as we get close to the end, and our questions about how it will end become stronger and stronger. We don't want to stop reading until we find out what happens. This is called *rising action*. The following diagram shows how events in story *rise* in importance and suspense as we read. The events of "Was It a Dream" are listed here. Use the listed sentences to fill in the boxes of the diagram to show the action *rising* toward the end of the story.

   a. I went out without knowing it, without wishing it, and toward the cemetery.

   b. I now saw: Having gone out in the rain one day, in order to deceive her lover, she caught cold and died.

   c. I had loved her madly!

   d. I wished to pass the night, the last night, in weeping on her grave.

   e. It appears that they found me at daybreak, lying on the grave unconscious

Rising Action -
What will happen next?

End of story

Storyteller's discovery

Storyteller's actions

Storyteller's problem

Beginning of story

9. Where in the *rising action* diagram would you place the title?

_____

10. What is the main idea in paragraph 4?

_____

11. Write five sentences from paragraph 4 that provide supporting details.

    a. _____

    _____

    _____

    b. _____

    _____

    c. _____

    _____

    d. _____

    _____

    e. _____

    _____

12. Write five words from the reading that contain a silent consonant.

    a. _____

    b. _____

    c. _____

    d. _____

    e. _____

13. Write five words from the reading that contain digraphs (consonants that work together to create one sound).

    a. _____

    b. _____

    c. _____

    d. _____

    e. _____

14. Write five words from the reading that contain two vowels that create one sound.

    a. _____

    b. _____

    c. _____

    d. _____

    e. _____

15. Write five words from the reading that contain the following prefixes.

    a. re   _____

    b. in   _____

    c. dis   _____

    d. un   _____

    e. fore _____

16. Write five words from the reading that contain the following suffixes.

    a. ly   _____

    b. ed   _____

    c. less   _____

    d. ing   _____

    e. tion   _____

17. Write five compound words from the reading.

    a. _____

    b. _____

    c. _____

    d. _____

    e. _____

18. Paragraph 19 contains several words that describe the persons buried in the cemetery. Choose five words that are new to you, look them up in your dictionary, and write the definition provided for each word.

    a. _____

    b. _____

    c. _____

    d. _____

    e. _____

19. Look up the word *adieu* in the dictionary. How many syllables does it contain? _____

20. What two vowel sounds are in the word *adieu*? _____

READER RESPONSE 8-9

Did you find the storyteller's words believable? Why or why not?

_____

_____

_____

_____

_____

_____

What was the most surprising event in the story? Explain why.

_____

_____

_____

_____

_____

_____

1. From reading the title and the first lines of paragraphs 1 through 6, what do you predict about the reading?

_____

_____

_____

The Tornado of the Century

By Pat Richardson

1   Sayler's boyfriend swung his Mustang into her driveway. "Thanks, Jake. Call me after work."

2   "Later, Babe," Jake replied as he leaned across Sayler to open her door. She plopped her roller backpack onto the driveway, leaned back into the car and gave Jake a quick kiss.

3   Sayler watched Jake's progress down the street, then turned and glanced at the dark sky to the west; another stormy afternoon and night, it looked like. That was nothing unusual for May in central Oklahoma. She rolled her backpack into the foyer, then crossed the front yard and headed for the neighbor's house two doors down.

4   "Hiya, Mrs. Luster. What's Izzie up to?"

5   "Oh honey, that little girl is a regular monkey. She climbed on top of my bookcase in the back bedroom a while ago, but right now she's playing 'cover the babies' in the computer room."

6   Saylor headed to Mrs. Luster's front bedroom, which was a bedroom, computer room, and playroom combined. She watched her two-year-old baby sister for a moment. Izzie had three dolls and three or four small stuffed animals lined up on the floor. She was covering them carefully with Mrs. Luster's tea towels. Izzie glanced up. "Sissy, Sissy, Sissy," she squealed. Sayler picked her up, grabbed Izzie's diaper bag, and said goodbye to the older lady.

7   "Honey, there's a cloud coming up," Mrs. Luster warned. "You turn on the TV and listen to the reports when you get back to the house. That thing started way off in Anadarko, and now it's heading for Chickasha. It's a tornado all right, but they don't know how bad it's going to be or where it's heading."

8   "Sure thing, Mrs. Luster," Sayler answered. She wasn't really worried or even interested. Storms came up all the time during this time of year, and her nervous neighbor overreacted as far as she was concerned.

9   At home, Sayler changed her sister's diaper, fixed them both a snack, and then took Izzie outside to the backyard play gym under the big elm tree. They swung and played Ring Around the Rosie, but finally got engrossed in a sandbox game, building a town with little people and houses, Sayler making up stories for Izzie as they built.

10   A cool wind hit Sayler's cheek. She glanced up and saw how black the western sky had become. "Come on, Izzie Busy. Let's go in now." Izzie was getting drowsy. It was almost time for her short afternoon nap. Sayler's and Izzie's dad went to work at the General Motors plant at 2:00 every afternoon. Their mom

worked for the county library system and didn't get home until 7:00. Sayler got home from school at 3:30. Her job was to pick up Izzie at Mrs. Luster's, take care of her, and start supper for their mom. Izzie usually took a short nap around 5:00 while Sayler talked on the phone, watched TV, and maybe thought about starting supper.

11   Sayler put Izzie down in her pink and white room, piling plenty of stuffed toys and her blankie around her. Izzie's eyes drooped shut. Back in the family room, Sayler turned on the TV. Before she even had a chance to switch it to cable, the loud, broken beep, which meant a tornado warning, filled the room. The weatherman on Channel 4 started talking quickly. The screen was filled with an ugly, big tornado, the biggest Sayler had ever seen on TV; she had never seen one in person. Gary Goodman's voice was full of suppressed tension as he pretended to be calm.

12   "It now looks like this system is headed for Moore. It has taken a 35-degree turn to the northeast. The first projections showed the main funnel heading east, northeast, from Chickasha to a little north of Lindsay, in the Dibble area. It is now heading for the metro area and will reach the edge of Moore within the next 40 to 45 minutes. Moore residents, take cover now! Go to the center of your home. . ."

13   Sayler clicked off the TV. She knew the drill. Oklahoma residents were trained from childhood to cope with severe storms. She ran to her parents' bedroom and gathered up pillows and blankets and piled them all into the hall. Hurrying into Izzie's room, she grabbed the twin-sized mattress from Izzie's "big-girl" bed, the bed Izzie didn't yet sleep in because she still preferred her baby bed. After dumping the mattress, pillows, and blankets into the hall bathtub, she paused a moment and then dashed into her parent's bedroom again. Feeling a little foolish, she grabbed her great-grandmother's Bible off the top closet shelf. Sayler didn't really think her house was going to be completely destroyed, but the Bible had all the family names written on the front pages. The Bible meant a lot to her mother. It was their family's history.

14   Taking a deep breath, Sayler decided to sneak a quick look outside. Standing in her back yard, she stared at the western sky. The sky was even blacker now, black tinged with green. The wind had died down, and the air was no longer cool. It was deathly still and quiet. The air was close, hot, and heavy and had a strange smell, like rotten eggs, like sulfur. Suddenly, the tornado sirens went off, and Sayler jumped straight up. The sirens made a loud, piercing, unbroken wail, which was enough to strike terror into even a nonchalant teenage girl!

15   Galloping back into the house, Sayler hit the remote as she whizzed into Izzie's room. Grabbing her baby sister and a few stuffed animals, she headed back down the hall. Gary Goodman on Channel 4 was almost shouting; in fact, he *was* shouting. "This is one tornado, folks, that cannot be survived above ground. We normally never give this advice, but if you are in the Moore or southwest Oklahoma City area, you need to either get below ground *now* or leave the area *now*! We repeat, this tornado *cannot be survived above ground*!"

16   "Great! That's just what I needed to hear," Sayler panted. She dashed into the hall bathroom, turned on the lights, and shut and locked the door. Izzie was still not really awake, but Sayler held her close as she climbed into the bathtub. With one arm, she cuddled Izzie; with her other hand and arm she carefully climbed

under the mattress and piled the pillows and blankets around them. She knew it was important to protect their heads. She was also glad that she and Izzie still had on their shoes. Normally, Sayler kicked off her shoes as soon as she got home, and she usually took off Izzie's shoes for her nap. Thank God, today she had done neither. If the windows were blown out and glass was everywhere, at least they would have on their shoes.

17   As they lay cuddled up with a stuffed rabbit and a "meow-meow" between them and the Bible under Sayler's feet, the air pressure dropped. The lights flickered twice and went out. There was a tremendous high-pitched roaring, like a killer hailstorm, but even louder. She felt an overwhelming pressure bearing down on the house, almost like it was going to explode.

18   Then it did explode!

19   Sayler screamed, clenched Izzie and sunk deeper into the tub, pulling with all her might to keep the mattress on top of them, at the same time pushing Izzie beneath her. She could feel and hear the house going to pieces around them. She started praying that nothing would hit them in the head or go through their bodies.

• • •

20   The next thing Sayler knew, it was pitch dark. Cold rain was pouring down on them; there was no roof, no walls, no house. The tub and half of the pipe wall seemed to be the only things left standing. Cries, screams, and sirens surrounded them. Every so often sparks would shower skyward from downed power lines, illuminating a landscape from hell. Sayler knew she was sobbing, but it seemed like her sobs and Izzie's shrill screams came from somewhere beyond her. A hand reached out of the darkness and touched her face. Terrified, she screamed, but the voice said, "It's OK. I'm a rescue worker. Are you OK? Is that a baby with you?" Izzie was still screaming her head off. "Is the baby OK? Don't worry, we will take care of you."

21   Hours later, Sayler lay in the fellowship hall of a nearby Catholic church. She was on a double-bed-sized mattress that was lying on the floor, and she was wrapped from neck to toes in lightweight blankets. Glancing over, she saw Izzie sound asleep underneath the blankets, her butt in the air, apparently unhurt. Sayler's mom and dad, Jake, and Jake's parents were sitting around the edges of the mattress, all of them looking like they had had a close encounter with a weed whacker.

22   "Mom?" Sayler whispered.

23   "Oh, honey, are you OK?" Her mother burst into tears. Sayler nodded weakly.

24   Her dad said, "Allie, she probably doesn't want to talk right now. We'll just fill her in. The house is gone, and Helen, Tom, and Jake's house is gone too. You have a mild concussion. Izzie is fine; she was just scared and upset for a while. We're proud of you, Sayler; you saved her life and yours as well."

25   "Sayler, I can't believe you thought of saving Grandma's Bible," her mother sobbed. "The rescue workers just scooped up everything in the tub, the stuffed animals, the blankets, pillows, and all. The Bible was there with all the other stuff. That was just so great of you to think of it. Aren't you proud of yourself?"

26   Somewhere nearby, a TV was blaring. The tornado was an F-6, winds up to 350 miles an hour. It had been more than two miles wide. Forty-six people

were dead; more were missing. Already, it was being called the Tornado of the Century.

27   "Mrs. Luster?" Sayler could barely get out the question.

28   "She's fine," her dad replied. "She has a cellar under her utility room, you know. Her house was destroyed, just like ours. The first thing she did was get on her cell phone and try to call you and everyone else she knows, but of course, cells aren't working."

29   Sayler smiled sleepily at Jake's folks. They smiled back, but there were tears in their eyes. Jake squeezed her hand, then pressed it to his lips. He looked awful, but she imagined she looked pretty awful too. She sighed, feeling safe, warm, and protected at last. About to close her eyes, she stole one last look at Izzie, her baby sister, before she drifted off again.

30   As a matter of fact, she *was* proud of herself! She had saved her little sister and her family's history. "I'm a survivor," was her last thought before sleep overtook her. She had survived the Tornado of the Century.

Comprehension and Skills Exercises

1. Why was Sayler not worried about Mrs. Luster's warning about a tornado?

_____

_____

2. What were Sayler's responsibilities at home?

_____

_____

3. How did Sayler safeguard herself and Izzie to get through the tornado?

_____

_____

_____

_____

_____

4. Why was the storm called the Tornado of the Century?

_____

_____

5. What details in the story tell about the warning system for tornadoes in Oklahoma?

_____

_____

6. Several Oklahoma towns are mentioned in the story (Anadarko, Chickasha, Moore, Lindsay, Dibble). What does this information tell you about the tornado?

_____

7. How did Mrs. Luster survive the storm?

   _____

8. Using context clues (and your dictionary, if necessary) define the following words.

   a. engrossed (paragraph 9)   _____

   b. suppressed (paragraph 11)   _____

   c. tinged (paragraph 14)   _____

   d. piercing (paragraph 14)   _____

   e. nonchalant (paragraph 14)   _____

   f. illuminating (paragraph 20) _____

   g. apparently (paragraph 21)   _____

9. For each of the following words, write C in the "Correct" column if the word is spelled correctly. If it is wrong, rewrite the word, spelled correctly, in the "Corrected" column.

Word	Correct	Corrected
a. tornadoe	_____	_____
b. carfully	_____	_____
c. engrosed	_____	_____
d. drooped	_____	_____
e. libary	_____	_____
f. survived	_____	_____
g. grabed	_____	_____
h. preferred	_____	_____

10. Listen to the syllables you hear as you pronounce the following words. Write the number of syllables for each word.

Words	Number of Syllables
a. weatherman	_____
b. pretended	_____
c. glanced	_____
d. tornado	_____
e. degree	_____
f. projections	_____
g. warning	_____
h. library	_____
i. ugly	_____
j. climbed	_____

11. Name the part of speech of each word underlined in the following sentence (noun, pronoun, verb, adverb, adjective, conjunction, interjection, preposition).

Suddenly, the tornado sirens went off, and Sayler jumped straight up.

Word	*Part of Speech*
a. Suddenly	_____
b. sirens	_____
c. went	_____
d. Sayler	_____
e. jumped	_____
f. straight	_____

12. Match words from the left column with the vowel sounds in the right column.

	Word	*Matching Vowel Sound*
_____	leave	a. long **a**
_____	grabbed	b. short **i**
_____	smell	c. short **e**
_____	climbed	d. long **e**
_____	gave	e. short **a**
_____	filled	f. long **i**

13. Analyze each word in the following list, and write its word parts (prefix, suffix, root word) on the lines provided.

Word	*Prefix*	*Suffix*	*Root Word*
a. coming	_____	_____	_____
b. biggest	_____	_____	_____
c. grabbed	_____	_____	_____
d. unbroken	_____	_____	_____
e. awhile	_____	_____	_____
f. describe	_____	_____	_____

14. Write the compound words in paragraphs 3 and 13 on the following lines. Record each word only once. Use a hyphen to separate each word as shown in the example.

Compound Word

Example: _____ back-yard _____

a. _____

b. _____

c. _____

d. _____

e. _____

READER RESPONSE 8-10

Sayler could be called an "ordinary hero," which is an ordinary person who displays bravery when faced with a dangerous situation. In three or four short sentences, describe Sayler's courage and level-headedness.

_____

_____

_____

_____

_____

_____

_____

Have you ever faced a dangerous situation when seconds count? If you have, describe what you did. If you haven't, think of a dangerous situation, and describe what you think or hope you would do.

_____

_____

_____

_____

_____

_____

_____

_____

ONLINE PRACTICE

Go to **MyReadingLab** at www.myreadinglab.com. Click on **Reading Road Trip** and select your textbook or the **Pioneer Level.**

1. For further practice using a **combination of skills** when reading, take a Road Trip to **Hawaii.**

2. For further practice using **active reading strategies**, take a Road Trip to **New Orleans.**

PROGRESS CHART

CHAPTER 8

SECTION ONE

Fill out the number of correct answers you have for each item below. Your instructor will tell you how to calculate your percentage score.

READING 8-1   Number right _____ out of a possible score of 5.   Percentage score _____

READING 8-2   Number right _____ out of a possible score of 5.   Percentage score _____

READING 8-3   Number right _____ out of a possible score of 5.   Percentage score _____

READING 8-4   Number right _____ out of a possible score of 10.   Percentage score _____

READING 8-5   Number right _____ out of a possible score of 5.   Percentage score _____

READING 8-6   Number right _____ out of a possible score of 5.   Percentage score _____

READING 8-7   Number right _____ out of a possible score of 10.   Percentage score _____

READING 8-8   Number right _____ out of a possible score of 5.   Percentage score _____

READING 8-9   Number right _____ out of a possible score of 10.   Percentage score _____

READING 8-10 Number right _____ out of a possible score of 5.   Percentage score _____

READING 8-11 Number right _____ out of a possible score of 20.   Percentage score _____

READING 8-12 Number right _____ out of a possible score of 5.   Percentage score _____

READING 8-13 Number right _____ out of a possible score of 5.   Percentage score _____

READING 8-14 Number right _____ out of a possible score of 20.   Percentage score _____

READING 8-15 Number right _____ out of a possible score of 20.   Percentage score _____

READING 8-16 Number right _____ out of a possible score of 20.   Percentage score _____

READING 8-17 Number right _____ out of a possible score of 20.   Percentage score _____

READING 8-18 Number right _____ out of a possible score of 15.   Percentage score _____

SECTION TWO

How do you feel? There are no wrong or right answers to how you feel about what you have learned. Circle Yes, Somewhat, or No in response to the following questions.

1. Do you remember to use prereading when beginning a new reading or assignment in another class?   Yes   Somewhat   No

2. Has your pronunciation improved by knowing how consonants and vowels sound?   Yes   Somewhat   No

3. Has your comprehension improved by understanding how root words and word parts make meaning?   Yes   Somewhat   No

4. Are you using your dictionary more often?   Yes   Somewhat   No

5. Does understanding context clues make your reading more enjoyable?   Yes   Somewhat   No

6. Has finding the main idea helped your reading comprehension in other classes?   Yes   Somewhat   No

7. Are you writing better sentences since learning about main ideas and supporting details?   Yes   Somewhat   No

8. Could you explain how to preview a text to a fellow classmate?   Yes   Somewhat   No

9. Has your personal and school reading improved since taking this course?   Yes   Somewhat   No

SECTION THREE

Take a minute or two to reflect on your reading development. Write a few sentences or discuss with other students how *Making Meaning* has changed your reading habits.

_____

_____

_____

_____

_____

_____

_____

_____

_____

_____

WORDNOTES and Student Vocabulary Log

Lines are provided after each alphabetical listing so you may add new words with their definitions as you learn them during the semester.

A

abscess   swollen area of the body containing pus

abstaining   doing without

adenine and guanine   two of the building blocks of DNA

adieu   farewell (French)

adolescents   people in their teens

adverse   harmful

affiliate   branch organization

agriculture   relating to the science of growing things

alms   money, food, or clothing given to poor people

amateur   one who studies a subject for pleasure instead of pay

ambition   strong desire for fame and power

anatomy   structure of the body

anesthesia   loss of feeling, especially from drugs

appropriate   suitable, fitting

articulate   able to communicate clearly

astrological   relating to the stars, moon, and planets

astronomy   the science of the stars, planets, and all other heavenly bodies

Atlantis   mythical sunken continent in the Atlantic Ocean

atmosphere   the mass of air surrounding the earth

attendants   those who help or support others

automatic   done by habit

autonomy   independence, the right to be self-directed

autopsies   examinations of dead bodies to learn the causes of death

autumnal   belonging to the fall season

avoid   keep away from

_____

_____

_____

_____

_____

_____

_____

_____

B

botany   science of plant life

breaches   breaks or separates

bromine   chemical element; usually, a reddish-brown corrosive liquid

bubonic plague   disease that is caused by bacteria and spreads quickly

buffer   anything that serves to deaden the shock of striking forces

bust   likeness of a person's head and shoulders

_____

_____

_____

_____

_____

C

Candide book by the French writer Voltaire about life in the 1750s

canopy roof, cover

captivated fascinated

captivity held within bounds

caregivers people who provide care for others

catastrophic great, sudden, ruinous

caulked spiked

ceaselessly constantly, never ending

character type or kind of behavior of a certain group

Chichen Itza ancient ruins of Mexico's Yucatan Peninsula

civil rights rights of citizens to legal, economic, and social opportunity

classical referring to Greece and Rome

cochlear implants prosthetic devices surgically set in place in the internal ear to restore partial hearing to the deaf

collaboration working together

colonoscopy examination of the inside of the large intestine using a fiber-optic device

complaining expressing pain

composition shape, structure

compromise settlement by mutual agreement

concentration camps camps set up for political and ethnic prisoners

consideration careful thought

contagious catching, spread by contact

contentious argumentative

contradictory opposite

contribution help given

conversion change into another form

coordinate bring into harmony or proper relation

Cozumel the largest island of the Mexican Caribbean

cross-examined questioned closely

culture habits, preferences, and behaviors of people in a given place and time

cunning clever, tricky, sly

_____

_____

_____

_____

_____

_____

_____

D

decades ten-year periods

deceived betrayed

dedicated set apart for a special purpose

delta triangular deposit of silt at the mouth of a river split into branches

design detailed plan

despairing giving up all hope

destruction ruin

detachment having no interest

devastation complete ruin, waste

diagnose recognize and identify a disease or problem

discrimination the act of being for or against a person or group based on feelings of prejudice

dispersed broken up, scattered

domestic tame

dramatic action or expression related to theater

dramatist one who writes plays

_____

_____

_____

_____

_____

_____

_____

E

economy system of managing monies and resources of a country

emancipation act of being set free

employment options job choices

enacted made into a law, accomplished

enhances improves, adds to

ensure make sure

envisioned imagined

episode happening

equinox   time of year when day and night are equal in length

ethnic   referring to a group of people having the same customs, language, religion, and culture

ethnically cleansed   words used to describe the killing of people of a certain race or culture

evacuation   withdrawal from

exclusivity   shutting out all others

exhibits   objects or collections of objects on display

exotic   foreign

expelled   driven out

exploited   taken advantage of, used

extravagant   extreme, wasteful

_____

_____

_____

_____

_____

_____

_____

F

familiar   common, ordinary, often met or seen

fantasy   imaginary, make-believe

fascinating   enchanting

fatigued   overly tired

features   parts of the face (eyes, mouth, nose)

filth   foul dirt

focus   adjustment for clear vision

foremost   first in place or time

forensic   relating to courts of law

founder   one who sets up, brings into being

frail   delicate, weak

_____

_____

_____

_____

_____

_____

_____

G

gallery   room or building used to display objects of art

generations   groups of people born around the same time (children, parents, and grandparents represent three generations)

generic   general, not specific

gesture   movement

globalization   bringing together common interests over the globe

gnawing   biting or wearing away with the teeth

gorget   fancy collar

granted   given

Great Depression   decline of business in 1930s

gynecological   referring to female diseases

_____

_____

_____

_____

_____

_____

_____

_____

H

heroine   female hero

hesitant   holding back in doubt

homogeneous   made up of the same parts

humid   damp, moist

hybrid   blend of two elements

_____

_____

_____

_____

_____

_____

I

ignorant   unaware, uneducated

imports   goods brought from another country

indecent   immoral

independent   taking care of yourself without the help of others

indicate   to point out, to show

infected   spread rapidly from one to another

infested   overrun in numbers large enough to be harmful

influence   power to affect others

insurmountable   not able to be overcome

intensity   having strong feelings or emotions

intent   plan

interaction   ongoing exchange of information

interactive   allowing two-way communication (e.g., an interactive video game)

interchange   meeting between highways where cars may enter and exit

interest rate   the amount of payment for the use of money

interned   detained or confined during a war

interpretation   explanation

intersection   place where two streets cross

intravenous   injected into a vein

introduced   brought in for the first time

isolated   set apart from others

_____

_____

_____

_____

_____

_____

J

jostled   bumped or pushed against

justice   fair, honest, and moral treatment

_____

_____

_____

_____

_____

_____

_____

K

kiosk   small open structure

_____

_____

_____

_____

_____

_____

L

levee   dam or dike to hold back water

logjam   jumble of logs jammed together in a stream

logrolling   ability to move logs downriver by balancing on them

Lorna Doone   romance novel by R. D. Blackmore

lumberjacks   workers who cut logs in the forest and move them to a sawmill

luminous   glowing

_____

_____

_____

_____

_____

_____

M

maintenance   preservation, upkeep, support

mammals   warm-blooded animals that suckle their young

maneuver   move skillfully

marathon   contest of great length that requires endurance

memento   something given or kept as a reminder of a person or event

merchant   one who buys and sells

Merida   a Spanish city founded in 1542

mesh   to fit together

microscope   an instrument that magnifies

migration   movement to another area or country

monument   something set up to keep alive the memory of one or more persons or an event

mortified   very embarrassed

_____

_____

_____

_____

_____

_____

N

noteworthy   worthy of attention

notorious   widely and unfavorably known

_____

_____

_____

_____

_____

_____

O

oath   statement to God and men that one will speak the truth and/or keep a promise

observation   noting and recording of facts, as for research

official   formal

optioned   purchased a right to buy later

originated   began

_____

_____

_____

_____

_____

_____

_____

P

pagan   nature based primitive religion

pageant   display or show

paramilitary   trained forces working with the regular army

permanent   lasting, unchanging

perspective   point of view

phase   stage

philosophy   view of life

piked pole   pole with a metal pick on one end

planetarium   room or building containing a device that projects images of astronomical bodies, such as the solar system, on a curved ceiling

plentiful   large supply of

pollute   to make impure or unclean

portfolio   collection of works

potential   possible

predators   animals that live by hunting other animals for food; people who prey on others

preferred   liked better

prevails   is used widely

primarily   mainly

proclamation   a formal public announcement

Progresso   a Mexican fishing village

protest   firm objection or disapproval

provisions   supplies

psychosocial   relating to the mind (psycho) and the world around us (social)

_____

_____

_____

_____

_____

_____

_____

Q

qualifier   something that restricts or limits

quandary   difficult choice

quaranting   enforcing isolation to prevent spread of disease

_____

_____

_____

_____

_____

_____

_____

R

recognized   noticed, known

recommendations   favorable proposals or advice

recurring   occurring again and again

refillable   able to be filled again

refinance   change a loan to get a better interest rate

refuge   shelter, safe place

regret   to feel sorry about doing or saying something

reign   period of rule of a royal leader

remarkable   worthy of notice, out of the ordinary

Renaissance   great renewal of art and learning in Europe in the fourteenth to sixteenth centuries

reproductive system   organs for producing offspring

reservoir   place where something is stored for future use

response   reaction

retreated   withdrew

rivals   competitors, people who try to be as good as or better than one another

river driver   lumber workers who move logs down a river

rural   relating to the country or country life

_____

_____

_____

_____

_____

_____

_____

_____

S

Saltillo   a Mexican town more than 400 years old

"Savez-vous planter les choux"   a traditional French folk song often used to teach French

scale   system of measuring or grading; a series of marks along a line at regular intervals

scams   swindles, cons, hoaxes

sculpted   carved or shaped

sediment   the matter that settles to the bottom of a liquid

segregation   separation from the rest of society

seized   took hold of, grabbed

shrine   a place that is sacred because of its associations

shriveled   shrunk, withered

sign   communicate using hand movements instead of speech, especially used by the deaf

slogan   catchy phrase used in advertising

sly   sneaky, cunning, shrewd

snipers   hidden shooters

somber   dark, gloomy

souvenir   a keepsake

sown   planted

sparsely   spread thinly

stash   to put away or hide

submitted   sent in

supernatural   not explained by known laws of nature; coming from God, ghosts, spirits, etc.

superstitions   beliefs not based on known facts or sensible thinking, especially belief in omens and the supernatural

symbol   something standing for something else

sympathizer   someone with compassionate feeling for a certain person or group

symptoms   signs of illness or disease

_____

_____

_____

_____

_____

_____

_____

urgent needed at once

urinary tract organs that make and store urine, one of the body's liquid waste products

_____

_____

_____

_____

_____

_____

_____

_____

_____

T

tactic particular approach to a problem

tame change from a wild state

Tenochtitlan ancient Aztec site in Mexico

theologically relating to religion

threat declaration of intention to harm

threatening intending to harm

topography surface features of land

torments miseries, pain

tragedy serious play with an unhappy ending as a result of the actions of a character or characters

transparent sheer enough to be seen through

trend general movement

tribute statement of gratitude, respect, honor, or praise

turban headdress formed by winding a long scarf around the head

typical average

_____

_____

_____

_____

_____

_____

_____

U

unanimously all in agreement

uniqueness quality of being one of a kind, rare

unrivaled cannot be beaten

V

vaccination injection with vaccine to prevent disease

vernal belonging to the spring season

veteran a person who has served in the armed forces

vicious very forceful, intense

vital essential; critically important

vivid lifelike, sharp, intense

volunteer one who offers to work without pay

vs. (versus) rather than, as opposed to

_____

_____

_____

_____

_____

_____

_____

W

wail to cry out in pain or frustration

wheezing breathing with difficulty, usually with a whistling sound

whimpered whined, cried

wonders amazing accomplishments

_____

_____

_____

_____

_____

_____

_____

_____

X

_____

_____

Y

yeti Abominable Snowman

yore time past, usually long past

_____

_____

Z

_____

_____

Appendix B

Glossary of Technical Terms

academic   related to school skills

adjective   a word that describes a noun or pronoun

adverb   a word that tells something about a verb, adjective, or another adverb

antonym clue   a word that means the opposite of the unknown word is used

appendix   a special section that is placed at the end of a textbook and contains specific information or activities related to the information and content of the book; plural is *appendixes* or *appendices*

autobiography   an account of a person's life written by that person

bibliography   a list of materials an author referred to when preparing a book

blends   consonants that work together to create separate but connected sounds

bold print and italics   methods of highlighting words to better understand the text

bullets   dots that signal important information

chapter structure   consists of an introduction, an outline, a list of objectives, and a brief summary of what is going to be discussed in the chapter

charts, diagrams, graphs   visual material showing information

compound word   two whole words joined to make one word

concluding sentence   a sentence that summarizes or comments on the information that has been presented

conjunction   a word that connects words or groups of words

consonants   21 letters that work by themselves and with each other to create various sounds (and sometimes no sound at all)

context clues   hints in the text that help the reader understand what unfamiliar words mean

credits   a list of the names of the people whose writing, photography, or artwork have been included in a textbook

definition   the meaning of a word

definition clue   the unknown word is defined following its use

diacritical symbols   symbols used to show how to pronounce words

dialogue   characters talking to one another in a play

dictionary   a book containing the words of a language, arranged alphabetically, and giving the meanings, pronunciations, and usually the origins of words

digraphs   consonants that work together to create one sound

entry words   the words listed on the pages of a dictionary

etymology   the origin and development of a word over time

example   one of a number of things that show the point of a happening

example clue   the unknown word is followed by one or more examples that help define the meaning of the word

facts   occurrences known to have happened

general sense of the passage   other words in the sentence or in the sentences before or after the unknown word give a general sense of what the word means based on the reader's knowledge and experience

Copyright © 2007 by Pearson Education, Inc.

329

glossary   a special dictionary that is placed at the end of a textbook and explains words with meanings that are particularly important to the book

graphic organizer   a diagram showing group of ideas

graphics   tables, figures, quotes, drawings, photographs, marginal notes, and captions that pro-vide additional information about topics discussed in a textbook

guide words   words in bold print at the top of each dictionary page; on the left-hand page is the word that begins the list of words on that page; on the right-hand page is the word that is the last word on that page

incidents   distinct occurrences

index   an alphabetized list of topics that is placed at the end of a textbook and gives page numbers to guide the reader to the page(s) on which each topic appears

infer   to reach a conclusion based on information presented and using prior knowledge and experiences

interjection   a word that shows emotion or surprise

introduction or preface   a special section that is placed at the beginning of a book, provides a brief roadmap for using the book, and describes special features of the book

italics and bold print   methods of highlighting words to better understand the text

main heading   first title seen at beginning of text, often in larger or different font

main idea   the main point the author is making about the topic

monologue   a character speaking to him- or herself

noun   a word that names a person, place, thing, or idea

origin of a word   a word's history

parts of speech   the eight groups that divide all the words in the English language: nouns, pronouns, verbs, adjectives, adverbs, prepositions, interjections, and conjunctions

predicting   guessing the outcome of a reading based on prereading, prior knowledge, context clues, and other reading strategies

preface or introduction   provides a brief roadmap for using a textbook and describes special features about the book

prefix   a word part that comes before the root word; each prefix has a meaning of its own and therefore changes the meaning of the root word

preposition   a word that shows how a noun is related to some other word in a sentence

prereading   looking over the text before beginning to read it word by word; reading certain material (titles, introduction, subheads, charts, etc.) in an organized way

previewing   another word for prereading; a strategy that helps a reader become familiar with a textbook before reading and studying in detail.

prior knowledge   connecting what is already known to new information and ideas

pronoun   a word used in place of a noun

root word   provides the core meaning of the word

schwa   an unstressed or soft vowel sound; it is pronounced *uh* as in *fun*

silent consonant   consonants or combinations of consonants not heard in pronouncing a word

skimming   reading for an overall idea by looking for major ideas and skipping over details

statistics   numerical data

subtitle or subheading   a secondary title under the main title

suffix   a word part that is added to the end of a root word and can be used to change the root's part of speech, its tense, or less commonly, its meaning

supporting details   examples, facts, or other information that support the main idea

syllabication   taking a word with more than one syllable and breaking it into separate syllables

syllable   a part of a word; each syllable in a word is pronounced separately and contains one vowel sound

synonym clue   a word that means the same as the unknown word is used

table of contents   a page that usually follows the title page and lists what a book covers, which topics are emphasized, in what order the topics are placed, and the special features each chapter contains

text boxes   information set off from the main text

thesis statement   the main idea of a long reading

title   the name of a book, magazine, article, chapter, picture, poem, or song

title page a page that lists the full title of a book, the author's name, the publisher of the book, and when the book was published

topic the general subject of a paragraph

topic sentence tells the reader what a paragraph is going to be about

transitional words or phrases used to link ideas together and help a reader understand and follow the connections between ideas

verb a word that expresses action or a state of being

visual material tables, maps, graphs, cartoons, photographs and other pieces in a college textbook that give you additional information

vowels five letters, *a, e, i, o, u,* and sometimes *y,* that work alone or with other letters to create sounds in words

Credits

Photo Credits

Text Credits

Chapter One

Chapter Two

Chapter Three

Chapter Four

Chapter Five

Chapter Six

p. 190   James M. Rubenstein, "What is Ethnic Cleansing?" from James M. Rubenstein, *An Introduction to Human Geography: The Cultural Landscape,* 8th Edition, © 2005, p. 250. Adapted by permission of Pearson Education, Inc.

p. 200   James M. Rubenstein, "Sports in Popular Culture" from James M. Rubenstein, *An Introduction to Human Geography: The Cultural Landscape,* 8th Edition, © 2005, p. 122. Adapted by permission of Pearson Education, Inc.

p. 217   "Gardner Rules!" excerpted and abridged from http://www.rulongardner.com Printed with permission of Danielle Marquis.

Chapter Seven

p. 237   Don K. Scott, "What Goes Down . . .?" Reprinted by permission of the author.

p. 243   Pat Richardson, "Lady of the Woods." Reprinted by permission of the author.

p. 248   "Of Horrors and Heroes," from *Episcopal Life* 15, No. 2 (2005). Written by Charles Ramsden with introduction by Jerrold Hames, pp. 1, 6-7. Printed with the permission of Charles Ramsden and *Episcopal Life*

p. 255   "Spring," by William Blake, 1789.

Chapter Eight

p. 260   Harold Whipple, "Omaha's First Water Company." Reprinted by permission of the author.

p. 262   Harold Whipple, "Sawmill Revenge." Reprinted by permission of the author.

p. 266   Christina Page, "Santa Claus Did Visit." Reprinted by permission of the author.

p. 267   Alice Doray, "Symbols of Christmas." Reprinted by permission of her daughter, Evelyn Eskridge

p. 271   Deborah Doray, "Wedding Charm." Reprinted by permission of the author.

p. 273   Vachel Lindsay, "The Flower-Fed Buffaloes," from *168 Poems written by Vachel Lindsay,* from http://www.americanpoems.com/poets/lindsay/#poems.

p. 276   Laura Eskridge, excerpt from "Internet College Journal." Reprinted by permission of the author.

p. 278   John Grisham, excerpt from *A Painted House,* by John Grisham, pp. 390–392. Copyright © 2000, 2001 by Belfry Holdings, Inc. Used by permission of Doubleday, a division of Random House, Inc.

p. 282   Debby Dobbs, "Language—A Code to Sail Dreams." Reprinted by permission of the author.

p. 284   Ruth Ozeki, "A Vacation with Ghosts." Copyright 2004, *New York Times.* Reprinted by permission.

p. 293   Monica Davey, "As Town for Deaf Takes Shape, Debate on Isolation Re-emerges," from *New York Times,* Monday March 21, 2005. Copyright © 2005 by The New York Times Co. Reprinted with permission.

p. 299   Michelle Andrews, "Next to the Express Checkout, Express Medical Care," from *New York Times,* Sunday July 18, 2004. Copyright © 2004 by The New York Times Co. Reprinted with permission.

p. 305   Guy De Maupasssant, "Was It a Dream?" 1891.

p. 312   Pat Richardson, "The Tornado of the Century." Reprinted by permission of the author.

Index